The Simple Guide to
Marine Aquariums
Second Edition

Jeff Kurtz
with David E. Boruchowitz

The Simple Guide to Marine Aquariums, Second Edition
Project Team
Editors: Craig Sernotti, David E. Boruchowitz
Indexer: Ann W. Truesdale
Series Design: Stephanie Krautheim
Design Layout: Stephanie Krautheim
Chapter 20 written by David E. Boruchowitz

TFH Publications, Inc.®
President/CEO: Glen S. Axelrod
Executive Vice President: Mark E. Johnson
Publisher: Christopher T. Reggio
Production Manager: Kathy Bontz

TFH Publications, Inc.®
One TFH Plaza
Third and Union Avenues
Neptune City, NJ 07753

12 13 14 15 16   9 11 13 12 10
Printed and bound in China
Library of Congress Cataloging-in-Publication Data
Kurtz, Jeffrey.
  The simple guide to marine aquariums / Jeff Kurtz with David E. Boruchowitz. -- 2nd ed.
    p. cm.
  Includes index.
  ISBN 978-0-7938-0672-0 (alk. paper)
  1. Marine aquariums. I. Boruchowitz, David E. II. Title.
  SF457.1.K87 2009
  639.34'2--dc22
                    2008037784

This book has been published with the intent to provide accurate and authoritative information in regard to the subject matter within. While every reasonable precaution has been taken in preparation of this book, the author and publisher expressly disclaim responsibility for any errors, omissions, or adverse effects arising from the use or application of the information contained herein. The techniques and suggestions are used at the reader's discretion and are not to be considered a substitute for veterinary care. If you suspect a medical problem consult your veterinarian.

The Leader in Responsible Animal Care for Over 50 Years!®
www.tfh.com

Table of Contents

Preface to the Second Edition

For many decades our civilization has been marked by a geometrically accelerating technology. Estimates such as Moore's Law for the number of transistors on a computer chip describe a doubling every two years or so, and such figures are often applied to all areas of technology. When I reflect on the advancements I have personally observed in the last 50 years, it seems as if the only thing that remains constant is that nothing remains constant!

The early days of the marine aquarium hobby featured epoxy-coated stainless steel tank frames, undergravel filters, coral skeletons, and a few hardy fish. I even remember an article or two that gave a recipe for a homemade salt water mix. Now if I were to list here some cutting-edge technology for the marine hobby today, the list would be conservative by the time this second edition is printed, and way out of date by the time the publisher prepares the third edition.

There are, however, trends that have remained significant for decades, even though the details change ever more rapidly. Some, like the survivability of particular species in captivity or the quality and variety of prepared foods for marine ornamentals, are tied more to the accumulation of research and experience than to increased technology. Others, like advances in filtration or lighting, depend heavily on the development of or improvements in available technology.

As in the world at large, some changes in the hobby are intellectual or philosophical—part of the gradual enlightenment that has accompanied the human species since its origin. Although the progress of this enlightenment has been fitful, plunging us into the occasional dark age, there has been a net gain, one marked by especially significant milestones. Milestones in the hobby include the concept of natural filtration, which led to the Berlin method and our current reliance on live rock, and the understanding of the need for sustainable sources of specimens, which fostered the development of captive breeding protocols even in the face of economics that still favor the use of wild-caught animals.

I expect great leaps to continue in these areas of research, technological advances, and enlightenment. It will not be long before we regularly see aquaria entirely stocked with aquacultured live rock and sand, propagated corals and other inverts, and captive-bred fish; they'll be lit with cool-running high-intensity LED units programmed for specific color temperature, as well as for nocturnal moonlighting on a lunar cycle to stimulate natural spawning for fish and invertebrates. Larval marine fish will be raised in special vessels and fed a variety of artificial plankton that in some cases will be species specific. And, if history has any predictive power, there will be many surprises as well—advances that appear out of the blue or from other technologies.

And then there are fads. Cultural changes in preference and style are typically unpredictable, and they tend to be cyclic rather than strictly progressive. The same is true in the marine aquarium hobby, where certain species come and go in popularity and where you can almost date a photo of a reef tank based on the type and placement of the live rock. I'm sure marine aquarists will continue to create bandwagons to jump onto and that it will be quite a ride!

Although a quick glance at the equipment available today for a marine tank might convince you that the hobby is more complicated than ever, the basics of marine aquarium husbandry remain the same, and the equipment available today actually makes it easier than ever for someone to get started in the hobby. At the same time, however, it is very easy for the newbie to get frustrated by the plethora of advice, equipment, and contradictory recommendations. In fact, if you read a lot of the descriptions of how to maintain a marine aquarium, sometimes it seems as if some marine aquarists are engineers, and the rest are chemists!

That's where this book comes in. Now revised and updated for its second edition, it still has the single goal of providing the new marine aquarist with all the information needed for success. Jeff has distilled all the confusion into an easy-to-follow set of instructions for the new marine aquarist. He sorts through the morass of tools and gadgets on the market and explains the minimal set needed. He guides you past the biochemistry to an understanding of just the vital concepts needed to keep your tank thriving. And he shares with you his knowledge and experience so that you can have an entertaining and educational first foray into the marine aquarium hobby. So if you are considering setting up that first saltwater tank, read this book.

Read the whole book before you buy anything. Then, armed with all you need, you can join the ranks of hobbyists who enjoy maintaining a little slice of the natural coral reef in their homes. As you progress in the hobby, you'll learn more and more, and soon you will be one of the people causing it to evolve into something even more exciting.

Read. Learn. Enjoy!

David E. Boruchowitz
Covert, NY
August 2008

Chapter 1

Thinking of Taking the Plunge into Salt Water?

Starting a marine aquarium is one of those undertakings that many people contemplate on and off for years before actually taking the plunge. Some hesitate because they feel overwhelmed by all of the high-tech-sounding gadgets and scientific terminology associated with the saltwater hobby. Others may find the relatively high cost of certain marine specimens and the equipment needed to properly maintain them to be prohibitive. Then there are those who are afraid to start another marine tank after trying before and failing. While each of these concerns has some validity, it would be a shame to allow them to become impediments to success in the marine aquarium hobby.

What Lies Ahead

- why we keep a saltwater aquarium
- marine hobby basics

There's no question that equipment plays an important role in maintaining a healthy marine aquarium, and many aquarists do take a shine to high-tech gadgets. You could also argue that much of the marine aquarium literature available today is long on technical jargon and short on clear, concise information written specifically for the beginner. But the truth of the matter is, regardless of your background or the size of your pocketbook, you can enjoy a thriving marine microcosm at home using only a minimum of equipment—and you won't need a doctorate in marine biology or chemistry to achieve it!

Throughout the pages of this book I'll attempt to clarify the most important technical aspects of setting up and maintaining a marine aquarium without burying you in a lot of scientific blather. I believe that the simplest explanation is usually the best explanation, and also I'm just not all that scientific-minded myself. Along with the technical stuff, we'll take a look at lots of interesting facts and anecdotes about the various creatures that inhabit the world's oceans. (See Fish Fact sidebars.) So with no further ado, let's get ready to get our feet wet in the fascinating world of the marine aquarium!

WHAT ARE THE BENEFITS OF A SALTWATER AQUARIUM?

Marine aquariums offer numerous advantages to those who maintain them. Of course, there's the simple satisfaction of creating a beautiful ocean ecosystem within the confines of five glass (or acrylic) panes—an achievement to be proud of when you consider the delicate balance of life that exists on the natural coral reefs. From a purely aesthetic angle, you'd be hard pressed to find anything more captivating in the home. What other decorative element can compare to the spectacular drama that is played out every day in a community of marine fish or the dazzling interplay of light, color, and hypnotic motion in the reef aquarium?

Making a Splash in the Classroom

Apart from its obvious beauty, the marine aquarium is also an excellent educational tool. While the closed system of the aquarium is not technically a natural environment, it is still the best way, without actually donning scuba gear, to teach children and adults alike about the interconnectedness of the coral reef ecosystem and the hazards of neglecting or abusing it. As an instructional tool in the high school or elementary classroom, the marine aquarium is unrivaled, especially when the students are encouraged to be directly involved in all aspects of setup and maintenance—cycling, testing water parameters, selecting compatible specimens, treating ailments, water changes, and so on—rather than just feeding the fish.

Of course, the educational opportunities provided by the marine aquarium don't stop at

The coloration of some marine fish is absolutely breathtaking. Pictured is the Red Sea eightline flasher wrasse, *Paracheilinus octotaenia.*

the classroom. Why not get the whole family involved in setting up a home aquarium, using the same educational approach? Assign age-appropriate duties to each child (and, of course, your spouse if he or she is willing), and try to link each maintenance task to its counterpart in nature. For example, give your kindergartner the responsibility for turning the aquarium lights on at the same time each day, and explain how the lighting system takes the place of the sun. Let an older child empty the protein skimmer's waste-collection cup, and draw a correlation between protein skimming and the effects of wind and waves on a body of water.

Conservation and the Marine Aquarium

In many ways, marine aquarium hobbyists are in the best position to promote the conservation of the world's coral reefs. After all, the first step toward preserving an endangered habitat is to develop an understanding of—and a love for—the organisms that exist within it. While the role of the scientific community in marine conservation is undeniable, it is often the private hobbyist who first observes unique behaviors that may have significant survival value for a particular fish or invertebrate species.

Take breeding, for example. It was once a widely held belief that getting marine fish species to successfully reproduce in captivity was next to impossible. Even if a captive-spawning event did occur, it was commonly assumed that raising the young to adulthood was simply not a viable proposition. This was attributed to two important characteristics held in common by the young of many marine fish species. One is that they have a prolonged pelagic stage during

Fish Fact

Food Fit for Marine Fry

In the not-so-distant past, one of the major obstacles to successfully rearing the fry of marine fish was finding a live food source small enough to fit into their tiny mouths. After hatching, the young of most marine fish species spend several days to several weeks drifting in the water column among the plankton. There they can choose from a wide variety of tiny prey items and feast to their hearts' content. However, this is not the case within the confines of an aquarium, where foods must be provided by the aquarist.

Commercial and amateur breeders alike have since found that perfect first food for many species in the marine rotifer—a minuscule multi-cellular organism about one-third the size of a newly hatched brine shrimp, which is extremely resilient and easy to culture.

But there's an amusing twist. Aquarists who wish to culture marine rotifers must also develop a culture of a particular single-celled alga (so-called green water) in order to feed the rotifers—a food to feed to the food to feed the fry. Marine rotifers are available along with the algae they feed on in starter cultures through many aquarium supply companies.

which they drift freely with the plankton rafts in the open ocean—a stage that can be very difficult to recreate in a closed aquarium system. The other is that they demand a steady supply of minuscule plankton as their first food—a daunting challenge for all but the most dedicated aquarist. But in spite of the gloomy odds, some amateur hobbyists have risen to the challenge and developed techniques for successfully breeding and rearing certain marine species. This happens sometimes by accident and sometimes through repeated painstaking experiments on the aquarists' part. Also, a staggering amount has been learned about the behavior, care requirements, defense mechanisms, and reproductive strategies of corals and other sessile (immobile) invertebrates by observing them over long periods of time in the aquarium setting.

A Saltwater Stress Reliever

Another important role played by the marine aquarium is that of pressure-relief valve. When the tensions of career, family, and the world at large combine to create an overwhelming wave of anxiety, a few minutes in front of a well-maintained aquarium will help restore your tranquility and sense of well-being. Of course, the emphasis in the preceding statement must be placed on the "well-maintained" part. If you've chosen an assortment of peaceful, compatible species and carefully provided for their different nutritional and environmental needs, your marine tank will indeed be a source of pleasure as well as a buffer against life's little anxieties. On the other hand, an aquarium that is out of balance in some way—that is, the fish are in poor health or constantly at each other's throats, or the corals and other invertebrates are mysteriously dying off—will quickly become a source of stress rather than a sanctuary from it.

THE MARINE AQUARIUM AND THE NOVICE AQUARIST

If you've never kept an aquarium of any kind before, you may be saying to yourself, "Maybe I'd be better off if I started with a freshwater aquarium before attempting a marine tank. After all, they're supposed to be much easier, right?" Well, you probably could make a convincing argument that many freshwater setups are easier and more goof-proof than most marine aquariums. However, you could also make the argument that some freshwater setups are just as complicated as a basic marine setup, if not more so.

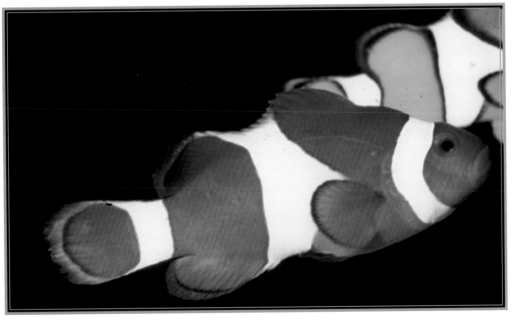

Unlocking breeding secrets of saltwater fish can take collecting pressure off wild stock. Pictured is the clownfish *Amphiprion ocellaris*, commonly available as captive-bred.

Go Ahead! Dive Right In!

As with the marine aquarium hobby, modern technology has made it much easier for the fish fanatic to get an up-close-and-personal view of life on the coral reef as a scuba diver. What was once an activity reserved only for the fittest adventurer or outdoor enthusiast can now be enjoyed by almost anyone, including your average couch potato.

While scuba diving has always been an equipment-intensive sport, it wasn't until the 1980s that the manufacturers of scuba equipment began to tailor their products to meet the specific needs and capabilities of the casual diver. Now scuba diving has become considerably safer as well as more democratic. With the advent of high-tech buoyancy compensators, low-cost and user-friendly dive computers, high-performance regulators, and ergonomically designed fins, men and women of all ages and fitness levels can experience the world beneath the waves.

If you've been wondering what it would be like to get in the swim so you can see some of those fascinating marine organisms firsthand, now may be the perfect time to give scuba diving a try. After all, why should the athletic types have all the fun?

Modern Equipment Favors Success for Beginners

The early days of marine fishkeeping were a logistical and technical nightmare for even the most seasoned aquarists, let alone for newcomers to the hobby. For one thing, there were no commercially manufactured artificial salt mixes to speak of. Hobbyists either had to create their own, using haphazard recipes, or make frequent trips to the shore to collect natural salt water, which likely contained a vast array of pollutants and pathogenic organisms. And that's if they happened to live in a coastal community; for many inland dwellers, setting up a marine aquarium was just about unthinkable. At the same time, very little filtration, lighting, and heating equipment was being manufactured specifically for the marine aquarium, and any products that were designed for use in salt water tended to be outrageously expensive. In addition, very little was known about the care requirements of most marine fish, so keeping them alive was a hit-or-miss prospect at best.

Today several factors favor success for the first-time aquarist, including the availability of high-quality synthetic salt mixes (used to mix up the tank's water; see Chapter 8), a vast array of modern life-support equipment manufactured specifically for the marine aquarium, and, of course, the wealth of information and literature about the marine aquarium hobby that has been accumulated through years of trial and error.

Starting With a Reef: Putting the Cart Before the Horse?

We've more or less established that there's no compelling reason for first-time aquarists to start out with a freshwater tank as a sort of apprenticeship toward salt water. But what about setting up a reef aquarium right off the starting block? Can a novice hobbyist succeed with a reef tank—arguably the pinnacle of achievement in the world of marine aquariums—without first gaining experience with a fish-only tank?

Before answering that question, it might be helpful to explain what the actual difference is between a FO tank and a reef tank. The FO tank is fairly self-explanatory. It's basically an aquarium housing either a community of compatible marine fish or a tank with a single specimen that is best kept alone because of its large size, aggressiveness, or predatory nature. Certain benign crustaceans and mollusks may also be included in the FO setup, although this may seem to be contradictory. The FO aquarium contains only motile animals (ones that move around). The reef aquarium, on the other hand, focuses mostly on various hard and soft

You will have a much greater chance of success with a reef tank if you set up a fish-only tank first to gain experience.

Aquarium Research in the Information Age

With the advent of the Internet, budding marine aquarists can have instant access to a staggering number of research sources with just a few simple keystrokes. Many aquarium-related websites provide very useful information for the beginner and expert alike, and some of the web forums are great places to go to get feedback and insights from fellow aquarists.

On the other hand, some of the information circulating out there in cyberspace is largely unsubstantiated or contradictory and must be taken with a grain of salt (excuse the pun). Remember, there are no Internet editors out there to separate the wheat from the chaff, so to speak, and there is no software that can filter out dubious or misleading claims.

So how can you be sure you're getting the straight story on the web? First, consider the source. Have you seen other written materials by the author in aquarium magazines, books, or newsletters? Secondly, look for agreement among supposed authorities. Does the information or claim jibe with what you've read on other webpages and in other sources? Finally, apply a little common sense. If the information strikes you as being out of line, it probably is.

corals and other sessile invertebrates (ones that stay put), many of which demand special high-intensity lighting for survival. If fish and motile invertebrates are included in a reef tank at all, they will be few in number and inoffensive toward the sessile invertebrates. Because fish waste and uneaten fish food tend to degrade water quality, some reef aquarists choose not to include fish at all.

Anyway, the answer to the question posed earlier is a very tentative yes. If you're willing to invest the time for research and you have the patience to take things one step at a time with no shortcuts, you may succeed in starting out with a reef tank. However, I would have to add the following caveat: reef aquariums demand absolutely impeccable water quality at all times, and fluctuating water conditions can spell disaster for your valued (and expensive) invertebrate specimens. Considering the fact that learning to control water parameters takes a little experimentation by most new aquarists, it's definitely a good idea to gradually build up to a reef as your experience and confidence grow. After all, you don't want your first foray into the world of the marine aquarium to end in frustration and disillusionment.

WHEN FRESHWATER AQUARISTS GO MARINE

Experienced freshwater aficionados who would like to have a go at keeping a saltwater aquarium will find that making the switch is relatively easy. In fact, most of the important principles that pertain to freshwater aquariums also apply to marine tanks. The process of cycling the aquarium is exactly the same. Proper stocking and feeding rates are just as important. The three basic forms of filtration—mechanical, chemical, and biological—still apply. Water changes are still the cornerstone of water quality maintenance. And, with a few notable exceptions, most of the necessary equipment can be carried over from fresh water to salt water as well.

Sticker Shock

One important distinction freshwater hobbyists will observe almost immediately is the relatively high cost of certain marine specimens when compared to the cost of the freshwater fish they're used to buying. I can still recall my first trip to a saltwater dealer to buy fish for my debut marine tank. I had been keeping freshwater tanks on and off for many years and was accustomed to forking over no more than a dollar or two for the various tetras, livebearers, and barbs that typically inhabited my tanks. Needless to say, when the total was rung up for my new marine specimens, my chin almost hit the floor. I also recall thinking at the time that the pressure was really on to keep those poor things alive. After all, it's one thing to lose a 2-dollar tetra, but losing a 100-dollar tang is another matter altogether.

So why the high cost? For one thing, most marine fish are still hand-collected in the wild. If you've ever attempted to keep pace with a frightened reef fish while diving or snorkeling, you can imagine how labor intensive and time consuming it is to actually net those little swifties. (Of course, some collectors use poisons and other destructive practices to make capture easier, but that's a topic for another chapter.) The high price tag can also be attributed to the high mortality rate during shipping and handling. With so many specimens coming all the way from the tropical Pacific and Indian oceans (often kept in the same bag and in the same dirty water throughout the long journey), it's not surprising that many perish in transit. Fortunately, hobbyist organizations have taken the initiative to create programs that have substantially lowered these losses and to educate both the trade and the hobby in the sustainable harvest of marine animals.

By contrast, many popular freshwater species are commercially captive-bred in large numbers, which helps to keep their cost down. Besides, some freshwater fish breed so readily in captivity and are so easy to rear (e.g., the popular livebearers: platies, guppies, and swordtails) that a small investment for a breeding pair (or even just a gravid female) yields more offspring than the average aquarist can handle. On a positive note for marine aquarists, captive breeding

Making the Switch From Fresh to Salt Water?

Items That Carry Over
- all-glass or acrylic tank
- wooden or acrylic stand
- newer submersible heater(s)
- floating or fixed thermometer(s)
- standard fluorescent lights
- canister, hang-on-tank, undergravel filters
- wet-dry filter system
- siphons, brushes, tongs, algae magnet, nets, etc.
- powerheads (must be safe for salt water)

Items to Purchase
- protein skimmer
- reverse-osmosis water purifier
- high-quality sea salt mix
- hydrometer
- crushed coral or aragonite
- substrate and rockwork
- ammonia, nitrite, nitrate, and pH test kits for saltwater tanks
- UV sterilizer (optional)
- high-intensity fluorescent or metal halide lighting (reef only)
- calcium and trace element supplements (reef only)
- All used equipment must be thoroughly cleaned and rinsed before transfer to new aquarium.

of certain saltwater fish is becoming more and more commercially viable, and the cost of captive-bred specimens is gradually coming down as technical advances are made in these programs.

Bread-and-Butter Beauties

In spite of their higher price tag, some of the more beautiful marine fish are surprisingly hardy and forgiving in captivity. The brilliantly colored clownfish *Amphiprion ocellaris* comes to mind, as do the stunningly beautiful angelfish *Centropyge bispinosus* and the wildly

Some of the things you need for a saltwater aquarium, including some fish, can be somewhat pricey. But if you're serious about the hobby, it's better to spend the extra money now for quality equipment and stock than have to shell out extra money later if there's a major problem.

patterned Picasso triggerfish, *Rhinecanthus aculeatus*. Not only are all of these fish strikingly attractive, but they are also amazingly resilient, which makes them ideal choices for the beginner. This stands in stark contrast to the freshwater side of the hobby, where it seems as if the more attractive a fish is, the more delicate and temperamental it is, and therefore the more difficult it is for a beginner to keep. Of course, as they say, beauty is in the eye of the beholder, and many freshwater enthusiasts would challenge my less-than-objective appraisal of the attractiveness of freshwater species.

THE INVESTMENT OF TIME AND ENERGY

One more factor that needs to be addressed before you start setting up your new marine aquarium is the amount of time and energy you'll need to invest to keep it running smoothly. In many ways, an aquarium is like a garden. There are certain regular gardening chores—weeding, pruning, fertilizing, and such—that simply cannot be avoided, no matter how hardy and resilient your plants are. If you leave the garden on autopilot, it will quickly deteriorate into an unsightly mess, and many of your prized specimens will perish. The same principle applies to the marine aquarium (or any other aquarium, for that matter). Failing to remove uneaten food, forgetting to replace water lost to evaporation, skipping water changes, or neglecting any other routine maintenance chore can have disastrous consequences on the condition of your tank and the health of the organisms within it—especially when it comes to a reef. This isn't to suggest that you can't squeeze a marine aquarium into an already chaotic schedule. After all, who among us has a light schedule nowadays? However, you may need to create daily and weekly maintenance checklists so you can physically mark off each task once it's been completed. Otherwise, like the garden on autopilot, your beautiful aquarium might start to deteriorate before your very eyes.

Getting the Whole Family Involved

Another way for a busy person to stay on top of aquarium maintenance is to delegate certain routine chores to other family members. Younger kids are generally very enthusiastic about being included in their parents' pastimes, so why not let them take over some of the

Captive-Bred Fish: Are They Worth the Price?

Considering the fact that captive-bred marine fish tend to cost substantially more than their wild-caught counterparts, you might ask yourself whether captive-bred specimens are really worth the higher price tag. Absolutely they are! Marine fish bred in captivity offer several advantages to aquarists, even though they may present no visible characteristics to distinguish them from wild-caught specimens.

Since captive-bred fish do not endure the stress of capture and prolonged transportation, their survival rate in the aquarium is much higher. They've also learned to accept such standard aquarium fare as flake, pellet, and freeze-dried foods, which means you're less likely to be faced with a fish that does not recognize anything you offer as food. In addition, buying captive-bred specimens takes some of the collecting pressure off the natural coral reefs, which are in decline in many parts of the world.

So what about the higher cost? Considering the ease with which captive-bred fish acclimate to aquarium conditions and the fact that they have a lower mortality rate than wild-caught specimens, you may actually end up paying less in the long run. After all, a less expensive fish that dies shortly after purchase is really no bargain at all.

Rhinecanthus aculeatus.

easier tasks like looking for sick or dead fish, wiping off salt creep, and turning lights on and off? Older kids and teens (if they aren't too ashamed to be related to a fish fanatic) can be tasked with testing specific gravity and water parameters, monitoring water temperature, and rinsing off prefilters. You might even be able to convince your spouse to assist by performing the occasional water change (although personal experience tells me that this is highly unlikely). You'll have to decide whether it's too risky to let anyone else feed your fish. Considering the impact overfeeding can have on your aquarium's water quality and the health of your fish, it might be better always to handle this duty yourself.

In any case, an informed decision to set up a marine aquarium can add a beautiful, entertaining, and educational piece of the natural world to your home. Even if there isn't a coast for thousands of miles in any direction, you can enjoy a coral reef microcosm on a daily basis.

Chapter 2

Basic Equipment

Okay, we've talked about the benefits of a marine aquarium, the special considerations for beginners and those making the switch from fresh water to salt water, and the amount of time and energy you'll need to invest in order to succeed with your new aquarium. Now it's time to start discussing some of the basic equipment you'll need.

What Lies Ahead

- tank considerations
- heaters and temperatures

FISH-ONLY OR REEF?

This basic equipment necessarily differs significantly depending on whether you want to start out with an FO tank or to plunge headlong into a reef tank. Again, I would be remiss if I didn't attempt to steer you in the direction of an FO tank for your first attempt at a saltwater aquarium. I want you to enjoy success in your new hobby right from the beginning so you'll be encouraged to stick with it for a lifetime, and I'm convinced that this is *much* more likely if you start with an FO tank.

An FO tank offers a much greater margin of error when it comes to water parameters and will help you to nurture the experience and skills necessary for ultimate success with the reef tank. Besides, you can always convert to a reef after you've gotten your feet wet with fish. On the other hand, if you're a quick study and feel confident in your ability to master reef-keeping techniques on the fly, I won't stand in your way. Just be sure to do some serious additional research utilizing books, magazines, the Internet, a trusted dealer, and other experienced reef aquarists before experimenting with costly invertebrates. For the rest of this book I will assume we are talking about an FO setup, but I will continue to add notes about reef setups as appropriate so that you will recognize places where a reef tank has different requirements and topics where you need to do more homework.

CHOOSING THE TANK AND STAND

The most fundamental piece of equipment you'll need for your new marine aquarium is the tank itself. It's critical to choose your tank wisely, since factors like the tank's construction, size, and shape will have an impact on the number and types of organisms you can house within it. Also, the style of tank you choose can either enhance or distort the clarity of the beautiful underwater vista that you're working so hard to cultivate.

All-Glass or Acrylic?

Tanks used for marine aquarium applications must not contain any materials that will either corrode or release toxic substances when they come into contact with salt water. This immediately rules out those old-fashioned metal-framed tanks, which will quickly rust with disastrous consequences. It's doubtful that you'd ever come across one of these near-antiques at your local aquarium store, but they still occasionally turn up in garage sales and at flea markets from time to time. If you should happen upon one of these garage-sale specials, or any other used tank of uncertain origin for that matter, do yourself a favor and pass it by—regardless of how irresistible the price may be. You have no way of knowing what was

The Leaky Tank: Use It or Lose It?

Just because a glass aquarium leaks doesn't necessarily mean that it's ready for the scrap heap. A more decisive issue is the actual location of the leak. If it occurs along one of the seams between two glass panes or at one of the corners where two side panels and the bottom come together, you may be able to seal the leak with a little silicone aquarium sealant (not to be confused with silicone caulk). However, if one of the glass panes is actually cracked, a repair should not be attempted, especially with larger tanks. In this case, the pressure exerted by the water could cause the pane to shatter, and the result could be a major flood instead of a minor slow leak.

Repairs using silicone aquarium sealant should be performed in a well-ventilated room or, better yet, outdoors where you won't be affected by the powerful fumes. After sealing the leak, give the silicone ample time to cure, according to the manufacturer's recommendations. Follow the manufacturer's directions about the removal of any excess sealant, and rinse the tank repeatedly with fresh water to eliminate any residue.

Even if your leaky tank has to be condemned for aquarium use, you might still find some good uses for it. For example, you could throw in a little potting soil and convert it into a terrarium filled with your favorite houseplants. Or you could cover it with mesh screening and use it as a habitat for a terrestrial pet.

previously kept in the tank or whether it contains some sort of harmful residue that may adversely affect the health of your fish or invertebrates. Of course, it's also difficult to rule out the possibility of leaks without filling the tank with water and observing it for several hours, which is highly impractical in a garage sale or flea market setting.

Given these restrictions, there are two types of tank that are ideally suited for the marine aquarium in terms of construction: all-glass and acrylic, both of which have distinct advantages and disadvantages to consider. Glass tanks are available for sale in a wider range of stock sizes (anywhere from 2.5 to over 200 gallons [10 to 800 liters]) and designs, and they are less expensive than acrylic. Glass is also more (but not entirely) scratch resistant. On the downside, glass tanks weigh significantly more when empty, and they are much more likely to shatter or spring leaks. Given their widespread availability and manageable price tag, however, glass tanks make an excellent choice for beginners.

A Tank for Sessile Invertebrates

Sessile invertebrates in the reef aquarium also do better when kept in a low rectangular tank. This is because the photosynthetic invertebrates that are commonly kept in these setups rely on high-intensity lighting of a particular spectrum in order to survive and thrive. In a tall tank the light cannot penetrate all the way to the bottom and will benefit only those organisms positioned at the highest point in the tank. To ensure that all of the light-hungry invertebrates get the exposure they need, it's a good idea to keep them in a tank no taller than 18 inches (46 cm).

Acrylic tanks offer superior shatter resistance, better thermal insulation, and, because they allow more light to pass through, better clarity with less image distortion. In addition, acrylic is colorless, while glass is actually green; the thicker the glass, the greater the green tint. The only real drawback to acrylic tanks, apart from the higher price tag, is the fact that they can be scratched very easily during handling or routine maintenance. Even the seemingly innocuous act of scraping algae off the walls of an acrylic tank can leave disfiguring scratches. It is possible to buff out any scratches from acrylic, but of course that requires dismantling the setup. Low-iron, super-clear glass can be used to produce large aquaria with a clarity comparable to that of acrylic tanks.

How Big Is Too Big?

The old adage about biting off more than you can chew can be misleading when it comes to the size of the tank you should buy for your first marine aquarium. In fact, "the bigger, the better" could be a more appropriate rule to live by. Degradation of water quality resulting from decomposing fish waste, overfeeding, overstocking, and the normal metabolic processes of the organisms in the tank is less dramatic in a larger volume of water. This is simply because there is more water to dilute any pollutants or toxic byproducts. Fluctuations in temperature, salinity, and other water parameters are also less pronounced in a bigger tank. Since water quality problems take longer to develop in a big tank, you'll have a greater opportunity to make any necessary adjustments or corrections to counteract them before they reach dangerous proportions.

On the other hand, in a small tank (for our purposes, 30 gallons/115 liters or less) changes for the worse can occur very quickly, especially when the temptation to stock too many fish wins out over common sense. Unfortunately, this is a very common occurrence among both beginners and experienced aquarists alike. For animals accustomed to life on the coral reef, arguably one of the most stable environments on earth, such rapid changes in water quality are a major source of stress, which can lead to poor health and, ultimately, death.

So how big is big enough? Of course, that depends to a large extent on how much space you have available in your home and how much weight your floors can support, but many experienced marine aquarists recommend starting with at least a 55-gallon (200-liter) tank. Others would argue for a minimum of 75 gallons (290 liters). Personally, I found 55 gallons to be just about right for my first marine aquarium. Does that mean you can't have a beautiful marine aquarium smaller than 55 gallons? Not at all! You'll just have to monitor your water parameters more frequently and perform those routine water changes with even greater diligence.

The Shape of Success

When shopping for your new tank, assuming you don't have one already, you'll have many different tank designs to choose from. Hexagonal, octagonal, triangular, and other nonrectangular tanks are available as alternatives to the standard rectangular kind. While these tanks are certainly attractive from an interior design standpoint, they aren't necessarily ideal for use as marine aquariums.

There is more of a chance for a small saltwater tank to crash than a large-sized tank. For your first marine aquarium, buy as large a tank as you can afford and accommodate.

Glass Versus Acrylic: Which Tank Should You Choose?

Glass

Advantages
- available in more stock sizes and designs
- less costly
- more scratch-resistant

Disadvantages
- heavier (empty)
- less shatter- and leak-proof

Acrylic

Advantages
- very shatter-resistant
- better thermal insulation
- superior clarity of image

Disadvantages
- more expensive
- scratches very easily

For one thing, they tend to be much taller than they are wide. This is a problem for the fish-only aquarium because it restricts the amount of space the fish can use for swimming and establishing territories. Remember, most fish species tend to occupy a particular section of the water column for most of their lives, depending on how their bodies are adapted for feeding. Some are bottom-dwellers, some occupy the mid-water region, and some remain near the surface. Rarely do they move among all three. It stands to reason, then, that a relatively low rectangular tank with lots of horizontal swimming space would be better for fish.

Another drawback to taller and irregularly shaped tanks is that they have a poor water-volume-to-surface-area ratio. In other words, the interface between the aquarium's water surface and the ambient air is much smaller than it is with a rectangular tank of the same volume. This reduces gas exchange between the water and air, which makes it harder to achieve proper oxygenation and to vent noxious gases from the system.

Again, this is not to suggest that you can't have a perfectly satisfactory marine aquarium in a hexagonal or octagonal tank. Just be aware that those tanks have certain design limitations that may affect the number and types of organisms you can safely keep together. Since they are constructed from multiple glass panes positioned at various angles to one another, another consideration is that the aquatic display may be distorted significantly depending on where you're standing in the room—a flaw that may not be readily apparent at the time of purchase.

The Stand: Buy It or Build It?

Once it's up and running, your new aquarium will contain many gallons of water, heavy rockwork and decorations, valued fish and invertebrates, lots of costly equipment, and all of your hopes and dreams of success in the hobby. In other words, it would be safe to say that there's an awful lot riding on the structural integrity of the stand you choose to support your new marine aquarium. Considering the critical (albeit unglamorous) role the aquarium stand

Copper Cures

Another reason to forgo a used tank is the problem of copper residues. Copper compounds are common in aquarium medications, but even tiny concentrations of copper are deadly to invertebrates. Lethal amounts can survive on tank glass, on aquarium ornaments, and in substrates, no matter how much they are rinsed. While you will probably not be starting with a reef tank full of sessile invertebrates, you might want someday to use the aquarium as a reef setup, and even in FO setups you may want a crab or a shrimp. Unless you are getting a used tank from the original owner who can assure you that no copper was ever used, a second-hand aquarium is a risky purchase.

plays, you should select it with the same amount of care you use when selecting the tank.

As a general rule, it's best to use a commercially manufactured stand designed specifically to support the weight of an operating aquarium. You could choose from the many wooden

Decide ahead of time what you want to keep in your tank. That way you will know what tank size is best for the fish or invertebrates you want. Pictured is a crab, *Neopetrolisthes* sp.

You should purchase a tank that comes with its own stand made by the same manufacturer. This should guarantee that the stand will be able to handle the tank's full weight once fully stocked.

cabinet-style stands, which blend in well with the interior design of many traditional homes. If you prefer a sleek, contemporary look, you could always go with one of the colored acrylic stands. In some cases, a suitable stand can be purchased as part of a package deal that includes the tank, the stand, and a matching lighted hood. Sometimes you're almost forced into taking a matching stand with the tank, because the tank might not be guaranteed if you don't buy the stand as well.

As far as building a stand goes, that is something best left to a professional. Even an experienced carpenter or cabinetmaker will not be used to dealing with the extreme weight-capacity requirements of an aquarium stand. In the same way, regular furniture such as tables, desks, and cabinets will not withstand the stress of supporting an aquarium setup.

Wrought iron and other metal stands are not appropriate for the marine aquarium. Just like metal-framed aquariums, metal stands will quickly rust when they come into contact with salt water. Even those painted with a protective textured coating are vulnerable to rust in areas where the coating has been accidentally scraped off. I can tell you from experience that once rust gets a foothold on a metal aquarium stand there's no practical way to sand it down and repaint it without getting dust and metal filings in your aquarium's water. (Okay, I'll admit that it sounds silly now, but it sure seemed like a good idea when it first popped into my head!) In addition, metal stands tend to concentrate all of the aquarium's considerable weight onto four small points on the floor, which may cause structural damage, depending on your floor's construction.

Location, Location, Location

When choosing a site in your home to place your new aquarium, there are several important factors to consider. These include the weight-bearing capacity of the floor, electrical access, the proximity of windows and heat sources, and the amount of traffic that usually passes through the room. You'll also want to take the not-so-remote possibility of water damage into account when picking a location. With any aquarium, occasional spills and drips are almost inevitable, which may rule out rooms with finished hardwood floors, fine rugs, or costly carpeting.

A WEIGHTY ISSUE

The first question you'll need to ask yourself about a possible location is whether the floor can support the weight of a functioning aquarium. Add to the weight of the water the combined weights of the substrate, the rockwork, the filtration equipment, the sump (if one is used), the stand, and the tank, and you've got a substantial amount of weight being exerted over a relatively small area of floor. As a general rule, you can calculate 10 pounds of weight per gallon (1.3 kg per liter) of tank capacity to arrive at the approximate total weight of an aquarium. Thus for a 55-gallon (200-liter) aquarium you can safely assume that your floor must be capable of withstanding a minimum constant weight of 550 pounds (260 kg)—and it must do so for (hopefully) many years.

If your flooring is of concrete or sturdy enough wooden construction, you shouldn't have any problems stemming from the weight of the aquarium. With any wooden floor, however, you should try to distribute the weight of the tank over as many joists as possible for maximum support. If you aren't sure about your floor's load-bearing capacity, especially if you're planning to set up a very large aquarium (or if you're considering putting the aquarium on the second floor), be sure to consult with a building contractor or structural engineer before getting under way.

HAVE YOU GOT THE POWER?

Even if you intend to set up a basic marine aquarium with very few bells and whistles, you'll still need convenient access to a reliable source of electrical power. At the very least you'll need to power your lights, heater, and filtration devices, and you'll want to have enough capacity left over so you can expand your equipment arsenal as needed. This last point is especially important if you plan eventually to convert from an FO tank to a reef.

I've found that two fully operational 110-volt outlets in close proximity to the aquarium usually are adequate for a basic setup. You can always add a power strip with a built-in surge protector if more outlets are desired. Avoid placing important life-support components on the

Do not underestimate the weight of your fully stocked tank. Be certain that your floors can take the weight.

same circuit with other energy-draining household appliances to avoid overloading the circuit. You don't want to have to make repeated trips to the breaker or fuse box because the circuit keeps blowing. Not only is this inconvenient for you, but it can also upset the delicate balance of your aquarium's water parameters.

It's important to remember that safety is a major issue any time electrical components are used around water. A ground fault circuit interrupter (GF[C]I), which will automatically disrupt the flow of current to a device in the event of a defect, should be used in conjunction with all powered aquarium equipment to reduce the risk of electrocution. In addition, it's a good idea to tie a small loop in the middle of your equipment power cords to prevent water and salt buildup (a.k.a. salt creep) from gradually traveling down a cord into an outlet and causing a short. However, this step is unnecessary if the outlets are positioned higher than the aquarium's water surface. In that case, the water and salt would have to fight against gravity to reach the outlet. I find it helpful to wipe off each power cord with a slightly damp cloth each time I perform a routine water change to prevent salt and other gunk from building up in the first place.

Try to avoid placing your aquarium in a room with lots of windows that let natural sunlight stream in. If you can manage it, avoid direct sunlight altogether. While you may be tempted to take advantage of natural light to illuminate your new tank for free, especially if your aquarium features photosynthetic invertebrates, this is not a good idea. For one thing, natural sunlight is unreliable and uncontrollable when compared to artificial lighting. It can also fuel unsightly algal blooms and cause your water temperature to fluctuate wildly out of control.

The relative position of heating vents, registers, and space heaters can also influence where you place your aquarium. If the tank is situated too close to any of those heat sources, you may have a difficult time regulating water temperature during the winter months. Similarly, a location too near an air conditioner or vent can also cause temperature swings in your aquarium. Of course, overheating during the summer can be a real problem, too, and you may need to consider air conditioning or a special aquarium chiller to keep your tank from becoming a stew pot.

Finally, try to select a cozy, relaxing location where there will not be a constant flow of foot traffic. Excessive activity in the area surrounding the aquarium can be very stressful for the fish within it, and stressed fish are more prone to disease and less likely to exhibit their natural behaviors. It's important that the area be comfortable for you the aquarist because, hopefully, you'll be spending lots of time in front of the aquarium, observing the fascinating interactions of the organisms and admiring the fruits of your labor.

THE HEAT IS ON!

As I've already mentioned (and likely will again before this book is finished), water parameters on the coral reef are remarkably stable. This applies to not only the chemical composition, salinity, and pH, but also the temperature of the water. I would recommend a water temperature in the range of 75° to 80°F (24° to 27°C). What the aquarist should strive for is to establish a particular temperature within that range that can be fairly consistently maintained, factoring in external influences like sun exposure, seasonal changes in air temperature, and the proximity of home heating and cooling appliances.

Avoid the Ups and Downs

The exact value of the water temperature is not as critical as the stability of the temperature. In fact, it would be better to maintain a consistent temperature of 82°F (28°C), which is actually outside the ideal range, than to bounce from 75°F (24°C) on one day to 78°F (26°C) the next day and so on. Some seasonal temperature fluctuation is to be expected,

This Fish Is Quick on the Trigger

The triggerfish (family Balistidae) are so named because of the locking spine located on their first dorsal fin. When frightened or pursued by a predator, a triggerfish can wedge its laterally compressed body into a crevice in the reef and erect this dorsal spine to lock itself in place. Once this spine is engaged, it becomes nearly impossible for the predator to extract the triggerfish from its refuge. This particular adaptation also makes it extremely difficult to net a triggerfish from an aquarium without first removing much of the rockwork.

however, and most marine organisms will readily adapt to these changes, provided they occur gradually and are not too pronounced.

It's important to note that prolonged temperatures in excess of 84°F (29°C) can be very stressful to fish and even more so to invertebrates in the reef aquarium, and appropriate steps should be taken to prevent this from occurring. If such a temperature spike is likely as a result of seasonal influences in your geographic region and you don't have an air conditioner to cool the ambient air, you may need to invest in a chiller to help keep the water temperature within the ideal range.

Heating Devices

Fortunately for budget-conscious aquarists, heating a marine aquarium is a fairly simple, low-cost proposition. Modern fully submersible heaters combine a thermostat and heating element in a very compact tube that can be attached via suction cups (usually included) to one of the glass walls of the aquarium—preferably adjacent to the return flow of either the mechanical or wet/dry filter for optimum heat dispersion. Glass heaters are available, but they can be problematic and potentially dangerous. Some better heaters today are made of titanium or are encased in a plastic sheath. Those who prefer to keep all gadgets out of sight for a more natural-looking aquarium can conceal a submersible heater within the rockwork in the main aquarium, with only the cord still visible, or in the sump beneath the aquarium (assuming a wet/dry system is being used).

Some heater models are designed to be clamped to the top edge of the aquarium so that the glass tube extends into the water while the temperature adjustment dial remains above the surface. These heaters operate on the same principle as the submersible kind, but they have one main drawback: because they cannot be fully submerged, they're more difficult to conceal than the submersible style. Also, they tend to be considerably more bulky, which further detracts from the aesthetics of the aquarium. Tank-mounted heaters do have advantages, however. The adjustment dial always stays high and dry, so it's easily accessible, and you don't have the problem of algae growing over and obscuring the calibrated temperature settings.

Whichever style of heater you choose, make sure it is constructed of sturdy glass so it can't be easily broken by shifting rockwork or the actions of the organisms in the tank. Also, look for a model that has easy-to-read temperature settings and can be easily adjusted while it is still positioned in the aquarium. You should also give careful thought to ease of access for adjustment and cleaning when deciding where to place the heater.

How Do Heaters Rate?

Aquarium heaters are rated by wattage. The higher the wattage of a given heater, the more rapidly it will raise the temperature of the aquarium water, and the larger the volume of water it can maintain at the proper temperature. How much heating capacity will you need for your aquarium? As a general rule, you'll want to provide approximately 5 watts of heating capacity per gallon of water for a smaller aquarium and approximately 3 watts per gallon for a larger aquarium. (Remember, temperature is more stable in a larger volume of water.) For a 30-gallon (115-liter) tank, you'd need a heater rated at 150 watts, while a 250-watt heater would be sufficient for a 75-gallon (290-liter) tank. According to some experts, it's better to use two

Avoid Gadget Overload

The marine aquarium hobby is rife with high-tech equipment and gadgets, many of which you can live without when you're just getting started—especially if you decide to go with a fish-only aquarium. For example, as you start shopping for equipment you'll probably hear about devices like ozone generators, ultraviolet sterilizers, calcium reactors, and ion exchangers. And that's just a small sampling! While each of these devices can play an important role in your overall water quality and the health of the specimens in your aquarium, they simply aren't necessary for a basic system. Besides, all of these bells and whistles can really take a bite out of your aquarium budget. You'll be much happier in the long run if you start out with just the basic equipment and add devices as your confidence grows and your budget allows.

Fish Fact

Uncouth Crustaceans

To the casual observer, barnacles look and behave more like feather duster worms than crustaceans, having numerous feathery appendages that withdraw with lightning speed into a protective calcareous shell at the first sign of danger. But make no mistake! Barnacles are crustaceans, related to crabs, lobsters, and shrimp. Those feathery appendages are actually their feet, which they use to capture drifting particles of food. Eating with their feet? Such manners!

Though barnacles are fascinating to observe in nature (unless you're a boat owner!), they aren't the best choice for the closed system of the aquarium. Their demand for large quantities of minuscule foods can be difficult for the average aquarist to satisfy, and it places a very heavy burden on the filtration system. That being said, some barnacle species have been known to make their way into the aquarium attached to corals or as stowaways on live rock. If they survive in your tank, they obviously find conditions satisfactory.

lower-wattage heaters, with each providing half of the necessary heating capacity, than one higher-wattage heater. That way you won't lose all of your heating capacity in the event that one of the units fails.

Beware the Hand-Me-Down Heater!

Considering the relatively low price of quality submersible aquarium heaters these days, you're better off purchasing a brand-new unit than using some antiquated model that has been moldering away in your basement or attic for years or one that was handed down from a well-intentioned friend who no longer has a need for it. The trouble with many older heaters is that when they break down they tend to fail in the "on" position. If this happens and you don't catch the problem soon enough, your aquarium's water temperature will rise precipitously, and you may end up cooking all of your valued specimens.

Modern heaters, on the other hand, are designed to fail in the "off" position, resulting in a gradual cool-down to room temperature. Since the average home is heated to somewhere between 70° and 72°F (21° and 22°C) during the winter months, all but the most delicate organisms will most likely survive until you have a chance to replace the faulty heater.

Monitoring Temperature

Daily monitoring of your aquarium's water temperature, using either a floating or fixed aquarium thermometer, will allow you to detect any trend away from the desired stable setting that you are trying to maintain and to catch any problems with the heater in time. Floating thermometers, as the name implies, are designed to be placed directly into the aquarium, where they tend to bob along at the mercy of the water current. The only drawback to the floating style is that they often drift into hard-to-reach places, which makes monitoring difficult. I find it convenient to corral my floating thermometer within the overflow box of my wet/dry biofilter. That way I always know right where to look for it when I'm in a hurry.

Fixed thermometers come in several styles, many of which attach to the interior glass of the aquarium by means of suction cups. (In fact, many floating models come with suction cups so they can be fixed to the glass as well.) These are handy because they can be positioned so the readout is always facing you instead of the interior of the tank. Also, you can place them at any depth in the aquarium rather than just at the surface—an important detail considering the fact that the temperature at the surface may not coincide with the temperature deeper in the tank, especially if

A constant temperature is best for your saltwater tank. Fluctuation can lead to serious illnesses or worse.

high-intensity lighting is used. In that case, it's a good idea to use two thermometers, one at the surface of the aquarium and one at the bottom, so you can easily determine whether the heated water is circulating properly or not.

Another style of fixed thermometer is the liquid-crystal variety, which is designed to adhere directly to the exterior glass of the aquarium like a sticker. These thermometers are very convenient in the sense that they are easy to read and readily accessible—attributes that have not gone unnoticed by many pragmatic aquarium dealers. One could argue that they aren't quite as accurate when it comes to reflecting the exact temperature as the different models that are designed to be placed inside the aquarium. However, they do reliably indicate whether

Fish Fact

What is Coral Bleaching?

There's no question that the phenomenon known as coral bleaching is occurring with increasing regularity on tropical reefs throughout the world. But even among the experts, there is major disagreement over the actual cause. Most fingers point to prolonged periods of excessively high water temperature as being the root of the coral bleaching problem. Other possible contributing factors include sedimentation, solar irradiation, exposure to air during extremely low tides, and disease.

You'd never guess it by looking at the beautifully colored invertebrates on a coral reef, but the tissues of corals are actually translucent. Their bright colors come from the symbiotic algae—called zooxanthellae—that reside within their tissues and provide the corals with nutrients through the process of photosynthesis. When corals are stressed, due to one or more of the previously mentioned factors, the concentration of zooxanthellae in their tissues may decrease. At the same time, the concentration of photosynthetic pigments within the algae may decrease. The calcareous skeleton of the coral then becomes visible through the translucent tissue—hence the bleached appearance.

However, not all bleaching events are fatal to the corals involved. If the stressor is eliminated or reduced in relatively short order, the zooxanthellae can rebound within a few weeks. Some experts even suggest that bleaching can promote the survival of corals by providing them an opportunity to replace weaker strains of zooxanthellae with more stress-resistant strains.

Temperature-Specific Species

It's important to know what temperature range is best for your fish and invertebrates, and that the specimens you're buying are actually what the dealer says they are. While most commonly available species do well with a temperature in the upper 70s, some actually require cool to coldwater systems. Some examples include the beautiful Catalina goby, *Lythrypnus dalli*, and the red rock shrimp, *Lysmata californica*, which may be sold under the name "peppermint shrimp" but doesn't eat *Aiptasia* anemones the way the true peppermint shrimp, *Lysmata wurdemanni*, does. The goby and the red rock shrimp will not survive for long in a tropical aquarium and require a dedicated setup with expensive chilling equipment. It is best to avoid them entirely.

the temperature remains stable or not, which, as I've mentioned, is more critical than the precise value.

That's it for the basics of tank, stand, and temperature control. Since lighting for marine tanks can be a bit confusing, we'll handle that in the next chapter, and since maintaining stable water quality is so important, after the chapter about lighting the following couple of chapters will go over what you need to know to succeed with your first saltwater aquarium.

Chapter 3

Let There Be Light!

Now we're moving into an area—the proper way to light the aquarium—that for many newcomers to the marine aquarium hobby is quite perplexing. I should note that the confusion is not limited to beginners; many a seasoned saltwater aquarist has shaken his or her head in utter bewilderment at the vast array of lighting options available today. With all those initials, from NO to VHO to PC to MH, and all the combinations thereof, it's no wonder that so many people are left in a state of befuddlement!

Fortunately, you probably don't have to worry at all about lighting, since it is only a significant issue for reef tanks. The lighting needed for a reef tank—not to mention the subsequent impact your lighting system will have on your pocketbook—depends on what type of invertebrates you will be keeping. By diligently researching the specific lighting needs of the marine organisms that you plan to keep (and soliciting the expert advice of a trusted dealer) you should be able to make educated, well-considered decisions when you're ready to invest in lamps and fixtures for your aquarium.

LIGHTING THE FISH-ONLY AQUARIUM

Fish and motile invertebrates require no special lighting. The only real requirement when illuminating these organisms is to provide sufficient light to display them to their greatest aesthetic advantage. In fact, if given overly intense light, some of the more shy and retiring organisms collected from deeper waters will tend to feel exposed and vulnerable, and they may be prompted to disappear from view whenever the lights come on—the exact opposite of the desired result. On the other hand, you wouldn't want to keep the aquarium so dark that the fish assume night has fallen and so remain perpetually hidden in the rockwork in an effort to evade predation.

You only really need specialized lighting in your tank if you are keeping sessile invertebrates (corals).

For the 55-gallon (200-liter) FO aquarium we've been using as our basic model, a standard reflective aquarium hood outfitted with a pair of 40-watt normal output (NO) fluorescent lamps is more than adequate. You can even get away with suspending an inexpensive fluorescent utility hood by chains above the tank, provided the top of the aquarium is securely covered with a glass sheet to prevent salt water from splashing onto the lamps.

In the previous chapter, I recommended that you avoid using certain obsolete equipment (i.e., metal-framed tanks and antiquated heaters) for your new marine aquarium. The same suggestion should also apply to those old-fashioned lighted hoods containing incandescent

Basic Lighting

Lighting in a FO setup is really only to enhance your viewing experience. You do not require any of the powerful, expensive lights you may hear about to view your fish or motile invertebrates. If you decide to move on to a reef tank, that is when you will need to buy special lighting.

bulbs that long ago fell into disfavor among most aquarists. Incandescent bulbs have two additional drawbacks apart from being less efficient than fluorescent tubes in terms of electric consumption to produce the same light output and therefore most costly to run. For one thing, most of the energy they produce is in the form of heat rather than light, which means the water temperature will tend to increase when the lights are turned on and decrease when they are turned off. Secondly, incandescent bulbs radiate heavily from the yellow-orange portion of the spectrum. Light of this color may create a warm and cozy atmosphere in your living room, but it won't do much to showcase the natural beauty of your fish.

Sunrise, Sunset

Now we are faced with another question: what is the optimum photoperiod for the FO aquarium? In other words, how long should the aquarium lights be left on each day in order for your valued marine organisms to survive and thrive?

For the average aquarium, a photoperiod of six to eight hours of light each day is ample. Remember, apart from establishing a predictable cycle of day and night and giving the fish a little light to feed by, the primary role of the lighting system in an FO aquarium is to enhance the aquarist's viewing pleasure. Restricting the photoperiod to between six and eight hours not only helps to keep the growth of undesirable algae in the tank to a minimum but also saves significantly on your energy costs.

Of course, if you want to maximize your enjoyment of the aquarium, it's a good idea to arrange to have the lights turned on—preferably with a little help from an electric timer—when you're most likely to be around. For example, if you usually work from 9 am to 5 pm, you might want to time your lights so they turn on around 3 pm and turn off at 11 pm. If you work nights, you could schedule them to be on from late morning until early evening. The fish have no preference as to which particular six- to eight-hour period you choose as long as it's regular, so it's entirely at your discretion.

There is one scenario where it would definitely be beneficial to leave the lights on for a longer period of time in an FO system—if you decide to keep tangs or other herbivorous fish in the aquarium. In this case you might want to allow the algae to grow in abundance on the glass (with the exception of the front pane) and rockwork of the aquarium, so the fish can continually graze on the algae throughout the day as they do in nature. You'll just have to be careful not to overfeed these fish so they don't choose to completely ignore the algae growing in the aquarium in favor of the tasty tidbits you offer.

That's It!

For an FO system, that's all you need to know, and you can go on to the next chapter. If you are contemplating a reef tank, or if you have come back to this book after enjoying an FO tank and are now ready to consider starting a reef, then the rest of this chapter will introduce the basics of lighting for reef tanks.

LIGHTING THE REEF

Light plays a much more complex and fascinating role in the reef tank than it does in the FO aquarium. In fact, if denied lighting of the proper spectrum and intensity level, many (but not all) of the organisms commonly kept in these aquariums simply could not survive. This dependence on light strikes many hobbyists as somewhat odd. After all, everybody knows that plants need light in order to produce food through the process of photosynthesis, but what does light have to do with the survival of certain sessile invertebrates, which, as we all agree, are animals? As a matter of fact, along with crystal-clear water conditions, light has almost everything to do with their survival!

Share and Share Alike

Many of the soft corals, hard corals, and tridacnid clams (the so-called giant clams) that are commonly kept in reef aquariums are considered to be photosynthetic invertebrates or light-hungry invertebrates. Strictly speaking, however, both terms are misleading. It's not the invertebrates themselves that need the light, but rather the symbiotic algae—known as zooxanthellae—that reside within their tissues, so the invertebrates rely on the light indirectly.

Zooxanthellae are specialized flagellates (unicellular organisms that move by means of a whip-like extension) that utilize the waste products released by invertebrates (carbon dioxide and ammonia) and energy from the sun to produce sugars and other carbohydrates through the process of photosynthesis. After utilizing some of these nutrients for their own survival, the algae then share the leftovers with their invertebrate hosts. Since the water around a coral reef tends to be very low in dissolved nutrients (as it should be in a reef aquarium as well), both organisms benefit significantly from this relationship. As long as adequate lighting is provided in the aquarium, supplemental feeding of photosynthetic invertebrates is considered by many to be unnecessary, the feeling being that the animals involved get all the nutrients they need from the zooxanthellae residing in their tissues. However, some—and there is disagreement about how many and which ones—zooxanthellae-equipped inverts need additional feedings as well. While their symbiotes produce plenty of carbohydrates, some if not all invertebrates need to feed on other animals (typically plankton) in order to get all the protein they need.

Artificial Sunlight

Photosynthetic invertebrates living on tropical coral reefs can rely on natural sunlight to provide lighting of the correct intensity level, spectrum, and duration. Unfortunately, since there's no practical and reliable way to focus natural sunlight on a reef aquarium, it's up to the aquarist to provide an artificial lighting system that replicates the intensity and spectral characteristics of the midday tropical sun as closely as possible.

So how can we go about defining the qualities of tropical sunlight, and how do these qualities relate to the aquarium lighting equipment that is available on the market today?

If you've ever spent too much time sunning yourself on a tropical beach without first

How much light some corals need to survive depends. Some are fine with moderate lighting, like this *Xenia* sp., while others require bright lights.

A well-maintained reef tank. Lighting is crucial in a setup like this.

applying a liberal dose of sunscreen, you've probably already gotten a good sense of just how intense the tropical sun can be—especially if you hail from a more temperate geographic region. But how do we determine the precise level of light intensity—in lumens or whatever unit of measurement lighting specialists use—that is necessary for photosynthetic invertebrates to thrive? The truth of the matter is, we don't have to. To keep things as simple as possible, which is the stated objective of this book, we'll limit our discussion of light intensity to the number of watts produced by a given light source.

One commonly cited rule is to provide a minimum of 3 to 5 watts of lighting per gallon (about 1 watt per liter) of aquarium water. This is a rudimentary rule at best because photosynthetic invertebrates differ markedly in their lighting demands. For example, this minimum amount of light would likely suffice for most soft corals or large-polyp stony corals, but it would be inadequate for most small-polyp stony corals. Still, the rule gives us a place to start. So, following this rule, we'll need between 165 and 275 watts for our 55-gallon tank. Right away, we know that the NO lamps recommended for FO aquariums would be inadequate for this setup, as four such tubes would provide a total of only 160 watts, and adding more tubes than this is highly impractical. However, there are several high-intensity lighting systems designed specifically for use on reef aquariums, which we will examine in short order.

As previously mentioned, the color spectrum of natural sunlight also plays an important role in maintaining the health of corals and other photosynthetic invertebrates. It stands to reason, then, that you'll want to provide light of similar, or nearly identical, spectral composition for your reef. In order to produce this with artificial lighting, you'll need to choose lamps with a minimum kelvin (a temperature scale) rating of 5,500 kelvins (5,500 K), which is nearly identical to the rating of the midday tropical sun on a cloudless day.

Kelvin temperature is not, as it would appear on its face, a measurement of the heat put out by a given light source, but rather an indication of the spectral output (or wavelength) of the light it produces. At one end of the spectrum you have red (long wavelength), followed by orange, yellow, green, blue, indigo, and violet (short wavelength). Light sources with a higher kelvin rating emit more of the deeper-penetrating blue-violet portion of the spectrum, which is desirable for most photosynthetic invertebrates, while those with lower ratings tend more toward the red-yellow portion. Lamps that radiate mostly red and yellow are best avoided, since these colors are the first to be filtered out by sea water and so will not support photosynthetic activity. This is also why reef aquarists often use lamps with very high kelvin ratings—10,000 K or more—because the intensity of the best lights is so much less than that of natural sunlight. The bluer light means more light energy actually reaches the organisms underwater.

Sunlight and Salt Water

The "white" light emitted by the sun and the artificial light sources we use over our aquariums is not really white at all. Rather, it consists of a spectrum of different colors, each of which corresponds to a particular electromagnetic wavelength and frequency. The longer the wavelength of the color, the shorter the frequency, and vice versa. Colors closer to the red end of the spectrum have longer wavelengths and lower frequencies, while colors closer to the blue end of the spectrum have shorter wavelengths and higher frequencies.

So what does any of this have to do with your marine aquarium? As light penetrates into salt water, the different wavelengths are filtered out or absorbed, at different depths. Red, which has the lowest frequency and longest wavelength, is the first to be absorbed, followed by orange, yellow, green, and blue. Blue penetrates the deepest. This information doesn't have much significance for the FO aquarium, but if you plan to set up a reef, understanding this characteristic of light will help you to choose lamps with the most appropriate spectral characteristics for photosynthetic invertebrates.

Strong lighting can produce a lot of heat. On this tank, a canopy has been built with a fan to cool the two powerful fluorescent tubes.

There are two forms of artificial lighting that reef aquarists commonly utilize to provide the correct intensity level and color spectrum for their light-hungry invertebrates—fluorescent fixtures and metal halide lamps. Both have distinct advantages and disadvantages, depending on the size of the tank they're used on as well as other factors. In general, fluorescent tubes are more convenient, less costly to purchase and operate, and produce considerably less heat while running. On the downside, they don't penetrate water very deeply and thus are used primarily on shallower tanks (20 inches/50 cm high or less). This drawback can be overcome, somewhat, by increasing the total wattage of the fixture.

Metal halides are the lamps of choice for deeper tanks, since they produce a very intense light that penetrates much deeper into water than fluorescent lighting can, but they too have their drawbacks. For one thing, metal halides run exceptionally hot, which necessitates the use of a cooling fan to maintain a stable water temperature. In addition, they can be significantly more expensive to purchase and operate than fluorescents. Which type of lighting is best for your aquarium? Let's take a closer look at both types before we attempt to answer that question.

FLUORESCENT OPTIONS

Fluorescent fixtures generate the most confusion among aquarists looking to light a reef because they are available in such a wide range of sizes, spectra, and power outputs. (Here is where we get into all of those initials I mentioned at the beginning of this section.) There's really no reason to let all of the choices overwhelm you, because having more fluorescent options simply means that modern reef enthusiasts have a greater capacity to tailor their lighting systems to meet the specific needs of their photosynthetic invertebrates.

Before we delve into the various fluorescent options for lighting a reef tank, it might be helpful to take a brief look at how these lamps actually function. A fluorescent lamp is essentially a glass tube filled with a mixture of inert gases, including argon, and tiny quantities of mercury, with an electrode attached to each end (only one end in the case of power compact tubes). The inside of the tube is coated with a powdery phosphor, the exact composition of which determines the ultimate color of the light. When electricity is applied to the tube, an arc of current passes through the gases and vaporizes tiny drops of mercury, causing them to emit ultraviolet (UV) light. The UV light then causes the phosphor coating to glow brightly, or fluoresce. The specialized high-intensity fluorescent tubes used for reef aquariums require the use of special electronic ballasts or transformers and cannot function in regular fixtures.

In terms of power output, fluorescent lamps are rated as being normal output (NO), high output (HO), or very high output (VHO), depending on the number of watts they produce. We've already established that 40-watt NO lamps are not adequate to support the photosynthetic activity of symbiotic zooxanthellae, so we can pretty much rule them out right away. HO tubes, at only 65 watts for a 4-foot (1.2-m) tube, are also inadequate for most light-hungry invertebrates. Besides, aquarium dealers seldom offer them for sale anymore. On the other hand, VHO tubes, which provide 110 watts each, are just about right. In fact, two 4-foot VHO tubes, totaling 220 watts, placed over our model 55-gallon (200-liter) aquarium will put us well within the desired minimum range of 3 to 5 watts per gallon of water.

VERY BRIGHT LIGHT FROM A VERY SMALL PACKAGE

Another fluorescent option that has gained considerable popularity in recent years is the power compact (PC—a.k.a. compact fluorescent) lamp. As the name suggests, power compacts are much smaller in size than regular fluorescent tubes, which means aquarists can install a larger number of lamps into a single hood for maximum light intensity. They also differ in that only one end of the tube connects to the electrical source.

The three most commonly sold PC lamps have power outputs of 35 watts, 55 watts, and 96 watts, respectively. Don't let these relatively low wattages confuse you, however. Because of factors like the size and shape of the tubes and the special electrical ballasts they require for operation, power compacts produce a much brighter light with less wattage than regular

Reef tank with the lights on, including a pair of 5,500 K metal halide bulbs to balance the color.

fluorescent tubes. For example, a 55-watt PC actually provides more light intensity than a 110-watt VHO. Needless to say, when using power compacts, the 3- to 5-watt-per-gallon rule doesn't apply.

A COMMON COMBINATION

One of the more commonly recommended fluorescent lighting combinations consists of VHO daylight (full spectrum) and actinic blue tubes. Daylight tubes provide the ideal light intensity and color spectrum (similar to that of the tropical midday sun) for light-hungry invertebrates from shallow coral reefs. The actinic blue tubes radiate (surprise!) more of the blue and violet portions of the spectrum that benefit invertebrates from deeper water. If we were to use this particular combination to light our model 55-gallon (200-liter) reef, one VHO tube of each style would be adequate. Many lighting manufacturers also offer fluorescent tubes that are half daylight and half actinic, so you can get the best of both worlds from a single tube. Of course, you can also put together a combination of fluorescent tubes and metal halide spots. Your aquarium dealer should be able to help you select the most appropriate combination based on the specific lighting needs of the organisms you intend to keep.

GETTING THE MOST FROM FLUORESCENT LAMPS

Whichever fluorescent lamps you decide to go with, you can maximize their output by installing them in a hood with a built-in reflector, which will capture light that would ordinarily be lost from the top and sides of the tube and direct it down into your tank.

You should be aware that all fluorescent tubes lose their lighting efficiency with use. The longer they burn, the more red their light becomes, and, as we've already established, the red portion of the spectrum is of little value to photosynthetic invertebrates. This shift to red is extremely subtle and cannot be detected with the naked eye. Your invertebrates, however, will feel the difference, and their overall health may begin to decline markedly. Fortunately, all you have to do to avoid this problem is replace your fluorescent tubes on a regular schedule, according to the manufacturer's recommendation. If no replacement schedule is provided, it's a safe assumption that your tubes should be replaced every six months.

MORE ON METAL HALIDES

Metal halide lamps are the best lighting choice for reef aquariums over 20 inches (50 cm) tall. Metal halides produce an intensely bright light that is capable of penetrating to the bottom of a home aquarium of virtually any size. Like VHO daylight fluorescent lamps, metal halides come very close to replicating the color spectrum and light intensity of the midday tropical sun. They typically are mounted in pendant fixtures and suspended above the aquarium, although some are designed for use in full-size fan-cooled hoods in conjunction with fluorescent actinic tubes or power compacts.

With some exceptions, metal halide bulbs look very much like oversized incandescent bulbs. Contained within each bulb are high-intensity discharge tubes that heat up a metal filament when an electrical current is applied. The filament then heats up the gases that are contained in the bulb's core, producing very intense light and lots of heat. The addition of a cooling fan usually is necessary to prevent the water temperature from rising precipitously whenever the lights are turned on. It's also important to keep water from splashing onto metal halide bulbs by placing a tight-fitting glass cover over the top of the aquarium. As with high-intensity fluorescent lamps, metal halides require the use of special electrical ballasts.

In terms of power output, metal halides pack quite a wallop compared to fluorescent lamps. They're most commonly sold in 175-watt, 200-watt, and 400-watt sizes, although lower wattages are available for shallower tanks. Kelvin ratings range from 5,500 K all the way up to 20,000 K. As a general rule, you should use one metal halide lamp for every 2 feet (60 cm) of aquarium length. This being the case, two 150- to 175-watt lamps would be just about right for our model 55-gallon (200-liter) aquarium.

Metal halide lighting is also very aesthetically pleasing. Whereas fluorescent lighting spreads uniformly throughout the aquarium, the light cast by metal halides can

Reef tank with only VHO actinic tubes, 7,100 K.

Fluorescent vs. Metal Halide

Fluorescent Pros
- less expensive to operate
- more convenient
- run cooler
- available in numerous spectra

Fluorescent Cons
- less effective on taller aquariums
- output may decline unnoticed
- require special ballast (except NO)

Metal Halide Pros
- ideal intensity level
- suitable for deeper aquariums
- enhance rippling effects
- create drama of light and shadow

Metal Halide Cons
- costly to buy and operate
- must be fan cooled
- not necessarily ideal in spectral output
- require heavy ballast for operation

be focused on different parts of the reef to create a dramatic interplay of light and shadow. Not only is this an eye-catching effect, but it also makes it easier to accommodate invertebrates with different lighting requirements in the same tank. For example, animals requiring brighter light, such as hard corals and *Tridacna* clams, could be placed directly "in the spotlight," while certain soft corals and other animals that prefer more subdued lighting could be placed in less intensely lit areas. Metal halides also have the delightful effect of enhancing the rippling movements at the surface of the water, much the way sunlight does on a natural coral reef.

As you delve further into the different lighting options for your reef, you may hear or read accounts of corals and other sessile invertebrates being burned by the intense light of metal halide lamps. But such claims are somewhat misleading. Even the brightest metal halide lamps can only approximate the intensity of the tropical sunlight that photosynthetic invertebrates are accustomed to. True, placing organisms that prefer subdued lighting under metal halides would have a detrimental effect on their health (if you've ever tried to grow shade-loving plants in full sun, you understand exactly what I'm talking about), but such problems stem more from human error rather than any inherent limitations of the lamps themselves.

WHAT'S NEW?

One of the most exciting technologies just making its way into marine aquarium lighting is LED (light-emitting diode) lighting. Cool-running lights of programmable spectral output almost sound too good to be true, but they are coming into the market, and advances will likely make them soon available at competitive prices and in a vast array of configurations.

As with virtually all other aquarium technology, LED lighting is not specifically for aquarium use, and its move from trivial uses like number displays to all types of major lighting needs will be revolutionizing many aspects of our lives. Who knows? Maybe the third edition of this book will relegate much of this chapter to historical interests and concentrate instead on LED lights!

Lighting Duration

In order for the light-hungry invertebrates in a reef aquarium to really prosper rather than just survive, their symbiotic zooxanthellae need to be photosynthesizing at peak efficiency. Not only do they require lighting of the correct intensity and color spectrum to accomplish this, but also lighting of the correct duration. In fact, even the most costly top-of-the-line combination of fluorescent and metal halide lamps will be of dubious value for a reef if it is turned on for only a short time each day.

A good rule of thumb is to light a reef aquarium for approximately 10 to 12 hours each day. You may need to tweak this lighting schedule somewhat, depending on how the organisms in your aquarium respond over the first few weeks. It's unlikely that photosynthetic invertebrates will react adversely to a 12-hour photoperiod, considering the fact that this fairly accurately mimics the lighting cycle of their native tropics. However, if they were deprived of adequate light for a prolonged period, such as during shipping or while with the dealer or both, they may need some time to adjust to the new lighting routine in your aquarium. If you know or suspect this to be the case, provide only a few hours of light exposure at first and then gradually increase it over several days until the desired level is reached.

The proliferation of algae is another factor that may influence lighting duration in a reef system. Algae pose no problem and may be beneficial in an FO aquarium, but if allowed to grow unchecked in a reef these minuscule plant-like organisms can really wreak havoc, growing over every surface in the aquarium and smothering the invertebrates themselves.

LEARN YOUR LIGHTING TERMINOLOGY

As promised, this was only a quick survey of lighting for the reef aquarium, but it should be enough to get you started. Knowing what is available and what the terminology is will guide you in your research and enable you to make informed decisions about what lighting will work best for your setup.

Chapter 4

Keeping It Clean

On a tropical coral reef the waste products of the fish and invertebrates are so efficiently utilized by the various indigenous organisms that they have almost no perceptible effect on the quality of the water surrounding the reef. In fact, a marine biologist once told me, "Every piece of fish poop goes through a minimum of three guts on the coral reef before its nutritional value is finally used up." This may be a bit of hyperbole, but there's no question that an incredible diversity of organisms inhabits the coral reef, forming a very complicated food web, and even the most insignificant scrap can play a major role in the survival of numerous tiny creatures. In addition, any waste matter that somehow manages to escape the attention of scavengers is quickly diluted by the vast quantity of water that the ocean comprises.

What Lies Ahead

- water quality
- mechanical filtration
- chemical filtration

In the artificial closed system of the marine aquarium, on the other hand, you cannot rely solely on foraging animals for the breakdown of solid waste products (although this may occur to a very small degree in a reef tank containing live rock and live sand), and there is no instant dilution of liquid waste, dissolved organic compounds, and the harmful byproducts of the nitrification process (much more on nitrification later) as there is in the open ocean. This means that without diligent intervention on the part of the aquarist, organic waste will decompose within the aquarium system, leading to the rapid deterioration of water quality.

WHAT'S SO IMPORTANT ABOUT WATER QUALITY?

In the FO aquarium, poor water quality usually leads to stressed fish, and stressed fish are much more susceptible to bacterial, viral, and fungal illnesses and parasitic infestation. Of course, when the fish get sick the aquarist usually goes into a panic and responds by dosing the aquarium with various and sundry medications, some of which are actually more harmful to the fish than the disease itself—a sort of vicious cycle that, more often than not, results in the heartbreaking loss of valued specimens.

In the reef aquarium, very exacting, almost pristine water conditions must be maintained at all times. As I've mentioned repeatedly, stability is the rule on the coral reef, and this applies

An Ounce of Prevention

When it comes to the health of your valued marine specimens, it's always better to be proactive than reactive. Taking the necessary steps to satisfy the three major forms of filtration—mechanical, chemical, and biological—and staying on top of those routine partial water changes will not only keep your marine aquarium's water looking crystal clear but also will help to keep your fish or invertebrates in excellent health. On the other hand, inadequate filtration and inconsistent water changes inevitably lead to the outbreak of disease, which usually sends the aquarist scrambling to the nearest aquarium store to buy an assortment of costly medications. If the disease is misidentified, as often happens, the wrong medication might be administered, and the cure may end up being worse than the disease.

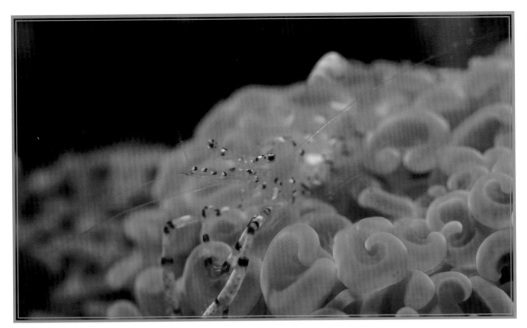

Maintaining a good water quality should be one of the top priorities for your saltwater aquarium. In a reef tank, water quality is paramount to success.

equally to the water quality in the reef tank. Even a slight degradation in water conditions, which would probably have little or no significant impact in an FO system, could spell disaster for an aquarium full of invertebrates—just another subtle hint that you might be better off getting your feet wet with an FO aquarium first!

So what steps can you take in order to maintain excellent water quality in your new marine aquarium? First, you'll need to familiarize yourself with the three basic forms of filtration and the different types of equipment you can use to achieve them. You'll also want to develop a basic understanding of the process of protein skimming, which is possibly one of the most significant technical advances the marine aquarium hobby has seen. Finally, it is very important to understand that no amount of filtration gadgetry can take the place of routine partial water changes. Whether you decide to go with an FO aquarium or a reef, the one sure way to remove pollutants before they begin to degrade water quality is to physically siphon out a portion of the dirty water and replace it with clean water. That being said, let's move ahead and begin our analysis of the three forms of filtration.

Is Mechanical Filtration Necessary?

Can you get by without mechanical filtration? To a certain extent you can—if you're extremely diligent about partial water changes. But you'll be much happier with your water quality and the look of your aquarium if you include some form of mechanical filter in your water purification system.

MECHANICAL FILTRATION

Mechanical filtration is the easiest of the three forms to understand, primarily because you can actually observe the process and its results with the naked eye. The job of the mechanical filter is a simple one—to physically strain out and remove particulate waste (fish feces, uneaten food, etc.) from the aquarium system. The step of eliminating particulate matter is important for two reasons. For one thing, debris clouding the water and accumulating on the rockwork and substrate detracts significantly from the beauty of the aquarium and therefore reduces the pleasure the aquarist derives from it. More importantly, any dirt and debris left in the system will decompose and foul the water. The two mechanical filtration devices most frequently used for marine aquarium purposes nowadays are the hang-on-tank filter and the canister filter, each of which has its pros and cons. A third—undergravel filtration—is less commonly utilized these days but is available.

Pros and Cons of the Hang-On-Tank Filter

The hang-on-tank filter is essentially a plastic box that hangs on the outside of the aquarium on the side or the back of the tank, depending on the configuration of the other equipment in the system. The box is divided into two chambers, one larger and one smaller. The larger chamber contains the various filter media (foam sponges, fiber pads, spun nylon floss, etc.), while the smaller chamber contains a siphon tube. One end of the tube is attached to an impeller, which is powered by a small electric motor located on the underside of the smaller chamber, and the other end of the tube extends down into the aquarium water.

When power is applied to the motor, the impeller begins to rotate rapidly, forcing the air out of the tube and drawing water up from the aquarium into the small chamber. From there the water spills over into the larger chamber, where it is filtered through the various media and then returns to the tank under the influence of gravity. You may encounter hang-on-tank models that deviate from this theme, but the same basic principle—take the water out of the tank and into the filter, strain it, and then return it to the tank—applies to all.

The biggest advantage of the hang-on-tank filter is its ease of use. Literally within minutes of removing the filter from its package you can have it up and running on your aquarium. All you have to do is hang the box in the desired location, snap a few lengths of plastic tubing together, attach the siphon to the impeller mechanism, add the desired filter media, fill the filter box with aquarium water, plug in the power cord, and you have mechanical filtration! Because hang-on filters are so easy to use, many beginners prefer them. They're also popular, because of their familiarity, with many experienced aquarists making the switch from freshwater to saltwater tanks.

However, hang-on-tank filters do have certain limitations. For example, since they mount directly to the side or back of the tank, they tend to detract from the natural beauty of the aquarium—not a major drawback, but an issue of concern if the tank is intended to be an important design element or showpiece in the home. Another drawback is that if the filter media become clogged with dirt and debris, the water may begin to flow over or around the media without being filtered effectively, an occurrence that may go undetected by the aquarist for a long time. Also, hang-on-tank filters lack versatility in that they aren't very efficient at performing chemical and biological filtration. In other words, hang-on-tank filters are best viewed as dedicated mechanical filters only.

Some aquarium stands come with built-in compartments that make the perfect out-of-sight home for filtration equipment.

Pros and Cons of the Canister Filter

If you want more versatility from your mechanical filter, an external (outside-the-tank) canister filter may be your best option. A canister filter is—as the name implies—a closed plastic canister designed to hold various filter media. Often several removable compartments are included with the canister to make the separation of media easier and more practical. Within most canisters is a pump containing a motor and impeller, although the pump is separate with some models. Water is gravity fed from the aquarium through a siphon hose down into the canister, which is situated below the water level of the aquarium. There it is pumped under pressure through the various filter media and back into the aquarium through a return hose.

The advantages of canister filters over hang-on-tank models are numerous. For one thing, they are much less disruptive in terms of aesthetics. In fact, they can be placed completely out of sight inside a cabinet-style aquarium stand (or any desired location in reasonable proximity to the aquarium, for that matter) with only the supply and return hoses showing. They're also much more versatile: by placing mechanical, chemical, and biological filtration media into separate compartments within a single canister, you can achieve all three forms of filtration with one space-saving unit. Also, some canister filters are designed so that multiple units can be plumbed together in a series and powered by a large external pump. So, for example, you could place mechanical filtration media in the first canister, biological filtration media in the second, chemical filtration media in the third, and so on. Such a setup is ideal for filtering very large tanks or several smaller tanks simultaneously.

Of course, canister filters also have their drawbacks. Whereas hang-on-tank filters are extremely easy to install and operate, canister filters can seem a little more complicated and off-putting to the beginning aquarist. This anxiety isn't completely unjustified. Water under pressure tends to follow the path of least resistance, so if a canister filter is not properly assembled and one of its O-rings fails, the result could be major flooding. Also, canister filters pose more of a challenge when it comes to routine maintenance. You can't simply shut off the system and pop off the hoses without spraying water everywhere, so it is necessary to install a series of cutoff valves that allow you to isolate both the canister and plumbing when it's time to clean the canister or replace the filter media. Newer canister filter models come equipped with the necessary shutoff valves.

Pros and Cons of the Undergravel Filter

Aquarists who are crossing over from fresh water to salt water are likely to be familiar with the undergravel (UG) filter. The UG filter, the old workhorse of aquarium filtration, was the filter of choice for many years among both freshwater and marine aquarists. However, it has recently fallen out of favor, largely due to newer filtration technologies that have since swept the aquarium industry. At this point, you might be asking yourself why, if undergravel filters were considered to be reliable and effective in the past, the same shouldn't be true now. Indeed, many experienced freshwater aquarists, and quite a few old salts returning to the hobby after being out of it for many years, might ask the same question. Actually, it's not that UG filters are any less reliable or effective, but rather that some of the newer filtration systems just tend to get the job done better, especially when it comes to mechanical filtration.

The basic UG filter system consists of a plastic perforated plate with transparent plastic lift tubes attached along the back edge at each corner. This unit is placed on the bottom of the tank and covered with a suitable crushed coral or aragonite substrate. A recirculating water current is created by either airstones, which are placed inside the lift tubes and connected to an air pump, or powerheads mounted on top of the lift tubes. Both methods cause water to flow up the lift tubes and be discharged from the tubes (or the powerhead) at the water surface; the upward flow of water from the bottom of the tank simultaneously causes water to travel down through the substrate into the filter plate. The main difference between the two methods is that powerheads pump the water much more forcefully, creating a fairly substantial current.

With a UG system, suspended particulate matter is drawn down into the substrate, where it is mechanically filtered out of the water. Biological filtration (more on this type of filtration in the next chapter) takes place at both the substrate level and in the perforated plate below the gravel. Ironically, the mechanical filtration aspect of a UG filter can actually work against its effectiveness as a biological filter. As more and more debris is drawn down into the substrate, the perforations in the filter plate can become clogged, thereby creating dead spots and discouraging the colonization of the beneficial aerobic bacteria necessary for biological filtration. Decomposing solid waste trapped within the substrate and filter plate can also have a serious impact on water quality—a fact that has not been lost on many reef aquarists, who typically shun UG filters in favor of other

Your filter will contain various types of media. All are designed to help you control dissolved organic compounds in your tank.

systems. For these reasons, it is very important when using a UG filter to vacuum the substrate frequently with a siphon hose.

If you're not discouraged by their limitations and still want to go with an UG filter, your best bet is to set it up as a reverse-flow system to prevent the filter plate from clogging in the first place. The most effective way to achieve this is by using the return hose of a canister filter to pump the water down through the lift tubes and up through the filter plate and substrate. This keeps particulate waste suspended in the water where it can be effectively eliminated by the canister filter. And since solid waste cannot accumulate to create dead spots, the biological filter has a chance to become fully established with no interference.

CHEMICAL FILTRATION

Contrary to what the name might suggest, chemical filtration does not involve adding chemicals to the water to eliminate or neutralize pollutants. Rather, when most aquarists discuss chemical filtration, they are referring to the use of a substance known as activated carbon to remove dissolved organic compounds from the aquarium water. You won't need to purchase any additional high-tech gizmos or gadgets to achieve this, since most standard filtration devices, including canister filters, hang-on-tank filters, and wet/dry systems, can accommodate activated carbon along with the various media needed for mechanical and biological filtration.

So what is activated carbon, and how does it filter your water? Essentially, activated carbon is a substance created by baking certain materials, such as wood, coal, and bone, at extremely high temperatures. As these materials bake, tiny pores are opened up, greatly increasing the surface area of the substance. At the same time, the surface of the carbon is chemically altered so that it has the tendency to attract the molecules of various dissolved substances.

When activated carbon is placed in your aquarium's filtration system—preferably sandwiched between two layers of filter floss or inside a nylon stocking to prevent the tiny pieces from being discharged into the aquarium—the water flows through the numerous tiny pores within the carbon, and the dissolved compounds are adsorbed (*ad*sorption should not be confused with *ab*sorption) from the water. That is, the compounds actually form a chemical bond with the surface of the carbon and are effectively eliminated from the system.

Heated debate sometimes rages over the value of activated carbon in the aquarium. Such disputes usually stem from the fact that activated carbon will attract and remove both desirable and undesirable compounds equally. In other words, it has no way to discriminate between those substances that are toxic to fish and invertebrates and those that would benefit them.

In addition, the incredible amount of surface area that activated carbon provides is highly attractive to the beneficial bacteria that perform biological filtration, which means that each

Beyond Activated Carbon

Activated carbon is not the only product on the market that can be used to chemically filter your aquarium water. There are also various resin-treated pads and granular filter media that are designed to eliminate specific undesirable compounds, such as ammonia, nitrate, phosphate, and silicate. These products can be effective as long as they are promptly replaced whenever they become exhausted and each one is used in conjunction with an associated test kit. However, it's important to remember that no form of chemical filtration can take the place of routine aquarium maintenance and, of course, regular partial water changes.

time the carbon is removed, a certain portion of the biological filter goes with it. This is not a significant problem, however, as long as you replace the carbon fairly frequently and provide enough biological filtration elsewhere in the aquarium system to compensate for the loss.

So how much activated carbon is needed to carry out the process of chemical filtration efficiently? Actually, there is no specific way to calculate an exact quantity that is appropriate for a given volume of water. This is due in large part to the fact that not all activated carbons are created equal. As a general rule, you should try to avoid carbons that look shiny and are relatively smooth to the touch. These carbons lack the large amount of surface area found in rough, dull-looking carbons. Sure, you can save a little money by using an inferior grade, but you probably won't be happy with the results in your aquarium. Also, the biological load (the number and size of the fish and/or invertebrates in the aquarium) will have a significant impact on how hard the activated carbon actually has to work to chemically filter the water.

Although there's no hard and fast rule governing the amount of activated carbon to use, it is important to replace the carbon regularly according to the manufacturer's recommended schedule. This will prevent the adsorbed toxins from being released back into the aquarium system to the detriment of the fish or invertebrates. It will also limit any impact on the aquarium's biological filtration capacity.

Now that we've covered mechanical and chemical filtration, we can tackle the most important one of all: biological filtration.

Chapter 5

Biological Filtration: Your Fish Just Can't Live Without It!

Technically, the concept of biological filtration belongs in the previous chapter along with mechanical and chemical filtration. However, since your ultimate success in the marine aquarium hobby depends to a great extent on how well you understand and apply this form of filtration, it deserves a chapter of its own.

What Lies Ahead

- beneficial bacteria
- wet-dry filter
- media
- NNR

Biological filtration—especially the part known as nitrification—is arguably the most important yet least understood of all the processes we will discuss in this book. For many aspiring aquarists, it's also one of the most mysterious—mostly because the actual nitrification process is invisible to the naked eye, but also because it's carried out by microorganisms, which we typically associate with filthiness and ill health. But, as you'll soon see, there's nothing mysterious about biological filtration, and you certainly don't need to be a microbiologist to understand it.

IT'S ALL ABOUT BACTERIA

Nitrification is carried out by beneficial aerobic (needing oxygen) bacteria, known as nitrobacters. The process begins with the release of ammonia into the aquarium water in the form of either excreted fish waste or decomposing organic material (usually uneaten food). Ammonia is the result of the natural metabolic processes of aquatic organisms. Ammonia in its pure form is extremely toxic to both fish and invertebrates and will quickly cause their death if it is permitted to accumulate in the aquarium water. Fortunately, there are bacteria that utilize ammonia as a food source and quickly convert it into a compound called nitrite. Nitrite, though slightly less toxic than ammonia, is still very harmful to fish and invertebrates, so it too must be eliminated from the aquarium water. That's where a second group of bacteria comes in. As soon as the ammonia is converted to nitrite by the first group, hungry colonies of these other bacteria break it down into nitrate.

Most marine fish can tolerate a moderate level of nitrate, provided it accumulates gradually over time, but nitrate is highly toxic to many sessile invertebrates even at low levels. Nitrate also functions as a source of nutrition and can promote blooms of undesirable algae—again, not necessarily a problem for the fish-only tank, but a potential disaster in a reef aquarium.

So how do you go about eliminating nitrate before it reaches a hazardous level? You can purchase special nitrate-removing granular filter media or resin pads to chemically filter it from the water, but you'll get mixed results at best with this approach. There is also a natural method you can use to reduce nitrate, which we'll explore later on in this chapter. But for all practical purposes, the only truly reliable way to eliminate nitrate from the aquarium system is to perform a partial water change. This partly eliminates not only nitrate, but also all other toxins and crud that have accumulated since the last water change. And since the water change is the simplest and most reliable solution to the buildup of nitrate, it's the one I would strongly recommend to the beginning marine aquarist. After all, this is supposed to be a simple guide, right?

The most important type of filtration is biological filtration. Beneficial bacteria change ammonia into nitrite, both very harmful to your fish and invertebrates, and more bacteria change nitrite into nitrate. Nitrate levels are controlled with regular water changes.

WHERE DO NITRIFYING BACTERIA COME FROM?

Okay, we now know that we need special nitrifying bacteria to perform the vital job of biological filtration for us. So how does one go about getting them into the aquarium? The beauty of it is, you don't have to do anything to get them there. They're already in there—on the glass, in the substrate, on the rockwork, and on any other available surface—albeit in relatively small quantities. All you have to do is give them adequate time to flourish and provide the three basic requirements for their survival: food, oxygen, and surface area.

Providing the food source for nitrifying bacteria is a relatively simple proposition, since they feed on the byproducts of fish waste and decomposing organic matter. The only time this becomes tricky is when you're first setting up the aquarium and you haven't introduced any organisms yet. But don't worry. We'll cover that in much greater detail in Chapter 9 when we discuss cycling the aquarium.

Since nitrifying bacteria are aerobic, they must be given oxygenated conditions in order to thrive. Usually this is accomplished by creating turbulence at the water surface, such as that produced by the water discharging back into the tank from the various filtration devices. If this is not adequate, oxygenation can be achieved through surface agitation by pumping air

Mandatory Filtration

Mandatory Filtration

You're asking for trouble if you add fish to a tank that does not have a functioning biofilter (another word for biological filtration). Once beneficial bacteria are established in your tank, you can begin to slowly add your fish.

through an airstone placed at the bottom of the aquarium. A bubbling airstone can also add to the overall aesthetic beauty of the aquarium if the stone is cleverly concealed within the rockwork or decorations and only the bubbles are visible.

Surface area is also easy to provide. As I've mentioned, nitrifying bacteria will colonize virtually every surface in the aquarium as long as oxygenated conditions and nitrogenous wastes are made available. You can give the bacteria even more surface area to colonize by inserting some sort of biological filtration medium into your mechanical filter or by including a wet-dry filter in your overall filtration arsenal.

But this brings up another important question: if nitrifying bacteria will colonize the aquarium anyway, why buy a special wet-dry filter to do the job? As with any other issue in the marine aquarium hobby, there are (at least) two schools of thought on the subject. Some insist that wet-dry filters are redundant and therefore unnecessary, while others believe that if a little biological filtration is good, more must be better. I personally fall into the "more is better" category when it comes to biological filtration.

WHAT IS A WET-DRY FILTER?

Wet-dry filters, also called trickle-down filters, might more accurately be called wet-moist filters, since there's no stage in the system where conditions are totally dry. The "dry" part of the name actually comes from the fact that the filter media are never completely submerged in water. Rather, the aquarium water is allowed to trickle gradually over the various filter media, keeping them constantly moist and highly oxygenated—perfect conditions to encourage the proliferation of nitrifying bacteria.

How do these systems work? Though there are many different styles of wet-dry filter available, each operates on the same basic principle. Since there's no reasonable way to describe the subtle distinctions between each type of filter without lulling you into a coma, I'll limit my analysis to one of the more common designs.

With this type of system, there is a two-chambered box hung on the side of the aquarium. One chamber hangs inside the tank, just slightly below the surface of the water, and the other hangs outside the tank. Water enters the first chamber through a series of slots along its front edge and is drawn into the outside chamber through a constant-level siphon. There the water may pass through a sponge pre-filter to remove any particulate matter before passing, under the influence of gravity, into a flexible tube connected to the bottom of the exterior chamber. The tube transports the water down into the biofilter, which usually sits beneath the main tank in a separate reservoir, or sump.

Once the water reaches the biofilter (a transparent glass or acrylic box divided into two chambers, one upper and one lower) it spreads onto a perforated filter plate located in the top chamber of the box and trickles down over the various bacteria-rich filter media, which are contained in the lower chamber. Additional mechanical and/or chemical filtration media can also be placed in the top chamber to keep the biofilter medium as free from impurities as possible. After being filtered by the nitrifying bacteria, the water collects in the sump and is pumped back into the aquarium through a return hose.

MEDIA FOR THE BIOFILTER

To encourage the establishment of aerobic nitrifying bacteria, the substance you choose as your biofilter medium must provide ample surface area. This means that the more porous the substance is, the better it will support bacterial colonization. Suitable media include, among other things, sponges, porous ceramic sandglass, spun nylon floss, and heavily grooved plastic spheres that provide an incredible amount of surface area for their size and, hence, ample opportunity for nitrifying bacteria to set up camp.

NATURAL NITRATE REDUCTION: HAVE WE FOUND THE HOLY GRAIL?

I mentioned earlier that there is a method, apart from frequent costly water changes (though regular water changes are encouraged regardless), that you can use to eliminate nitrate from your aquarium without the need for any chemical resins or granular denitrifying filter media. This method, called natural nitrate reduction (NNR), requires the installation of a so-

It's somewhat unclear how beneficial bacteria get into the home aquarium, but once a source of ammonia is introduced they always seems to show up.

How Do the Different Filter Types Rate?

Type of Filter	Mechanical	Chemical	Biological
Hang-On-Tank	Good	Fair to Good	Poor to Good
Canister	Excellent	Good	Good
Undergravel	Fair	Poor	Excellent
Wet/Dry	Poor	Good	Excellent

called plenum system beneath the substrate of your aquarium during the initial setup phase. Since such a system has considerable limitations in terms of how much nitrate it can process, it is normally used only for reef aquariums with very light fish loads.

NNR, a process conceived in the 1980s by Dr. Jean Jaubert of the University of Nice, made a pretty big splash a few years back, with much of the popular aquarium literature heralding it as one of the most significant advances the hobby had seen since the development of synthetic sea salt mixes. Jaubert's method gained even wider popular acceptance with the endorsement of aquarium industry heavy hitters. However, as with so many advances in the marine aquarium hobby, it wasn't long before articles questioning the value of NNR and plenum systems began to pop up.

So which viewpoint is more accurate? I would suggest that both are correct to a certain degree. In fact, I would argue that every form of aquarium technology has both its selling points and its drawbacks, and all we aquarists can do is to try to make the most educated decisions possible when it comes to the technology that is available to us.

Is NNR the Best Approach for Beginners?

So the question is: should you attempt to use Jaubert's method of nitrate reduction in your first marine aquarium? Well, for an FO setup, the answer is probably no. For a reef system, it depends. Reef invertebrates are very sensitive to nitrate and may benefit significantly from a system that reduces nitrate before it can accumulate to even moderate levels.

Another question you have to ask yourself concerns whether you are confident enough in your tinkering ability. In other words, are you certain that you'll be able to design and assemble the plenum system correctly? Using improper materials for the plenum or simply putting the materials together the wrong way can result in disaster. For example, if you decided to use a different screening material that tends to clog easily instead of the recommended fiberglass window screening, you could end up creating an anaerobic (no oxygen) rather than anoxic (low oxygen) state in the lower sand layer. This could potentially lead to the buildup of hydrogen sulfide gas and the poisoning of the animals in the aquarium.

It's not really recommended in most cases for the novice marine reef aquarist to use a plenum system. You are probably better off relying on regular water changes for nitrate reduction, but if you want more information, what follows is a very sketchy overview.

What is a Plenum?

The Jaubert method utilizes a stagnant area, known as a plenum, beneath a sand substrate. The plenum is created using a grid material like eggcrate or a standard undergravel filter plate. The grid should be elevated a minimum of 1 inch (2.5 cm) off the bottom of the tank (the larger the tank, the deeper the plenum), and there should be a 1-inch gap between the grid and aquarium glass on all sides so the plenum is not visible from outside the aquarium. To achieve the desired height and provide sufficient support for the overlying sand and rockwork, you'll need to affix sections of half-inch-diameter (1.3-cm-diameter) PVC tubing to the bottom of the plenum, using aquarium-safe silicone adhesive or plastic cable ties. Next, wrap the plenum with a sheet of fiberglass window screening to keep the sand from sifting down into the stagnant area, which should remain open water.

If you plan on keeping a reef tank, your biological filter will have to be well established. Corals are very sensitive to nitrate. Be sure to stay on top of your water changes.

A Case of Mistaken Identity

It's not unusual for larger predatory fish to line up at coral reef cleaning stations, waiting their turn to be picked clean of parasites by cleaner wrasses, *Labroides dimidiatus*, and other cleaner organisms. The trusting host fish may even allow the diminutive cleaner wrasses to explore inside its oral cavity and gill covers in search of edible tidbits.

But in some cases, what looks like a cleaner wrasse actually turns out to be a false cleaner, *Aspidontus taeniatus*—a predatory blenny that cleverly mimics the shape and color of the cleaner wrasse. The false cleaner uses this disguise to win the trust of its unsuspecting host and rewards it by promptly biting off a chunk of flesh—a painful case of mistaken identity!

After the plenum is assembled and put in place, it's time to put in the first layer of substrate. This layer should be approximately 2 inches (5 cm) deep and ideally should consist of aragonite or crushed coral sand. Finally, place a second sheet of screening on top of the first sand layer, and top it off with two additional inches of sand. The dividing screen between the two layers of substrate prevents digging or burrowing organisms from disturbing the lower substrate, which would lead to an imbalance in the relationship of aerobic and anoxic zones.

Once your aquarium is up and running, you'll need to practice a little patience while the sand becomes colonized with denitrifying bacteria. You can accelerate the process by adding a few handfuls of sand from an established plenum system or by using live sand, which is essentially sand harvested from the ocean floor that contains an array of tiny benthic (bottom-dwelling) marine organisms, including the desired nitrate-reducing microbes.

How Does NNR Work?

Although the plenum system is technologically simple, the chemistry of its operation is quite complex. In very simple terms, the plenum serves as a reservoir for small amounts of various chemicals. Bacteria of various types inhabit zones in the sand defined by their relative oxygen concentration. Denitrifying and other bacteria recycle chemicals, primarily nitrate, which diffuses into the sand layer above the plenum, where the denitrifying bacteria convert it into free nitrogen gas. The gas rises through the sandbed and is released at the surface of the aquarium. Other beneficial processes attributed to the plenum method include the supplementation of calcium and certain trace elements without the need for commercial additives. Of course, I must emphasize that this is a very rudimentary explanation of the nitrate reduction process and that there is much about the way these systems function that is yet to be fully understood—even among experts.

Live Rock NNR

One of the many benefits of live rock, whether in an FO tank or a reef, is that its pores provide a full range of microenvironments, from oxygen-rich to oxygen-poor. Thus both nitrifying and denitrifying bacteria reside in the rock. This adds a considerable amount of biofiltration to your system. In a lightly stocked reef tank, live rock sometimes is able to process all the nitrogenous wastes, and nitrate does not accumulate, but in most cases live rock does not support enough biofiltration to manage absolutely all of the wastes produced, though it certainly helps.

SUMMARY

Nitrifying biofiltration is extremely important for all aquariums, and some denitrifying biofiltration takes place in any aquarium with live rock. Live rock filtration is vital for reef tanks, and dedicated denitrifying filters like plenums can sometimes be beneficial in a reef aquarium. We'll revisit biofiltration when we talk about tank cycling.

Damselfish are a hardy species and are sometimes used to cycle a new aquarium. The word "cycle" here is just another way of saying "maturing your tank's biological filter."

Chapter 6

More is Better:
Skimming and Living Filters

Next to the biofilter, the single most important piece of equipment for the marine aquarium is the protein skimmer, or foam fractionator. In fact, one could conceivably maintain a tank full of marine organisms in superior health using only these two forms of water purification in conjunction with frequent partial water changes. When the biofilter is live rock, this is the well-known Berlin System for maintaining a marine aquarium.

The purpose of the protein skimmer is to remove dissolved organic waste from the water before nitrifying bacteria act upon it, thereby taking some of the load off the biofilter and slowing the accumulation of nitrate. Protein skimmers are especially efficient at removing surface-active compounds (surfactants), which can sometimes be seen as an oily film on the surface of the aquarium water. The molecules of these surfactants are bipolar, with one end of the molecule being attracted to water and the other being repelled by water and therefore attracted to the surface—an interface between air and water. The key to the function of a skimmer is the production of bubbles that provide enormous air-water interface or surface area.

ANATOMY OF A PROTEIN SKIMMER

A protein skimmer is essentially a tall cylindrical chamber through which aquarium water is pumped at the same time that a mass of tiny bubbles is generated. The bubbles are produced by pumping air through a very fine airstone (usually made of limewood) or by a motor-driven venturi valve. As the bubbles rise through the chamber, the surfactants adhere to the bubbles and are transported to the top of the chamber, where they accumulate in a thick brown foam. As the foam continues to build in volume, it spills over into a collection cup located at the top of the unit and collapses into a foul-looking brown liquid. The aquarist can then simply detach the collection cup, empty and rinse it out in a sink, and replace it on the skimmer unit. Various skimmer designs work to maximize the contact time between the aquarium water and the bubbles, since it is while the bubbles and the water are in contact that the removal of dissolved wastes occurs.

Protein Skimming, Nature's Way

Virtually every process that is carried out in the closed system of the marine aquarium has a parallel component in nature. For example, while aquarists use mechanical protein-skimming devices to remove dissolved organic compounds from aquarium water, the forces of wind and waves generate the same effect in natural bodies of water. If you've ever noticed dirty foam collecting on a beach or at the base of a pier, weir, or waterfall, you've seen this natural protein skimming at work.

Airstone-Driven Skimmers

There are several different styles of protein skimmer available on the market, and each has its distinct advantages and disadvantages. The most basic and least costly is the airstone-driven columnar kind that is designed to be placed directly into the aquarium. This style is relatively simple to use and reasonably efficient, although you may need to repeatedly adjust the height of the skimmer chamber relative to the water surface to achieve the proper foam consistency, especially just after replacing the airstone. These skimmers are also somewhat bulky, so they may detract from the aesthetics of the aquarium unless you go to great lengths to conceal the chamber behind rocks or decorations.

The most efficient form of tank-mounted protein skimmer is the counter-current style. With this type of skimmer, the water flows in through slots near the top of the chamber and travels down toward the bottom. Since the water flows in the opposite direction to the rising stream of bubbles, the contact time between water and air is maximized.

A quality protein skimmer is one of the best investments you can make for your tank.

An external airstone-driven skimmer is a good alternative if you don't want a big unsightly cylinder taking up space in your aquarium. However, this type of skimmer is slightly more costly because it must be made watertight. Also, these skimmers are, by necessity, much taller than the tank-mounted kind in order to get sufficient contact time between the rising bubbles and the water in the chamber. This means that in some cases the appropriate external skimmer for a larger tank would be too tall to fit beneath the aquarium in a cabinet-style stand. It's important to remember that with both the tank-mounted and external airstone-driven protein skimmers, the airstone will clog over time and must be replaced on a regular basis to ensure proper bubble size and to keep the protein skimmer operating at peak efficiency.

Rating the Skimmers

In-Tank Airstone-Driven Skimmers
Advantages
- least costly
- easy to use

Disadvantages
- require frequent height adjustment
- bulky and detract from aquarium aesthetic
- airstone clogs over time
- least efficient

External Airstone-Driven Skimmers
Advantages
- don't disrupt aquarium aesthetic

Disadvantages
- more costly than in-tank models
- taller and harder to conceal
- airstone clogs over time

Venturi Skimmers
Advantages
- produce whirling vortex of bubbles for optimum contact time between air and water
- smaller and easier to conceal than external airstone-driven models
- no airstone to clog

Disadvantage
- most costly, but worth the added expense

Venturi-Driven Skimmers

Unless you're operating on a very restricted budget, I would suggest that it's worth paying a few extra dollars at the outset for a venturi protein skimmer. These skimmers have several advantages over the kind that utilize airstones. For one thing, the venturi valve produces a whirling vortex—rather like a tiny tornado—within the chamber, which optimizes contact time between air and water. For this reason, venture models can be much smaller and more easily hidden than airstone-driven models while producing better results. Also, you don't have to worry about constantly replacing clogged airstones if you decide to go with a venturi skimmer.

LIVE ROCK: WHO YOU CALLIN' AN OXYMORON?

Ask the average nonaquarist whether he or she has ever heard of live rock and you're likely to get an expression of utter bewilderment in response. I must confess that the first time I heard an aquarium dealer mention live rock, the first thing that popped into my head was the venomous stonefish. In my defense, I was much younger then and had kept only freshwater aquariums up to that point. After all, a stonefish is living, and it does look rather like a rock, right? But as I soon discovered, live rock is not as big an oxymoron as it might seem, and it plays a very significant role in a marine aquarium.

In simple terms, live rocks are pieces of coral rubble that have broken off the reef under the influence of storms and heavy surge. As they lie in the sand around the base of the reef, they become heavily colonized by various beneficial microorganisms, a host of tiny invertebrates, pink and purple coralline algae, and certain forms of macroalgae. In other words, it's not the rocks themselves that are alive, but rather the great number of organisms that encrust their surfaces and inhabit every crack and crevice. Live rocks also carry with them an amazing potential for future life in the form of numerous eggs, larvae, and spores, which are deposited by various means into the tiny pores of the rocks as they rest on the ocean floor.

Live Rock Aquaculture

The ecologically minded reader might be concerned about the sustainability of wild live rock collection and the potential for damage to the coral reefs by unscrupulous collectors. Both of these concerns are well justified, and steps are being taken in many parts of the world to encourage the practice of live rock aquaculture in order to satisfy the ever-growing demand from the aquarium industry without placing additional collection pressure on the reefs. In fact, federal law currently forbids the collection of live rock in all of the waters surrounding the

A jumble of live rock can provide many hiding places for your fish, which can help them feel more secure and therefore they will be seen more often out and about.

George Scores a Direct Hit

To give you some appreciation of the impact hurricanes can have on live rock aquaculture projects and why "just rocks" can cost so much, consider what happened when Hurricane George hit the Florida Keys. In the summer of 1997 I helped a personal friend who leases a live rock aquaculture site off Plantation Key to install 18 tons (16 MT) of coquina rock on the ocean floor. First we built a large "patio" out of concrete slabs to keep the rock pile from sinking into the sand. Then, under the hot Florida sun, we painstakingly lowered the rocks onto the concrete pad one small load at a time (loading the rocks and patio stones onto the boat was no picnic either, I might add).

A little over one year later, with no regard for our toil and sweat, Hurricane George passed through, swept the rock off the patio, and unceremoniously buried it in the sand—in 56 feet (17 m) of water! The nerve of that hurricane! The real tragedy is that the rock pile was just starting to develop a nice coating of coralline algae and a diverse assortment of encrusting organisms. Oh well, if at first you don't succeed, try, try again.

continental United States. This ruling has encouraged a number of environmentally conscious entrepreneurs to set up commercial aquaculture sites around the Florida Keys and in other suitable locations.

Live rock aquaculture is a relatively straightforward, albeit time-consuming, process. The operator chooses a desirable site on the ocean floor in strict accordance with governmental regulations and builds a sort of artificial reef—basically a big pile or several piles of rock—on the site. The rock pile is usually placed on top of some kind of environmentally friendly underlayment (concrete patio blocks, untreated wood lattice, etc.) to keep the lower portion of the pile from sinking into the sand. In most cases, limestone rock is used, but any highly porous, irregularly shaped rock will work just as well; many use coral rock mined from inland quarries—remnants of long-extinct reefs from prehistoric oceans. Once the rock pile is in place, all the operator can do is wait for nature to take its course. Within approximately two years, unless a tropical storm or hurricane scores a direct hit on the pile (a more common occurrence than you might think), the rock is usually fully inoculated with desirable organisms and is ready to be harvested and shipped to dealers.

Transporting and Curing Live Rock

Live rock is traditionally shipped out of water, wrapped in wet newspaper, although I know of at least one operator who is developing a method for keeping the rock completely submerged from the time of collection until the time of delivery. The problem with the standard shipping method is that a certain percentage of the organisms encrusting the rocks will die off before they ever reach the dealers' tanks. Needless to say, you'd never want to place rocks covered with dead or dying organisms into an established aquarium. The resultant pollution would completely overload the biofilter and likely wipe out every animal in the tank. Instead, the rock needs to be cured before it can be safely introduced into the aquarium. In some instances, dealers will cure their live rock before putting it up for sale, but since this adds to the price of the rock, many will leave the curing to the customer as a cost-cutting and labor-saving measure.

Prior to curing the rocks, it's a good idea to clean them of any obviously dead or dying organisms. Carefully brush off any sediment that may still be clinging to the rocks as well as any undesirable algae or slimy, discolored patches. It's also a good idea to remove any sponges from the rocks, as they are very unlikely to survive in the aquarium, especially if they have spent any time in the open air. Some reef aquarists suggest spreading the rocks out on a waterproof tarp or plastic sheet at this stage so you can check each one out thoroughly. This technique may also reveal any nasty live rock stowaways (mantis shrimps, for example) that you don't want in your aquarium. Believe me, it's much easier to catch and destroy unwelcome pests before they find their way into your aquarium. Just be sure to keep the rocks moist during the cleaning process by spraying them frequently with salt water.

The actual curing process simply involves storing the rock in a separate container filled with salt water while the aforementioned die-off process occurs. Large plastic storage tubs or even plastic garbage cans make ideal curing vats. Numerous water changes are performed to eliminate the ammonia and nitrite produced by the decomposing organisms. The more efficiently you clean the rocks prior to curing, the shorter the actual curing time will be, but you can expect it to take somewhere in the vicinity of two weeks before the rock is ready for the aquarium. A fairly reliable way to determine whether the rock is fully cured is to perform a smell test. If you take a whiff of the curing vat and detect the scent of rotten eggs, you'll know that the die-off process is still taking place, and additional water changes will be necessary. The water should test zero for ammonia and nitrite when the curing is complete.

What Do Live Rocks Do?

In the FO aquarium, aquascaping can be achieved with less costly base rock or artificial corals, but, as aficionados of FOWLR (Fish Only With Live Rock) systems can attest, live

Live rock is notorious for bringing unexpected and interesting organisms into your tank. This photograph was taken with a red light at night and captured a tiny hitchhiking octopus!

rock provides excellent biofiltration, a wonderfully naturalistic setting, ample places of concealment, and opportunities for the natural foraging and grazing behaviors of fish. In the reef aquarium, live rock performs all these and more very important functions. One of these functions is to serve as a physical platform to which the assorted sessile invertebrates can attach themselves. But in any setup, due to its extremely porous nature, high-quality live rock provides ample surface area for nitrifying and denitrifying bacteria to colonize. For this reason, many reef aquarists feel that it's redundant to add a wet-dry filter or some other commercially manufactured biofilter to a system containing live rock. However, one could also argue that no real harm can come from having a super-abundance of biological filtration.

Keep in mind that if adequate water circulation is provided in the aquarium, live rock can also aid in the denitrification process. The same microbes that form the basis of Jaubert's plenum system can colonize the interior portions of live rock, provided the rock is sufficiently porous. A high level of porosity is necessary for two reasons. First, it allows just enough oxygen to penetrate deep into the rock to create the anoxic (low oxygen) conditions favored by the denitrifying bacteria. Second, it provides a pathway for nitrate-rich water to reach the bacteria, which then convert the nitrate to free nitrogen gas.

The Mini Cleanup Crew

Live rock also supports a large population of miniature motile invertebrates (tiny crustaceans, brittlestars, etc.) that emerge from their tiny burrows, usually at night, and scavenge through the rockwork and substrate for anything remotely resembling food. Some will even glean whatever scant nutrients they can derive from the waste material of the larger organisms in the aquarium. As a result of the efforts of this miniature cleanup crew, the aquarium water remains remarkably low in nutrients, which is very similar to the water conditions on a natural coral reef and very desirable for sensitive corals and other sessile invertebrates.

BERLIN SYSTEM

In the previous chapter we examined the process of natural nitrate reduction using a plenum. But the natural approach to maintaining a reef aquarium is not limited to Jaubert's technique. Another method, known as the Berlin method (conceived in Germany during the 1970s), relies heavily on the use of live rock (and in later versions, live sand) to carry out the important processes of biological filtration and denitrification. With this approach, no plenum is used, and the only additional filtering device used is a high-quality protein skimmer, which eliminates dissolved organic compounds. Since such systems seldom include fish or house only a few small ones, there is very little particulate matter to contend with, which makes mechanical filtration largely unnecessary. Any debris that does make its way into the aquarium can be vacuumed out easily during routine partial water changes.

Live Sand

We've already discussed live rock and how it contributes to nitrification and denitrification, but what is the role of live sand? As was mentioned in the previous chapter, live sand is sand harvested from the ocean floor that contains an array of tiny creatures, ranging from beneficial microorganisms to sand-sifting crustaceans and echinoderms. When the proper depth of sand is used (a minimum 2 to 3 inches [5 to 7.5 cm]) in the aquarium, anoxic conditions favorable to denitrifying bacteria tend to prevail deep within the sand. The sand-sifting creatures continually turn the top layer of the sand over, thereby fostering the proper oxygen gradient throughout the sand. Without these creatures, the sand would eventually compact and become anaerobic, which would undermine the denitrification process.

Not all Live Rock (or Live Sand) is Created Equal

It's important to keep in mind that spending time on the ocean floor is not the only criterion necessary for rock or sand to be considered "live" and therefore suitable for aquarium use. Remember, you're looking for a full complement of beneficial encrusting organisms, not just a batch of very costly base rock. On several occasions I have seen bargain "live rocks" for sale that had not a single organism visible on their surfaces. Perhaps such rocks would suffice for aquascaping an FO aquarium, but they would be grossly inadequate for a reef—especially one that relies exclusively on natural filtration. If all you're after are rocks to be used for aquascaping purposes, you can easily get by using inexpensive terrestrially mined limestone. Even though these rocks will be devoid of life when you buy them, they will in time support colonies of beneficial nitrifying bacteria and provide ample hiding places for the fish in your aquarium. You must of course avoid the use of rocks that could leach harmful chemicals into the water.

Live sand is another excellent addition to your tank.

The particular site on the ocean floor from which live rock or live sand has been harvested can also have an impact on quality. If collected from areas within close proximity to shore, there's a strong probability that the rock or sand will contain various harmful pollutants resulting from boat traffic, the discharge of sewage, chemical runoff from farmers' fields, and a host of other sources. Live sand from such areas has also been known to harbor—in addition to these pollutants—disease-causing microbes that can wreak havoc on your valued aquarium specimens. Reef aquarists must be especially wary of live sand collected close to shore, as it is a known source of *Vibrio* viruses, which are a major killer of small-polyp stony corals in the aquarium.

So how can you be sure that you're getting the best quality live rock or live sand possible? Actually, there's no way to be 100-percent sure, but buying from a reputable dealer is certainly a step in the right direction. And don't be afraid to ask questions about the source of the rock or sand, the manner in which it was collected, and the way it was handled after collection. A trustworthy dealer should be able to answer most, if not all, of those questions. More importantly, you should trust your own senses when selecting live rock or sand. If a particular dealer is offering discount live rock with no visible signs of life, or live sand that is coated with cyanobacteria (a.k.a. slime algae, or blue-green algae), you'll want to take your business elsewhere.

BEWARE OF ROCKS BEARING PESTS!

Thus far in our discussion of live rock I've made repeated allusions to "beneficial encrusting organisms." However, as I briefly indicated earlier in the section about cleaning and curing the live rock, there are several organisms that have been known to stow away on live rock that can become quite troublesome within the confines of an aquarium. Some of the more irksome pests that fall into this category include mantis shrimps, fireworms, and *Aiptasia* anemones. Unfortunately for aquarists, some of these organisms may arrive in the form of unhatched eggs or tiny larvae obscured within the pores of the rock, so they may escape detection during the processes of cleaning and curing.

Thumb-Splitting Shrimps

Some of the more volatile of the live rock stowaways are the mantis shrimps, known by fishermen and live rock collectors as thumbsplitters. Mantis shrimps are so named because of their large stalked eyes, elongated bodies, and hooked feeding appendages (chelae), which make them look for all intents and purposes like terrestrial praying mantises. They get the thumbsplitter nickname from their propensity to lash out with lightning speed at prey items and predators with their formidable chelae. When accidentally disturbed or handled by unwary aquarists, they can deliver a serious and painful wound. They have even been known to crack aquarium glass with their powerful punch.

Mantis shrimps are extremely efficient predators of fish, some sessile invertebrates, and other crustaceans, so securing a meal in a well-stocked aquarium is rather easy for them. Also, since they are primarily nocturnal feeders, aquarists are often unaware of their presence until prized specimens start to disappear. Unfortunately, most mantis shrimps remain hidden within holes in the live rock during the day, so locating and eradicating them can be problematic.

If you can't pinpoint the daytime refuge of a mantis shrimp, your best bet is to try to catch the stowaway using a baited trap, which you can purchase through your local aquarium dealer or from various online sources.

That being said, I should mention that not all mantis shrimps are equally harmful in the aquarium, and catching sight of one of these critters is not necessarily cause to tear the aquarium

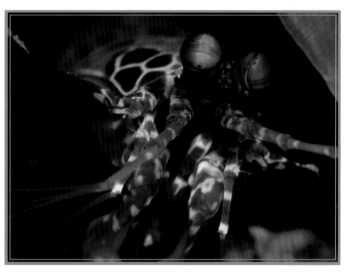

Mantis shrimps can be kept in a single-specimen tank, but make sure the tank is acrylic, not glass. Adult mantis shrimps can break glass.

apart in order to locate the shrimp. In fact, some of the larger mantis shrimp species are rather exquisitely colored, which makes them attractive to certain hobbyists who have a penchant for unusual marine species. Of course, given their predatory nature, it is necessary to give these thumbsplitters an aquarium all to themselves.

Don't Get Burned by Fireworms

Another live rock stowaway that can wreak havoc in the reef aquarium is *Hermodice carunculata*, one of the polychaete worms of the family Amphinomidae, generally called fireworms because of the venomous nature of the bristles covering their bodies. Fireworms are easily identified by the rows of fuzzy-looking bristles along their sides. But don't be fooled! Those fuzzy bristles are actually needle-like spines that can inflict a painful sting—even if the aquarist makes contact by accident.

It's important to keep in mind that most bristleworms are detritus feeders and harmless to reef invertebrates. *H. carunculata*, on the other hand, is known to feed on corals and other sessile invertebrates, as well. Fortunately, commercially manufactured traps are available on the market that can be effective in eradicating these pests.

Also, certain fish, including various triggerfish and tilefish, will happily devour any bristleworms unfortunate enough to cross their paths. However, introducing either of these fish to a reef aquarium for the purpose of bristleworm control is not recommended, since they enjoy nibbling on certain cnidarian polyps as much as *H. carunculata* does. A more reef-safe alternative for biological bristleworm control is the banded coral shrimp, *Stenopus hispidus*, which, I might add, is quite interesting and attractive in its own right.

Some Anemones You Don't Want in Your Reef Tank

Much to the dismay of many reef aquarists, some of the most desirable anemone species are notoriously difficult to keep alive in the reef aquarium because of their exacting water quality and lighting requirements. On the other hand, there is one group of anemones that not only thrives under less than ideal conditions but also resists almost any effort to eliminate them from the aquarium. These are the *Aiptasia* anemones, also called rock anemones, or glass anemones, which usually make their way into the aquarium concealed within the pores of live rock.

Aiptasia are small, drab brown or transparent anemones that can spread like wildfire throughout a reef aquarium if left to their own devices. Now, you might be asking yourself, what's so bad about anemones that are easy to care for and propagate? Isn't that the perfect type of organism for the reef aquarium? Well, if *Aiptasia* were attractive and kept their tentacles to themselves, that would be true, but unfortunately they aren't, and they don't. That is to say, *Aiptasia* add nothing to the reef in terms of aesthetics, and they have a nasty habit of

Aiptasia anemones.

repeatedly stinging desirable invertebrates, occasionally to the point of death, in order to make room for themselves among the rocks.

DEATH BY LETHAL INJECTION

Aiptasia are nearly impossible to kill through mechanical means. Any attempt to cut them off the rock merely prompts them to withdraw back into their holes out of reach. Even if you're quick enough to cut away a portion of one of these animals, it will merely re-grow as if nothing happened. In fact, shredding these animals actually propagates them, since each tiny piece has the potential to re-grow as a separate anemone! These troublesome anemones can be eliminated by injecting or coating each individual animal with various chemicals or commercial formulations, but this is an extremely tedious and painstaking process that often must be done repeatedly in order to be effective.

ANIMALS THAT EAT AIPTASIA

If you'd rather not fool around with needles and chemicals, you might want to try introducing one of the animals known to feed on *Aiptasia* in the wild. One of these is the copperband butterflyfish, *Chelmon rostratus*, which has been used successfully by many reef aquarists to eradicate *Aiptasia*. Unfortunately, this fish's taste for invertebrate flesh doesn't necessarily end with *Aiptasia*, and it may expand its menu to include your prized specimens. In addition, it can be very difficult to net and remove a butterflyfish from an aquarium if things don't go as planned. A better choice of predator might be the red-legged hermit crab, *Dardanus megistos,* or the peppermint shrimp, *Lysmata wurdemanni*, both of which have been known to consume *Aiptasia* while being generally (though not always!) trustworthy around other sessile invertebrates. They may, however, ignore the pest anemones unless deprived of other foods.

Another control option is the *Aiptasia*-nibbling nudibranch *Berghia verrucicornis*. However, as with any biological control method, hobbyists report mixed results from this species. Also, *B. verrucicornis* is an obligate *Aiptasia* feeder. In other words, its diet consists solely of these irksome anemones. That means that once (if) it eradicates all the *Aiptasia* in one aquarium, it must be moved to another aquarium containing *Aiptasia* or it will starve to death. In some cases

Like Rock Pests and Control Methods

Suspect	Wanted For	Controls
Mantis shrimps, (a.k.a. thumbsplitters)	Devouring tankmates and wounding aquarists	Search and destroy, commercial traps
Fireworms	Devouring tankmates and stinging aquarists	Commercial traps, banded coral shrimp
Aiptasia anemone, (alias rock or glass anemone)	Killing neighbors and being ugly and prolific	Chemical injections, commercial formulations, dopperband butterflyfish, red-legged hermit crab, peppermint shrimp, *Berghia verrucicornis*

The peppermint shrimp, *Lysmata wurdemanni.*

aquarists pass the animals around once they've done their job in one tank so that everyone can benefit and so that the nudibranchs can thrive.

SUMMARY

As you can see, the combination of protein skimming and living filtration can make a significant contribution to the marine aquarium. Even many pests can be controlled biologically by including predators of the pests among the livestock. The benefits from live rock and live sand make their use in an FO system (making it an FOWLR one) very substantial, and they are basic to a reef system.

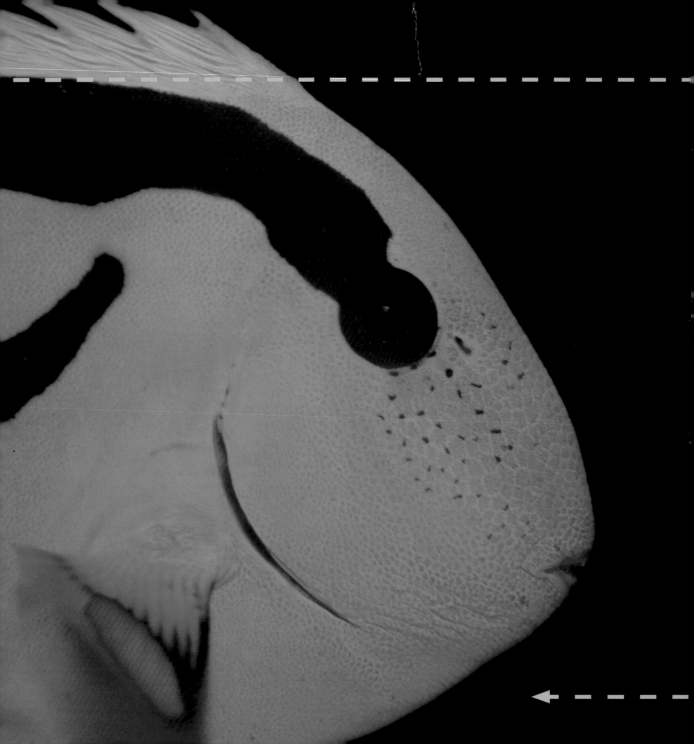

Chapter 7

Water Changes: The Ultimate Key to Aquarium Success

Up to this point, we've examined several methods of filtering and purifying the water in your aquarium, each of which relies heavily on specialized equipment or certain biological processes within the aquarium system. But in this chapter we'll discuss the critical role that routine partial water changes play in the management of healthy, thriving marine fish and/or invertebrates.

What Lies Ahead

- the benefits of water change
- more is better
- how to change your water

The water change is arguably the most important of all maintenance tasks carried out by the aquarist. In fact, I would suggest that no amount of expensive high-tech filtering gadgets and gizmos can completely eliminate the need for water changes, although there are some who would disagree with this assessment. The beauty of water changes is that they are completely within the control of the aquarist, and to a certain extent they serve as a safeguard against a wide range of water quality blunders common to novice aquarists (and quite a few experienced ones, I might add), such as overfeeding and overstocking.

CHANGING TIMES

In the good old days of the marine aquarium hobby—before the benefits of water changes were fully understood and before low-cost, high-quality synthetic sea salt mixes had arrived on the market—water changes were generally postponed for as long as possible. In fact, utilizing the same aquarium water for a prolonged period of time was considered to be a bragging point by many pioneer hobbyists. And who could blame them? If I had to concoct my own salt mix out of various chemical elements or make repeated trips to the beach to collect buckets of natural sea water, I probably wouldn't bother with water changes either. But nowadays modern one-step salt mixes make it extremely easy, and relatively inexpensive, for marine aquarists to give their charges all the clean salt water they need.

GUARANTEED NITRATE REDUCTION

Of all the methods of nitrate reduction available to aquarists, the only 100-percent guaranteed method is the water change. It's also the safest. There is really no downside to changing the water. But if a predictable water change schedule is put in place immediately after the aquarium's biological filter becomes fully established, the nitrates and other undesirable compounds should remain at a constant low level.

I should mention, however, that in some cases nitrate might be present in tap water, which means you could be adding low levels of nitrate to the aquarium with each water change. With an FO aquarium, the amount of nitrate added in this way would probably be inconsequential, but it could make a difference in a reef, where little or no measurable nitrate should be present. To safeguard against this eventuality—or if a call to your local water utility reveals that nitrate is indeed present in your municipal water supply—you will definitely want to process your tap water through a reverse-osmosis unit (a good idea anyway, but more on that later) or a denitrifying filter before mixing in the salt and adding the water to the aquarium.

Nothing helps the overall health of your tank more than regular water changes.

PHOSPHATE REDUCTION

Phosphate is another dissolved compound that can accumulate to harmful levels if not diluted through regular partial water changes. Phosphate is a compound that is present in all living things. It is usually introduced into the aquarium with fish foods, as a result of various biological processes, or via low-quality synthetic salt mixes. Like nitrate, phosphate can also be found in some tap water. In the aquarium, high levels of phosphate can fuel blooms of filamentous algae and unsightly cyanobacteria (slime algae or blue-green algae). Fish are not especially troubled by phosphate, but invertebrates respond poorly to even minuscule amounts. Stony corals are especially sensitive to phosphate, as it interferes with their ability to manufacture their calcareous skeletons.

Detecting phosphate is relatively easy, since it typically makes its presence known by the proliferation of algae. You can also test for it with a phosphate test kit available at any aquarium store. On the other hand, eliminating phosphate altogether can be a much trickier proposition, since it can arrive in the aquarium through so many different sources. If your water supply is the suspected or confirmed (by testing) source of phosphate, you can usually

An Underwater Odd Couple

The various shrimp gobies, which are members of approximately five different genera in the enormous family Gobiidae, get their name from the peculiar mutualism that they develop with pistol shrimps (family Alpheidae). With each shrimp/goby team, the shrimp uses its outstanding digging skills to maintain the tunnel that both occupy, and it won't hesitate to drive off intruders with an audible snap from its impressive claws. Fortunately (for the goby), it will never turn its claws against its goby companion. The almost-blind pistol shrimp also benefits from the relationship because the goby stands guard for predators as the shrimp cleans the burrow or sifts the sand for food. The only question is, can two completely unrelated marine organisms occupy the same burrow without driving each other crazy? Apparently yes!

take care of the problem by filtering your tap water through a reverse osmosis unit. You should also check the package of your synthetic sea salt mix to make sure it contains no phosphate. With high-quality mixes, this information should be clearly emblazoned on the package. If neither your tap water nor your salt mix is the culprit, you may need to cut back on the amount you're feeding or reduce the number of specimens in the aquarium. Of course, stepping up your water change regimen is the most efficient way to keep phosphate levels under control.

THE EFFECT OF WATER CHANGES ON AQUARIUM LIVESTOCK

In order to truly understand the importance of water changes for your fish and invertebrates, try to imagine being locked in a poorly ventilated room for a month with several of your closest friends. Assume that you have a full bathroom and that you'll still be given three square meals each day and possibly television privileges, but no one will be allowed to leave the confines of the room. Under such circumstances, everyone's nerves might get a little frayed, but it would, perhaps, be tolerable. Now imagine being confined to that same poorly ventilated room, but with no functional plumbing and no provision for garbage removal. Now things are getting a bit dicey! Within a matter of days, everyone in the room would likely be pleading with their captors (just for the sake of illustration, let's assume they're giant fish, keeping humans as pets) for a window or door to be opened to allow for at least a partial exchange of air. That's essentially what we put our fish and invertebrates through when we put off water changes for a prolonged period of time. Sure, the aquarium's filtration system can eliminate many of the pollutants, but harmful compounds will ultimately accumulate until they reach intolerable levels.

It's not surprising, then, that both fish and invertebrates exhibit much better overall health, superior coloration, and a heightened level of activity after a partial water change is performed. In fact, after observing the almost joyful response of my fish to a long overdue water change, I really feel guilty for not performing them more frequently.

HOW MUCH AND HOW OFTEN?

In most cases, frequent smaller water changes are preferable to infrequent larger ones. A good rule of thumb for a minimal water change regimen is to change approximately 10 percent of the tank volume every two weeks, although some aquarists favor a 20-percent water change once a month. In a larger system containing very few specimens, a monthly water change might be adequate, but I would strongly encourage bi-weekly changes—especially while you're still getting accustomed to the ins and outs of your new aquarium. Of course, changing more than the minimum is always better!

Make sure that the salinity, temperature, and pH of the water you're adding to the tank during a change is equal to the water already in the change. Wild fluctuations can damage your fish and invertebrates.

Fish Fact

Nature Abhors a Vacuum—But Remoras Don't!

One of the more unusual adaptations exhibited by a marine fish is the suction disk located atop the flattened head of the remora (family Echeneidae). The remora comes by its nickname, "shark sucker," honestly. Its first dorsal fin is modified into a disk that is covered with a series of ridges—actually modified dorsal spines. When a suitable chauffer swims by, the remora glides beneath it and attaches its disk to the underside of the shark (or turtle, or whale, or boat—they're not picky!) through a series of muscle contractions, forming an almost unbreakable vacuum seal. Contrary to popular belief, remoras do not clean parasites from the bodies of their hosts. Rather, they use their hosts to get where they want to go and will detach to hunt for themselves whenever suitable food items are spotted—often the scraps of their ride's meals.

Remember, the conditions on tropical coral reefs are highly stable, and changing the water more often ensures that the water parameters will not fluctuate markedly. Frequent changes also ensure that the various trace elements found in synthetic salt mixes, which are necessary for the healthy functioning of marine fish and invertebrates, are replenished in a timely manner.

SOMETIMES BIGGER IS BETTER

There are certain events that might demand a very large water change, such as a sudden precipitous rise in ammonia or nitrite levels. However, in a case like that you can't just change the water and call it a day. The spiking ammonia or nitrite would most likely be a symptom of some major problem in the system, such as a decomposing dead animal hidden in the rockwork or a broken-down filter. Whatever the source of the problem, you need to locate and correct it with dispatch once you've saved your livestock by changing the water and getting the accumulated toxins under control.

Occasionally you might want to perform larger water changes in order to keep your aquarium's nitrate level within the acceptable range. Even when performing routine 10-percent water changes, the nitrate level can rise over time, depending on the biological load in the aquarium. For example, if the nitrate level in an FO system measures 40 parts per million (the approximate upper limit for most marine fish) prior to a 10-percent water change, it would only be reduced by 4 ppm following the change. In other words, the nitrate level would only be diluted to approximately 36 ppm, which is still dangerously close to exceeding the safe range. If more specimens are added following that water change, or if the aquarist overfeeds the fish on several occasions, the nitrate level could rise well beyond the safe level before the next scheduled water change, and then changing only 10 percent of the water volume probably would not be adequate to bring the nitrate level back into the safe range.

A STEP-BY-STEP WATER CHANGE

Performing a routine partial water change is a fairly straightforward proposition, but it won't hurt for us to examine the process in detail anyway. When I first got started in the marine aquarium hobby, I found it extremely helpful to work from a checklist whenever I did a water change. That way I could be sure that I hadn't missed any important steps. I also included several additional maintenance tasks in my water change checklist to ensure that they would be completed in a timely manner. The list looked something like this:

- Disconnect power to filters and pumps.

- Remove and clean cover glass.

- Clean algae from the front glass pane with an algae magnet (I allow algae to grow on the sides and back as "tang fodder").

- Siphon the goal (at least 10 percent) of the aquarium's water volume into bucket while vacuuming the substrate.

- Rinse out prefilters and filter media, using aquarium water in bucket.

- Clean patches of slime algae from rockwork.

- Inspect all equipment for proper functioning.

- Clean and rinse protein skimmer, filters, pumps, hoses, and attachments using assorted brushes and aquarium water.

- Clean salt creep from power cords, top edge of the aquarium, etc.

- Use already prepared new salt water, made with dechlorinated tap water processed through reverse-osmosis and a high-quality salt mix.

- Make sure the temperature and salinity of the replacement water match that of the aquarium water.

- Very gradually add the replacement water to the aquarium.

- Power up the equipment and replace the cover glass.

Of course, there's no law that says you have to follow this list exactly as I've outlined it. You can modify it in any way that makes sense to you. And if you're not as forgetful as I am, there's no need to make a list at all.

You may also have noticed that I didn't mention anything about replacing filter media on the checklist. That's because it's best to change filter media a couple of days before or after a water change so you don't disrupt the biological filter too much. Remember, nitrifying bacteria will proliferate on any suitable surface in the aquarium, including the sponge or floss in your mechanical filter and any activated carbon that you might be using in the system. If all of these media are removed from the aquarium simultaneously, you may be eliminating a substantial portion of your biofilter, which could precipitate a dangerous spike in ammonia or nitrite.

HOW TO AVOID A MOUTHFUL OF DIRTY SALT WATER

One aspect of water changes that literally leaves a bad taste in many aquarists' mouths is having to get the siphon started by placing one end of the hose in the aquarium and sucking on the other end. Those who don't react quickly enough once the water starts flowing usually receive a mouthful of dirty salt water for their trouble. While this is not likely to result in any major health problems, it's certainly not a pleasant experience!

Fortunately, there's a technique that you can use to start the siphon without ever putting the hose to your lips. In order for this method to work, the bucket used to catch the wastewater must be positioned well below the level of the aquarium, but not so low that the hose can't reach. All you have to do is place one end of the siphon hose inside the bucket and hold the end with the wide vacuum attachment over the aquarium with the opening facing up. Slowly submerge the vacuum attachment into the aquarium water until it is completely filled with water. Then raise the vacuum end out of the aquarium, allowing the water to rush down into

Fish Fact

Tool-Wielding Crustaceans

Scientists typically associate the use of tools with humans and other higher primates. But the minuscule boxer crab, *Lybia tessellata*, a mere crustacean, has been known to carry a tiny anemone in each claw and to brandish them threateningly as a warning to potential predators. To the casual observer, this is an absurd spectacle, looking rather like a crabby cheerleader with miniature pompons, but to the crab the anemones can mean the difference between life and death. In fact, the only time the boxing crab puts aside its tentacled weapons is when it's preparing to shed its exoskeleton.

Decide on a schedule for your water changes (every Wednesday before dinner, every Saturday morning, etc.) and stick to it.

the bucket. Just before all of the water drains from the vacuum end, submerge it into the aquarium again in the same fashion as before. If you time it right, the water will continue to flow into the bucket. You can then position the vacuum so that the opening faces the bottom of the aquarium and begin vacuuming the substrate. Don't be concerned if it takes you a few tries to get the hang of this method, but rest assured, once you've mastered this method, you'll never want to go back to siphoning by mouth.

SUMMARY

Regular water changes are the easiest and best tool you can use to maintain water quality. In addition, massive water changes are the only feasible way to address a sudden water quality problem, but they will only remove the danger—you still need to discover the cause and remedy it.

Chapter 8

Getting the Aquarium Up and Running

Now that we've explored the major life support systems for your new marine aquarium, it's time to put all the pieces together. After testing for leaks by filling the tank with fresh water and examining the seams over a 24-hour period, your tank should be completely drained, secured on its stand, and carefully leveled. Be sure to leave adequate space at the back and sides for cords, tubing, and any equipment to be added later on. Also, all of your heating, lighting, and filtration equipment should be in place and ready to be turned on when the time comes. Soon you'll be ready to start mixing salt water! But before you can begin filling the tank, you'll need to install your substrate, rockwork,

What Lies Ahead

- how to properly set up your tank

and decorations (if you choose to include any), making sure that everything is firmly affixed so nothing can tumble over and crack the glass or scratch the acrylic. Believe me, you'll be surprised at how efficiently some fish and invertebrates can upset seemingly stable piles of rock with their wanderings—which often include burrowing that can undermine structures much larger than the fish.

SUITABLE SUBSTRATES

Using a substrate in a marine aquarium has its advantages and disadvantages. I prefer to use one for purely aesthetic reasons. That is, it creates the natural look I've grown accustomed to seeing when diving on coral reefs. An appropriate substrate also has the benefit of buffering the pH of the water. In other words, substrates suitable for use in salt water will continually leach calcium carbonate, which helps stabilize the pH within the desired range of 8.2 to 8.4. A substrate is necessary if you intend to keep burrowing or sand-sifting organisms in the aquarium.

However, some would argue, especially those reef aquarists who don't favor natural filtration methods, that the substrate merely serves to entrap particulate waste, which causes the nitrate level to rise as the waste decomposes. The bottom line is that the decision whether or not to use a substrate is entirely up to you. As long as you're prepared to vacuum it gently during each partial water change, you shouldn't experience any water quality problems associated with the substrate.

So which materials are suitable for use as marine aquarium substrates and which are not? The best choices include crushed coral, dolomite, and aragonite gravel. Not only are these materials excellent pH buffers, but they also offer that pristine natural appearance that makes the aquarium look like an authentic slice of coral reef. Fine-grain sand can also be used as a substrate, provided you're not using an undergravel filter. The fine grains would tend to clog the filter and reduce its effectiveness. If you decide to use sand, it's very important to stir it occasionally to keep it from becoming anaerobic and to keep particulate matter from getting trapped. Anaerobic conditions coupled with decomposing waste can lead to the production of hydrogen sulfide gas, which, as you are now aware, is highly toxic to most living organisms. This is not such an issue when live sand is used, because the sand-sifting organisms that inhabit the sand will turn it over continually through their feeding activities.

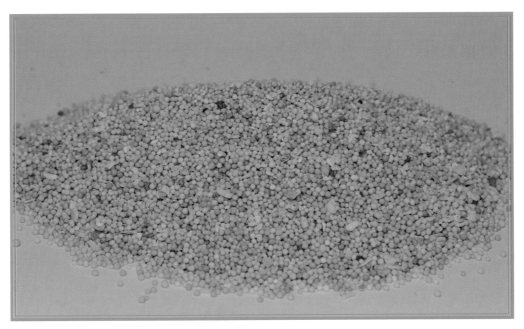

You can use certain substrates, like this aragonite gravel, to help maintain your tank's pH.

No Brightly Colored Gravel, Please!

As far as I'm concerned, the various gravels that are popular in the freshwater side of the hobby have no place in marine aquariums. Not only do they lack the buffering capacity of most marine substrates, but they also create the wrong aesthetic impression. The earth-toned gravels that are most commonly used in freshwater tanks create a look reminiscent of a riverbed or lake bottom rather than the ocean floor. As far as those garish, fluorescent-colored gravels are concerned, there may actually be laws against their use on the books somewhere, probably under the heading, "Crimes Against the Senses."

Substrate Depth

In the FO aquarium, a substrate depth of 2 to 3 inches (5 to 7.5 cm) is generally more than adequate, and there's certainly nothing wrong with using less. The only reason you might want to make the substrate deeper is if you intend to keep certain burrowing fish, such as the different species of jawfish (family Opistognathidae), which require enough sand or gravel to completely conceal their elongated bodies while "tail-standing" in a vertical position. But if no burrowing or tunneling fish are present, the substrate is primarily decorative in purpose, and the depth is fairly arbitrary, although it will, in due time, contribute to the biological filtration of the aquarium.

In my very first FO system (a 55-gallon [200-liter] tank), I placed approximately 1 inch (2.5 cm) of aragonite gravel in front of the rockwork, while leaving the area beneath and behind the rocks free of substrate. I also affixed a powerhead to the back pane near the bottom with its discharge directed along the back of the aquarium. With this configuration, I could readily siphon out any debris that collected in the substrate at the front of the aquarium, and the powerhead prevented debris from settling beneath and behind the rocks. Unfortunately, because I didn't properly screen the powerhead intake at the time, it was responsible for the death of a banded coral shrimp, which got stuck on the intake and couldn't break free. You live and learn!

How deep your substrate is depends on what fish you keep. Jawfish will require a deeper substrate because they will dig burrows.

Rinsing the Substrate

Whichever type of substrate you choose, be sure to rinse it out thoroughly in clean fresh water before placing it into the aquarium to eliminate most of the fine dust that is invariably packaged along with the gravel. To accomplish this, simply place the gravel in a clean plastic bucket and add water to the bucket until it rises well past the level of the gravel. Then swirl your hand through the gravel repeatedly and drain off the dirty water. Take care not to dump any of the substrate in the process. Repeat these steps until the water remains relatively clear. Depending on how much you buy, it may be necessary to divide the gravel into manageably small quantities for cleaning. If you fail to rinse the substrate ahead of time, your aquarium water will assume the color of milk for several days until the dust completely settles out. Of course, live sand requires no rinsing and should never be treated in this manner.

CHOOSING THE ROCKWORK

Once you've settled on an appropriate substrate, you'll want to select an assortment of rocks to be fashioned into an artificial reef wall for an FO system or used as a foundation for the live rock in a reef tank. Some of the better choices include tufa, limestone, coquina, and lava rock, each of which is adequately porous to promote the proliferation of nitrifying bacteria and to minimize the displacement of water. These rocks are generally soft enough so that their shapes can be altered as needed through mechanical means. Try to choose uniquely shaped rocks that can be stacked in a natural presentation without creating the look of a contrived stone wall.

Installing the Rockwork

In order to ensure the stability of the rockwork in the aquarium, it should be installed on top of the bare glass bottom prior to installation of the substrate. An exception is live rock, which should be placed in the tank only after the tank is partially filled with water. It's highly recommended that the rocks be secured to the bottom of the tank and to each other with dabs of aquarium-safe silicone to minimize the likelihood of mini-avalanches.

Some aquarists prefer to stack the rocks right up against the back pane of the aquarium to achieve maximum support and to gain the greatest amount of space at the front of the tank. And, indeed, this is a good technique to employ in a reef if you want to display the invertebrates to their greatest advantage. However, in an FO aquarium it is desirable to leave a gap between the back glass and the rockwork so the fish have plenty of room to hide. Although it seems counterintuitive, they'll actually spend more time out in the open if they know that ample refuge is close at hand (fin?). Leaving a gap at the back and on either side of the rockwork also creates a nice circular swimming pattern, so the fish don't have to reverse

If your rockwork is not set up properly it can fall and crack your tank's glass, which will lead to a big wet mess.

direction continually as they move about the tank. The open space at the back of the tank also makes it easier to conceal submersible heaters, undergravel filter uplift tubes, filter return hoses, and any other equipment that must be placed directly into the main aquarium.

Another important factor to consider when arranging the rockwork is the number of caves, crevices, nooks, and crannies that are provided for the fish. Again, the more hiding places and bolt holes you provide, the more safe and secure the fish will feel, and the more they'll make themselves available for your viewing pleasure at the front of the tank. If you select irregularly shaped rocks rather than uniformly slab-shaped ones, you'll be able to create a honeycomb effect, similar to what the fish would find in their natural surroundings on the coral reef. This honeycomb layout also makes it easier for the invertebrates in a reef aquarium to find suitable ledges and outcroppings on which to secure a foothold.

ARE DECORATIONS REDUNDANT?

The decision whether or not to include decorations in a marine aquarium is largely based on personal preference and aesthetic sensibility. Some would suggest that tropical marine fish and invertebrates are so strikingly beautiful that there's little need for additional accents in the aquarium. Others feel that aquascaping with a few tasteful and judiciously placed decorations only serves to enhance the natural beauty of the marine organisms. If you fall into the latter category, by all means feel free to experiment with a few decorative elements. Just be sure that any ornament you're thinking of placing into the aquarium, whether it's natural or artificial, is completely safe for use in a marine aquarium.

Play it Safe When You Decorate

Some of the more whimsical decorations that are commonly sold for freshwater aquariums—you know, those plastic deep-sea divers, sunken ships, skeletons, treasure chests, castles, and the like—may not be suitable for use in marine aquariums. In some instances, they may even contain paints or other materials that will release toxins when they come into contact with salt water. To play it safe, check the label of any artificial aquarium decoration to verify that it is specifically manufactured for use in salt water, and if there is any question, don't risk it. As a general rule, you can immediately disqualify any decorations that contain metals, since the metal will react with the salt water.

Make sure your decorations don't have any sharp edges that can harm your fish, especially fish like this hawkfish that likes to perch on objects in the aquarium.

Even Better Than the Real Thing!

Some of the better decorative choices for marine FO aquariums are the synthetic reproductions of sessile invertebrates, such as stony corals, sponges, and sea fans, that are manufactured out of environmentally friendly resins. Compared to similar products of the past, which were rather garishly colored and clumsily fashioned, the modern versions come in naturalistic tones and are very intricately and convincingly designed. Once these products spend a little time in the aquarium and begin to develop a natural patina of algae, it can be hard to tell them apart from the real thing.

The Trouble With Coral Skeletons

In the early days of marine fishkeeping, no aquarium was complete without at least a few bleached coral skeletons. At that time they provided the only means of creating anything approximating a naturalistic reef setting. Nowadays the popularity of using natural coral skeletons as decorations has waned among aquarists for several reasons.

For one thing, the wild collection of coral skeletons can have a serious impact on the health and sustainability of the reefs, depending on the particular collection method that is used. For another, the heavily convoluted skeletons, which are usually considered the most attractive, can be difficult to clean thoroughly. This means decaying polyps may be introduced into the aquarium, where they will continue to decompose to the detriment of water quality. Finally, coral skeletons tend to trap uneaten food, fish waste, and other detritus with remarkable efficiency, again, leading to the degradation of water quality. Large univalve seashells are also big detritus trappers. Though some shells are extremely beautiful and great fun to collect, your best bet is to leave them out of your aquarium unless they serve as alternate homes for a resident hermit crab.

TIME TO GET WET!

Now that your substrate, rockwork, and decorations are in place (with the possible exceptions of the live rock and live sand, which should be added after the tank has been partially filled with water), and all your heating, lighting, and water purification equipment is installed and ready for operation, it's time to mix up your first batch of salt water. However, you should be aware that your municipal tap water supply might contain various contaminants, such as nitrate, phosphate, copper, lead, and aluminum among other things, that may be hazardous to marine life, even if they are of little consequence to humans. Also, tap water is usually treated with a chemical like chlorine or chloramine to make it safe for human consumption.

In order to ensure that no harmful contaminants or dissolved organic compounds are introduced into your aquarium, it is highly recommended that you purify your tap water with a reverse osmosis (RO) unit prior to adding the synthetic salt mix, especially if you intend to set up a reef tank. No matter what, you must also remove the chlorine or chloramine from the water with some sort of chemical dechlorinator or

Some local fish stores will sell you premixed salt water. Check to see if your store offers this.

dechloraminator before it is suitable for aquarium use. Such products are relatively inexpensive and simple to use. Usually adding a drop or two per gallon of water is all that is necessary.

WHAT IS REVERSE OSMOSIS?

The process of reverse osmosis involves forcing the water from your tap through a semi-permeable membrane that retains most of the contaminants that might either poison marine organisms directly or contribute to the overall degradation of water quality. To a certain extent, the RO membrane even excludes bacteria and viruses, although this is no guarantee that certain aquatic diseases won't be a problem. Pathogenic microorganisms can still make their way into the aquarium, especially whenever new fish or invertebrates are introduced.

RO-purified water should be used every time you prepare replacement salt water to be used after a partial water change and every time you replace fresh water lost to evaporation. Fresh water, rather than salt water, is used to compensate for evaporation because the salt that is mixed with the water does not evaporate; only the water evaporates. If you top off the evaporated water with salt water, the salinity will rise beyond the desired level.

MIXING THE SALT WATER

Adding the synthetic salt mix to the RO-purified and dechlorinated/dechloraminated water is a simple procedure. Considering the significant volume of salt water that is needed to completely fill a large aquarium, you might find it easier to mix the water and synthetic salt in the tank itself during the initial setup phase. Of course, if you prefer, you can also mix up the salt water in separate buckets and then carefully pour it into the aquarium one bucket at a time. Once the aquarium is operating and the fish and/or invertebrates have been added, you'll need to mix all of your salt water for partial water changes in separate buckets. Never add salt mix to an established tank.

Be sure any buckets you use are made of plastic (preferably food-grade) and have never been contaminated with any household cleaners, detergents, or any other substance that might potentially be toxic to marine organisms. It's also a good idea to clearly mark your buckets as "clean salt water only" or "aquarium use only" with an indelible marker so that you never have to worry about someone accidentally using them as mop buckets. These buckets can be purchased from any hardware or department store. Of course, empty synthetic sea salt buckets are ideal for this purpose, as well.

That being said, let's get back to mixing our salt water. At this stage, you'll need a high-quality synthetic salt mix, a hydrometer (either the swing-needle variety or a standard floating one—more on this in a moment), a plastic or wooden stirring stick, and RO-purified tap water. Begin adding water either directly to the tank or to a separate bucket. The tank should be filled no more than three-fourths of the way. The remaining 25 percent of tank volume can be used to make any minor specific gravity adjustments as needed. You can fill the bucket as high as you like, as long as you can lift it over the aquarium without losing control and spilling some of the water or, worse yet, dropping the entire bucket onto the tank.

Slowly start stirring in the salt mix, pouring very gradually and making sure that each

Fish Fact

Handle Me With Care!

The common names chosen for marine fish are often based on a particular fish's color pattern, body shape, or some natural behavior it is known to exhibit. When it comes to the various members of the family Acanthuridae—the surgeonfish—the common name should be taken as a warning to aquarists to "handle with care." All of the members of this family, though relatively peaceful in the aquarium, are equipped with scalpel-like retractable spines on the caudal peduncle (the base of the caudal fin). These razor-sharp spines are capable of inflicting nasty lacerations on the fingers and hands of careless aquarists, so care must be taken when moving these fish and during routine aquarium maintenance to avoid injury.

batch dissolves completely before adding more. If you add the salt too quickly, it won't dissolve properly, and you'll tend to get inaccurate hydrometer readings. It's a good idea to measure out approximately one cup at a time with a plastic measuring cup so you'll have at least a vague idea of how much salt must be mixed with each gallon of water in order to reach the desired salinity level. You should also test the water with your hydrometer after each addition of salt so you'll know when the correct salinity has been reached.

Specific Gravity and the Role of the Hydrometer

I just mentioned that you should test the salinity of your water with a hydrometer as you mix it, but this isn't entirely accurate. A hydrometer measures specific gravity, not salinity. So what's the difference? The salinity is a measure of the total amount of dissolved salts in a saltwater mixture, which is read in grams per liter, or parts per thousand. Specific gravity is an indirect measure of salinity. A hydrometer actually compares the weight of a sample of salt water with the weight of an equal volume of distilled water. The more dissolved salts that are present in the sample, the higher the specific gravity and, for all intents and purposes, the higher the salinity. For example, a water sample that has a specific gravity of 1.020 at 77°F (25°C) has a salinity of 29.8 g/liter, while a sample with a specific gravity of 1.024 at that same temperature has a salinity of 35.5 g/liter. The two scales may measure something completely different, but there is a direct correlation between the results.

Both the swing-needle hydrometer and the traditional floating hydrometer will give accurate measurements of specific gravity, but I would recommend that you stick with the swing-needle style. I've tried both, and I find that the swing-needle models are simpler to use and much easier to read. After all, it's hard to mistake the reading when there's a big needle pointing directly to it. With floating hydrometers, on the other hand, you have to squint your eyes to see which graduated mark on the float lines up exactly with the surface of the water in the beaker.

What is the Correct Specific Gravity?

As I've mentioned time and time again, the water parameters in the world's oceans, especially around tropical coral reefs, are remarkably stable, and this applies equally to the specific gravity. That's not to suggest that a hydrometer reading taken in the Caribbean would be perfectly identical to one taken in the tropical Pacific or one taken from the Red Sea. Indeed, you might get significantly different results from each location (up to 1.035 in the Red Sea!). On the other hand, if you were to take several measurements over the course of many years in the same location, you would get nearly identical results each time. So what does this tell us about the correct specific gravity for a marine aquarium?

As with all other conditions, it's not the exact value of the specific gravity that is most

Why Is the Specific Gravity in My Dealer's Tanks so Low?

I mentioned that the ideal range for the specific gravity in a marine aquarium is between 1.022 and 1.024. Why, then, do so many dealers keep the specific gravity of their aquarium water much lower than this? (My dealer keeps his around 1.018.) The reason is that they're trying to minimize the number of parasites and pathogenic microorganisms that are present on the fish. Wild-caught fish, along with the various pests that are found on their bodies, are accustomed to the relatively high specific gravity of the ocean. While the fish can adjust to a considerably lower specific gravity (provided the transition takes place very gradually), many of the pathogenic organisms cannot, and they are subsequently killed by the osmotic shock.

important; it's the stability. A good target range for the specific gravity in an FO marine aquarium is 1.022 to 1.024. Ideally you should choose a value within that range and keep your water stable at that value. In a reef tank, a stable value at the higher end of this range (or even slightly higher, up to 1.025) is preferable. Even a seemingly slight variation, say from 1.022 to 1.023 over the course of 24 hours, would be excessive and could adversely affect the health of your livestock. To prevent such dramatic swings, it's very important to top off any fresh water lost to evaporation on a daily basis and to make sure the specific gravity of the clean salt water you add after a partial water change exactly matches that of the water in your aquarium.

What's Wrong With Using Natural Sea Water?

Readers who live on or near the coast may be asking themselves, "Why go through all the trouble of purifying tap water, measuring and mixing synthetic sea salt, and testing the specific gravity over and over again, when all I have to do is make a quick trip to the beach to collect a few buckets of natural sea water?" The truth of the matter is that using natural sea water in the aquarium is fraught with problems. For one thing, you probably wouldn't have much choice but to collect it from very close to shore, which means you'd likely be getting water contaminated with pollutants introduced through boat traffic, the dumping of raw sewage, agricultural runoff, and a host of other sources. Also, natural sea water can introduce a wide range of parasites and pathogenic microorganisms into the aquarium, some of which may be extremely difficult to eradicate once they get established. And truth be told, lugging heavy buckets full of water from the shore to your car and then transporting them home without any major spills is a logistical nightmare. You're better off mixing your own salt water, using RO-purified tap water and a high-quality synthetic salt mix. That way you can be sure that you're starting off on the right foot.

Tweaking the Specific Gravity

Let's assume that you've decided to mix the salt water for your marine aquarium in the tank itself. You've filled it three-quarters of the way with water, and you've gradually been adding synthetic salt mix one cup at a time, aiming for a target specific gravity of, say, 1.022. What happens if your last hydrometer reading indicates that the specific gravity is actually 1.023? Do you drain all of the water and start all over again? Not at all! This is exactly what you should use that remaining 25 percent of aquarium volume for. Consider it your margin of error. All you have to do is gradually dilute the water in the aquarium with a little fresh water (dechlorinated/dechloraminated and RO-purified, of course) until the specific gravity comes down to the desired level. On the other hand, if your hydrometer reading is too low, simply continue to add salt until the specific gravity reading is high enough.

ADDING LIVE ROCK AND LIVE SAND

As I've already indicated, live rock and live sand should be installed only after the aquarium has been partially filled with water. To ensure that the beneficial encrusting and sand-sifting organisms are not exposed to wildly fluctuating salinity levels, it's highly recommended that you mix your salt water to the correct specific gravity in a separate container, rather than in the aquarium itself, if you intend to use live rock or live sand. As a general rule, you'll want to use 1 to 1.5 pounds of live rock per gallon of water. This amount of rock can displace a considerable amount of water, so the tank should be no more than half full when you add the rock. Be sure to have extra salt water mixed and ready in the likely event that you'll still need to top off the aquarium after adding the rock.

When positioning the live rock on top of its base-rock foundation, keep in mind that every live rock technically has an upside and a downside. In other words, the side of the rock that was exposed as it lay on the ocean floor should be facing upward in the aquarium as well. Why? That portion of the rock likely will be more heavily encrusted with organisms requiring oxygenated conditions and at least some exposure to sunlight. The side of the rock that was in contact with the ocean floor (perhaps even partially buried in the sand), on the other hand, should face downward in the aquarium. Reverse this position and you risk losing most of the desirable encrusting organisms, the whole reason you paid the long dollar for live rock in the first place.

When adding live sand, it's very easy to cloud the aquarium with tiny white particles. This can be avoided, or at least minimized, by very slowly lowering the plastic bag containing the sand until it comes to rest on the bottom of the aquarium. Pinch the top of the bag closed

Live rock and live sand will help you cycle your tank, and is a more humane option than using a damsel, like the one pictured, as a source of ammonia.

with your fingers so none of the sand can escape as you lower it. Once you have it resting on the bottom, gently tip it over and pour out the contents. The slower you pour, the less water clouding you'll experience. Then very gently and evenly spread the sand across the bottom of the tank with your hands. Once the live rock and/or sand are in place, and the aquarium is filled to capacity with salt water of the correct specific gravity, the protein skimmer should be turned on immediately to remove any dissolved pollutants introduced with the rock or sand. No matter how diligently you may have cleaned and cured the rock ahead of time, it's still very likely that some die-off will continue to occur within the aquarium, and the skimmer will help to minimize the impact to your water quality.

MAKING SURE ALL SYSTEMS ARE GO

Okay, your rockwork, substrate, and decorations are in place, your protein skimmer is skimming along nicely, and your aquarium is finally filled with salt water. It's time to fire up the rest of the equipment to make sure everything is working as it should be. But before plugging anything in, carefully examine all of the equipment power cords to make sure none is damaged or frayed. Try to arrange the cords in a neat, organized fashion, so they are easily accessible but still hidden from view as much as possible. Also, make sure there is a bend or loop in the middle of each power cord so salt water cannot travel straight down the cord into the power outlet, causing a short. If your light fixture is suspended over the aquarium, make sure it is high enough so that water cannot splash onto it easily, or place a tight-fitting cover glass over the aquarium.

If you haven't done so already, consider using a ground fault circuit interrupter (GF[C]I) in conjunction with all of the electrical equipment. A GF(C)I will instantaneously disrupt the flow of current to an electrical device in the event of accidental immersion. I was extremely grateful to have this technology several years back when I accidentally dropped a fluorescent hood—lit, of course—into a freshwater aquarium. Knowing full well that electricity and water are a lethal combination, out of reflex I tried to grab the fixture as it fell into the water. The hood was a total loss, but I luckily escaped unscathed thanks to the GF(C)I.

A GF(C)I outlet or power strip is a mandatory piece of equipment.

Once you've taken all necessary steps to minimize the danger of electrocution, it's safe to plug in your heater, lights, and filtration equipment. Give everything a thorough once-over to make sure there are no malfunctions, excessively loud motors, leaky connections, and so on. If you're using a wet-dry biofilter, you might need to adjust the height of the intake chamber up or down slightly at this point in order to keep the water level in both the aquarium and sump in equilibrium. When you're satisfied that everything is operating as it should, you can leave all the equipment up and running as if the fish or invertebrates are already in the aquarium. Before too long, you'll be ready to introduce your first specimens, but there's one major hurdle yet to be overcome: the cycling process. We will cover cycling in the next chapter.

Chapter 9

Hurry Up and Wait:
Cycling the Aquarium

It's at this stage of the set-up process that many budding aquarists begin to lose patience and choose to rush headlong into the introduction of animals. After all, why wait? All of the equipment is fully functional, the temperature and specific gravity are right on target, and the water looks crystal clear. What better time to add the fish or invertebrates? Actually, this is the worst time to introduce them. In fact, to do so now would likely result in the death of all the desired creatures in the tank and, subsequently, despair and loss of interest on the part of the aquarist.

What Lies Ahead

- New Tank Syndrome
- the different ways to cycle your tank

NEW TANK SYNDROME

Unfortunately, this sudden and seemingly unexplainable loss of newly introduced specimens—known in the hobby as New Tank Syndrome (NTS)—occurs more often than it should among novice freshwater and marine aquarists. It's also a huge confidence buster for newcomers, many of whom simply abandon the hobby in frustration after all of their efforts and expenditures come to naught.

But the good news is this: NTS is completely avoidable. All you have to do is give your new marine aquarium adequate time to cycle before introducing any valuable specimens. If you're making the transition to salt water from fresh water, you're probably already familiar with the concept of cycling, and the process is, for all intents and purposes, identical. For those unfamiliar with the concept, cycling simply means allowing the beneficial nitrifying bacteria—the same ones we examined in the chapter on biological filtration—to become fully established within the aquarium. Remember, without ample colonies

Fish Fact

Is Conspicuous Coloration a Drawback?

It somehow seems counterproductive for so many reef fish to be brilliantly colored. With hordes of hungry predators about, one would think that brightly colored fish would be easily preyed upon. Surprisingly, however, brilliant coloration is not necessarily a handicap on the coral reef. For one thing, brighter colors can help fish identify other individuals of the same species for spawning purposes—a major plus when you consider the vast number of fish that live on and around the coral reef. Also, many of the sessile invertebrates inhabiting the reef are fairly brightly colored themselves, so the fish don't necessarily stand out against the backdrop of the coral reef.

As far as predators are concerned, most of them emerge at dusk to feed, and in the twilight all those brightly colored fish become, for all intents and purposes, invisible. Besides, the red-yellow portions of the visible light spectrum can only penetrate a few feet into salt water, so fish sporting those particular colors will tend to look grayer at depth, even when the sun is at the highest point in the sky.

of nitrobacters to convert ammonia to less harmful compounds, any specimens that you place in your aquarium are at risk of literally being poisoned by their own waste.

IS CYCLING A CATCH-22?

Right now you might be asking yourself, "If nitrifying bacteria use fish waste as a fuel source, how can I get them to proliferate without first introducing some fish? Isn't that a catch-22?" Indeed, it would be if fish waste were the only source of ammonia; fortunately, it is not. You can jumpstart the cycling process just as easily by adding a pinch of flake food or a little liquid invertebrate food to the water each day. As the food decomposes, it will produce the necessary ammonia to initiate the cycle. Another tried-and-true method is to add ammonium chloride, an inorganic source of ammonia that can be purchased at any chemical supply store, to the aquarium. The bacteria don't care what the source is, whether organic or inorganic, as long as they have ammonia as a fuel to get the cycle going.

DAMSELS AS GUINEA PIGS

It was once common practice among marine aquarists (and probably still is for some) to introduce one or two inexpensive, hardy fish—usually damsels—to initiate the cycling process. The poor creatures would be forced to endure spiking ammonia and nitrite levels as colonies of nitrifying bacteria became established and began to do their work. Those lucky enough to survive the ordeal might then be traded to another aquarist. who would likely use them to cycle yet another aquarium, and they'd find themselves right back where they started—swimming in toxic water. If the fish survived and were left to inhabit the newly cycled aquarium, a different problem would often arise. The highly territorial damsels would claim the entire tank for themselves, making the introduction of additional specimens extremely problematic. While there's no question that the damsel method was (is?) a fairly reliable way to cycle a new marine aquarium, one could certainly make the argument that using fish this way is not the most ethical approach to cycling—no matter how expendable we may think they are.

Cycling an aquarium is just another way of saying you are maturing your tank's biological filter, or biofilter.

HAND-ME-DOWN COLONIES

A third way to help the cycling process along is to "borrow" some existing colonies of nitrifying bacteria from an established aquarium. This can be done by taking a filter medium (sponge, spun-nylon floss, etc.) or a scoop of substrate from the mature aquarium and placing it into your new system. The source of the existing colony can be a fellow marine hobbyist or a friendly dealer. As long as you also provide oxygenated conditions, ample surface area, and a source of ammonia, this hand-me-down colony will quickly spread throughout the rest of the aquarium. Of course, high-quality (extremely porous) live rock is also an excellent source of beneficial nitrifying bacteria, and the more pieces you add, the more rapidly the aquarium will cycle. Just be sure to clean and cure the live rock as previously described or you may end up overwhelming the system with pollutants produced by decomposing organisms.

Consider the Source!

It's very important to consider the source when borrowing gravel or a filter medium from an existing tank in order to inoculate a new system. Under no circumstances should you accept such materials from an aquarium that has recently contained a sick or dying animal, especially if you intend to use it to cycle a reef tank. It's not that you need to worry so much about introducing parasites or pathogenic microorganisms into your new system. Few if any of these organisms will survive the entire cycling period, which can take up to a month or more, without a host organism's being present (i.e., a fish or invertebrate to infect). A more serious concern is that you may inadvertently release traces of medication into your new aquarium, some of which can be harmful to some fish and invertebrates and very difficult to eliminate completely from the system.

Over-the-Counter Colonies

Yet another way to kick the cycling process into high gear is to use one of the numerous liquid- or dry-media cycling products, which can be purchased by mail order or from your local aquarium dealer. These products contain live cultures of beneficial nitrifying bacteria, which can easily be added to the aquarium water to supplement the existing microbial population. However, it's important to keep in mind that you can't just dump one of these products into the aquarium on the first day after filling it with salt water and assume the cycling process is complete. Without oxygenated conditions and a sufficiently high level of ammonia to sustain them, the bacteria would simply die off, and you'd be back to square one.

LIVE ROCK CYCLING

As I've already mentioned, live rock can be a substantial biofilter. Curing live rock is in large part cycling. As the die-off begins to decompose, ammonia is produced. As bacterial colonies establish themselves in the porous rocks, ammonia will begin to decline, and nitrite will spike. Later nitrite will decline while nitrate begins to accumulate. Once the rock is cured, it hosts a mature biofilter. In a reef tank, or in an FO tank that has a substantial amount of live rock, this should be all the biofiltration you need.

If you now put it into an aquarium and let it sit, the biofilter will die off from lack of food, but if you immediately stock the tank with fish, the bacteria will have plenty of ammonia to feed on. You should not put all the fish in at once, just in case, and you must test for ammonia and nitrite daily. If they remain at zero for a few days, you can add the rest of the fish, but keep testing daily. If after a few more days levels are still zero, you're done!

TESTING

We've established that cycling an aquarium can take as long as a month or more, but isn't there some way to determine the exact number of days or weeks we must wait for cycling to occur? If all things were equal from one aquarium to the next, perhaps we could establish some precise time frame, but such is not the case. Even subtle differences in the filtration media used, the type of substrate and rockwork, the amount of turbulence that is created at the surface of the aquarium, and the amount of nitrogenous food that is introduced into the water can have a significant impact on the rate of the cycling process. Simply put, the better job you do of providing the three essential elements that nitrifying bacteria need for survival, the faster the cycling process will go.

While we cannot predict exactly how long it will take to cycle a given aquarium, we can certainly monitor the process by testing the water regularly with ammonia, nitrite, and nitrate test kits.

Cycling doesn't have to take very long. You can borrow live sand or a filter from a mature tank, plunk it into your tank, and you're ready to slowly add fish.

These relatively inexpensive kits are available at any aquarium shop, and they are remarkably easy to use—even for us nonscientific types. Though the instructions will vary slightly from test kit to test kit, typically all you have to do is fill a small vial with aquarium water, add a predetermined amount of the test chemical—either in tablet or liquid form—to the water, shake the vial, and wait a few minutes for the water to change color. Then you simply compare the color of the water to the color chart included with the kit (preferably against a white background). Each color on the comparator chart will match a specific level of ammonia, nitrite, or nitrate, depending on what you're testing for, which will be indicated in parts per million (ppm) or milligrams per liter (mg/l).

During the first several days of the cycling process, you should get very high readings of ammonia. As colonies of nitrobacters begin to flourish in response to the elevated ammonia level, testing will eventually indicate a precipitous drop in the ammonia level and a spike in the nitrite level. The nitrite level will continue to rise until the nitrifying bacteria begin to proliferate. At that point, the nitrite level will drop and the nitrate level will begin to climb. The aquarium is considered fully cycled once testing indicates no measurable ammonia or nitrite. A large water change—at least 50 percent, though some would suggest changing as much as 100 percent of the water—should be performed at this stage to dilute the nitrate. Fish can generally tolerate nitrate levels up to approximately 40 ppm. However, for the reef, nitrate should never be allowed to accumulate beyond 20 ppm at the very most. Some of the more delicate sessile invertebrates will even suffer at that concentration, so the best bet for reefkeepers is to maintain the nitrate level as close to zero as possible.

Be sure you are constantly testing your water to monitor ammonia and nitrite levels, as both can seriously harm your fish.

A VERY DELICATE BALANCE

Once cycling is complete, it's safe to begin adding livestock to your new marine aquarium. This should be accomplished very gradually. Add no more than two or three fish or invertebrates at first, and give them a few weeks to get adjusted to their new surroundings before adding more specimens. If you introduce too many organisms too quickly, the bacteria that make up your biological filter will not be able to keep pace with the excessive "bioload," and you may experience a sudden ammonia spike. On the other hand, if you introduce additional specimens every few weeks, while continuing to test for ammonia and nitrite, you won't upset the delicate balance that exists between

Tips for Ensuring Accurate Test Results

- Always use test kits from the same manufacturer and product line. There is some variability in accuracy between different manufacturers' products.
- Avoid using outdated test kits. The chemical reagents are viable for only a certain amount of time. A use-by date should be listed on the product's packaging.
- Follow the manufacturer's instructions to the letter.
- Always test at the same time of day. Some water parameters will vary slightly depending on the time of day.
- Store your test kits out of direct sunlight in a cool, dry location to increase their longevity.
- Keep a record of your test results in a log or journal so you can monitor any changes that take place over a long period of time.

the biofilter and the bioload, and your new fish and/or invertebrates will have a much better chance of surviving the transition. This is very important not only from the standpoint of conservation but also because early success in the saltwater hobby can make the difference between sticking with it for a lifetime and quitting prematurely out of frustration.

Another factor that can upset the delicate balance of the biological filter is the amount of food that you provide for your new charges. Overfeeding is a very common mistake among novice and experienced aquarists alike. It's just so hard to resist dropping in another pinch of flake food or another helping of frozen brine shrimp when the fish keep giving you those puppy dog eyes that seem to say, "I know you just fed me an hour ago, but I'm feeling faint with hunger." The problem is that most fish will give you that look every time you pass the tank (after all, they know on which side their bread is buttered!), and consistently giving in to their begging will not only overwhelm the biofilter but also will lead to significant health problems for your fish further down the road.

SUMMARY

As important as cycling is, it is not difficult. The main requirement is patience and the right test kits. The use of plenty of live rock can significantly shorten cycling, but it is still very important to keep testing the water daily until you are certain that the biofilter is fully established and able to handle the bioload in the tank.

Chapter 10

Important Water Parameters

Thus far we've discussed the importance of stability in the marine environment as it applies to temperature, specific gravity, and various aspects of water-quality management. In this chapter we'll take a closer look at certain characteristics of salt water and the specific water parameters you'll need to maintain with a high degree of stability in order to achieve success with your new marine aquarium. We'll also discuss some of the important supplements and trace elements that you'll need to be familiar with if you intend to keep a reef system.

What Lies Ahead

- pH
- supplements
- calcium
- iodine and strontium

At the risk of sounding redundant (although it may be too late for that already!), the water parameters in the world's oceans, especially in the areas around coral reefs, are remarkably stable in quality and chemical composition (that is, if you discount the presence of the various pollutants introduced through human activities). Our main responsibility as aquarists is to replicate the conditions that marine fish and invertebrates have adapted to in their natural environment as closely as possible and to take all necessary steps to prevent them from fluctuating to a significant degree.

pH AND ALKALINITY

One of the more important parameters you'll need to become familiar with and monitor carefully is the pH of your aquarium's water. Readers who have a background in chemistry will bristle at the following definitions, but we're trying to keep things simple, right? A pH value is a measure of how acidic or basic the water is. Any pH measurement below 7.0 (neutral) is acidic, while measurements above 7.0 are basic.

Coral reefs are some of the most stable environments on the planet. You should do your best to replicate this stability so your fish will thrive.

Saltwater fish
and invertebrates
require a basic pH.

Technically, alkalinity is a measure of the buffering capacity of the water. Although alkalinity is often called "carbonate hardness," this is a misnomer that can lead to confusion. In simple terms, buffering capacity can be defined as the water's ability to resist a change in pH. Dissolved substances, most notably carbonates and bicarbonates, react with the acid that is produced by metabolic processes, neutralizing the acid and preventing the pH from dropping. In most cases when a drop in pH occurs, the problem can be rectified through the addition of buffering compounds. Fortunately, buffering compounds are normally included in most high-quality synthetic sea salt mixes, so each time you perform a partial water change these compounds are re-introduced. Frequent small water changes, using a quality salt mix, will go a long way toward maintaining the water's alkalinity, and therefore its pH, at the desired level.

The question then becomes: what is the desired level? The pH of natural sea water ranges between 8.2 and 8.4, which is relatively high compared to most freshwater habitats. One notable exception is the fresh water found in Africa's Rift Lakes, whose pH is similar to that of sea water. And while freshwater habitats range in pH from 3 (peat bogs) to 9 (Africa's Lake Tanganyika), marine habitats are—yes, again!—boringly stable at about 8.3. The exact value of the pH in your new marine aquarium is not as important as the stability of the pH, as long as it remains within the desired range with little or no fluctuation.

No Deadbeat Dads Here!

Can you guess the name of the fish that has a tail like a monkey, a pouch like a kangaroo, and the head of a horse? If you answered "the seahorse," you guessed right! Seahorses (*Hippocampus* spp.) do indeed seem to be an odd assemblage of spare parts taken from various members of the animal kingdom. In fact, their appearance is so strange (albeit irresistible) that many people are unaware that they're actually fish. But their strangeness doesn't end with their appearance. In the world of the seahorse, it is the male that becomes pregnant and gestates the young. The female deposits her eggs into a specialized pouch on the male's belly, where the male fertilizes them. The male then protects and nurtures them within his body until they are ready to be born!

FACTORS INFLUENCING pH

As I've already mentioned, most high-quality synthetic salt mixes contain buffering compounds that will keep the pH of your water properly elevated. However, several factors can cause pH to drop in spite of the presence of these buffers. For example, the waste materials and the byproducts of the metabolic processes of various marine organisms tend to be highly acidic and will gradually use up the water's buffering capacity and lower pH over time if allowed to accumulate. Decomposing food items and the acidic compounds produced during the nitrification cycle will also contribute to this pH-lowering trend. It stands to reason, then, that crashing pH levels can be a major problem in an aquarium that is overstocked and overfed. So what can you do to counteract this trend? Obviously the most important thing you can do is to avoid overstocking and overfeeding, but the next best thing is to stay on top of those routine partial water changes! The more often you change the water, the less pronounced the swings in pH will be, even if you tend to overfeed on occasion or you sometimes fall victim to one-more-pretty-fish syndrome.

Other factors affecting pH are completely natural and have nothing to do with neglect or poor husbandry on the part of the aquarist. For instance, certain invertebrates utilize the same elements that buffer pH to build their calcareous shells and skeletons, which effectively reduces the buffering capacity of the water and hence lowers the pH. Also, photosynthetic organisms in the aquarium, including various marine algae, whether cultivated or unintentionally introduced, can contribute to pH fluctuations through their natural photosynthetic activity.

During the day they utilize carbon dioxide and produce oxygen. However, when night falls or when the lights are no longer on to promote photosynthesis, they stop using carbon dioxide. Dissolved carbon dioxide can form carbonic acid, so the pH in the aquarium will tend to drop whenever the lights are turned off and rise again when photosynthesis resumes in the morning.

Again, water changes are the key to overcoming these problems. Frequent water changes will not only help to replenish the buffering agents that are routinely used up for shell and skeleton production by certain invertebrates but also will also keep the dissolved nutrient level in the aquarium low, thereby minimizing the proliferation of unwanted algae and decreasing the accumulation of pH-lowering carbon dioxide at night.

TESTING FOR pH

Of course, in order to stay on top of any changes in pH you'll need to test your aquarium's water routinely with a test kit. Be sure to buy a kit formulated specifically for testing salt water rather than fresh water, as the two are not interchangeable. In addition, freshwater pH test kits generally measure from 6.0 up to 7.6, while most saltwater kits measure from 7.6 to 8.4. Testing for pH, which should be performed on a weekly basis, is done in exactly the same fashion as are the tests for ammonia, nitrite, and nitrate. You simply fill the vial with aquarium water, add a few drops of the test chemical liquid, shake the vial, and compare the color of the water to the color comparator chart included with the kit. As I mentioned previously, any stable reading within the range of 8.2 to 8.4 is acceptable. If the pH should fall below that range, you'll need to determine the cause of the problem and make the necessary correction immediately. This may mean cutting back on the amount you're feeding, reducing the number of specimens in the tank, or locating and removing a dead animal from somewhere in the aquarium system.

SHOULD YOU USE SUPPLEMENTS?

As I said, certain elements and minerals that occur naturally in sea water, such as calcium, iodine, strontium, and others, are drawn from the water and utilized by various marine organisms for a wide range of biological processes. It stands to reason, then, that these same elements in nearly the same concentrations should be provided for the fish or invertebrates in the marine aquarium in order to keep them in optimum health. The only difference is that in the closed system of the aquarium the organisms gradually deplete these elements, but there is no natural means of replacing them. The processes of protein skimming and chemical filtration with activated carbon can also remove necessary substances from the water. So how do you go about putting these vital elements back into the aquarium system once they're all used up? In the FO aquarium, these elements are replaced in sufficient amounts whenever a partial water change is performed, provided a high-quality synthetic salt mix is used. In the reef tank, however, stony corals can extract some of these elements from the water so rapidly that partial water changes cannot keep pace, and it may become necessary to replenish them with supplements.

CALCIUM

Calcium is the element of greatest concern, as it is required for the health of all marine organisms. It is especially important for organisms that produce skeletons, exoskeletons, or shells out of calcium carbonate, including certain corals, crustaceans, tubeworms, mollusks, echinoderms, and fish—in other words, most of the organisms of interest to the reef aquarist.

The desired calcium level for the marine aquarium is approximately 400 mg/liter (roughly 400 ppm), which can be monitored routinely and easily with a calcium hardness test kit available at any aquarium shop. Whenever testing indicates that the calcium concentration is beginning to dip below the desired level, you can bring it back up by adding a commercial liquid calcium supplement to the aquarium. If you enjoy tinkering with chemicals, you can also produce your own calcium additive, which is known in the hobby as kalkwasser or limewater. But you must be cautious during the entire process. Both the calcium hydroxide powder used in making the limewater and the limewater solution itself are extremely caustic, so goggles, gloves, and a dust mask are necessary attire when making the solution or handling the powder. Also, limewater is akin to lye and extremely alkaline (with a pH around 12!) and must be added to the water very gradually to avoid raising the pH beyond the desired range. Considering the dangers involved and the hit-or-miss nature of supplementing calcium with homemade limewater, you are better off using an off-the-shelf calcium additive, at least at first. It may end up costing you a little more, but the added certainty and peace of mind are worth a few extra pennies.

The addition of marine algae, like this *Chaetomorpha* sp., can help you maintain a healthy tank.

IODINE AND STRONTIUM

Two elements that are also vital to the health and well-being of marine organisms are iodine and strontium. Iodine is especially critical if you intend to cultivate certain marine macroalgae, such as the various species of *Caulerpa* and *Halimeda*, which are very popular among reef aquarists. The desired levels are 60 micrograms per liter for iodine and 7.9 mg/liter for strontium. Both can be supplemented with easy-to-use liquid additives, but neither can be monitored with a commercially manufactured test kit. This means that it is very important to adhere strictly to the manufacturer's recommendations when determining the rate and frequency of supplementation.

There are several additional trace elements found in sea water that are vital to the metabolic processes of various marine organisms—in fact, all of the elements known to science are present in small amounts in sea water. Most of these important trace elements are available in the form of liquid supplements, either singly or combined with other elements. However, since there is much yet to be learned about how individual trace elements affect the health of different marine organisms (not to mention the fact that many trace elements do not have corresponding test kits), it's very important to use them judiciously.

If you want to get seriously into the reef hobby, you should research this area thoroughly, since even the experts do not agree. To learn more, consult the references listed at the back of this book.

The most important thing to remember about using trace element supplements is that even the best additives on the market won't compensate for poor maintenance practices or a lack of timely water changes.

SUMMARY

The stable conditions of the coral reef need to be maintained in the marine aquarium with regard to water chemistry. Most important are pH and alkalinity, or buffering capacity. Regular water changes using a quality salt mix will in most cases do the job for an FO system. In a reef tank containing rapidly growing stony corals or tridacnid clams, you will almost certainly need to supplement calcium and other elements. Obviously, testing and supplementing go hand in hand.

Chapter 11

The Payoff!

You've finally made it through the tedious set-up and cycling phases; all of your filtration, heating, and lighting systems are up and running; and testing indicates that your water parameters are well within the ideal range. Now it's time for your patience to start paying off! It's time to add some animals to your new marine aquarium!

What Lies Ahead

- do your research
- the best specimens for your first tank
- compatibility
- stocking rate
- territoriality
- acclimation
- the hunger strike

Selecting organisms is far and away the most fun and satisfying stage of putting together a marine aquarium. There are so many delightful fish and invertebrates to choose from that it can seem almost impossible to narrow down your options to just a handful of specimens.

However, it's critical to proceed with caution when deciding which specimens to include in your aquarium. The stocking decisions you make at this stage will determine whether you will ultimately experience a beautiful assortment of peaceful and compatible species or a tank full of mismatched organisms that are constantly squabbling at the slightest provocation. The key to achieving the former and avoiding the latter is to do a little advance research. But where to begin?

RESEARCH SOURCES

Your best bet is to head for the library or bookstore to check out or buy a few additional marine aquarium reference books. I've tried to include all of the vital information about livestock selection within the pages of this book, but it's always helpful to read what other authors have to say on the subject as well. There are many excellent books out there that are well suited for beginners interested in learning about the characteristics and requirements of different marine species. Aquarium magazines and journals are also excellent sources of information on species selection. If you haven't done so already, you might consider getting a regular subscription to one of these publications. You can also gather lots of useful information about fish and invertebrates online. Just keep in mind that there is no editor looking over Internet materials to verify accuracy. In other words, a lot of wacky information and spectacular claims can make their way onto some websites, so you have to be wary of your sources. The references at the end of this book include a lot of sources to get you started.

LEARNING FROM FELLOW AQUARISTS

Another way to learn about different marine organisms is to consult with other fish enthusiasts or invert aficionados who may have hands-on experience in keeping some of the species that interest you. You can connect with fellow marine aquarists through your local aquarium society or, perhaps, through Internet chat rooms or forums. Your dealer might even be able to help you get in touch with other marine aquarists in your area who will be willing to share the benefit of their experience. Who knows, you might have a tremendous source of information living right next door to you!

Research will help you learn everything you need to know to keep the fish or invertebrates that interest you alive.

FINDING A REPUTABLE DEALER

The surest way to end up with a peaceful and compatible community of marine organisms is to solicit the advice of an experienced, reputable dealer. Look for someone who is willing to spend a little time—even when business is hopping on a weekend afternoon—to help you find the right fish or invertebrates for your needs and who is capable of giving thoughtful and thorough answers to any questions you might have about the organisms offered for sale. You can also tell a lot about a dealer by the condition of his aquariums. If every other tank has a dead fish floating in it, or the water in the tanks is the color and consistency of pea soup, it's probably a wise idea to shop elsewhere. On the other hand, you can safely assume that a dealer who devotes lots of time and attention to aquarium maintenance will be equally inclined to lavish attention on customers.

More often than not, the right dealer will be the sole proprietor of a small aquarium shop who has had many years of personal experience in keeping both fish and invertebrates. I'm not suggesting that the young sales clerk at The Discount Fish-O-Rama doesn't know

The High Cost of Cyanide Collection

The collection of tropical marine fish with sodium cyanide, which though illegal is still going on in certain parts of the world, is both destructive and self-defeating for those who practice it. Not only does cyanide collection exact a heavy toll on tropical marine fish sought after by aquarists, but it also destroys scores of fish and other marine organisms that have no value to the aquarium industry but are nonetheless vital to the ecology of the reefs.

Even more discouraging is the toll that cyanide collection takes on the coral reef itself. When cyanide collectors squirt this noxious solution into the cracks and crevices of the reef in order to subdue the fish they're after, they unwittingly destroy the corals and other sessile invertebrates that compose the reefs, hence undermining their own livelihoods. Once the corals are destroyed, the fish that live among them soon vanish, and a once-thriving habitat disappears forever.

what he's talking about. Who knows, he may only be working there to pay the bills while he finishes his degree in Marine Biology. It's just that I've generally gotten better advice, more encouragement, and fewer bum recommendations from small-business owners over the years.

WHERE IN THE WORLD DO THE FISH COME FROM?

Experience isn't the only important criterion you should look for when shopping for a dealer. A qualified dealer should also be able to tell you with a good degree of certainty where and how his specimens have been collected. This is important because in certain parts of the world reef fish are still sometimes poisoned with a sodium cyanide solution to make them easier to capture. As you can imagine, fish collected in this manner seldom survive for long in the aquarium. Cyanide-poisoned fish often seem perfectly healthy at the time of purchase and may even eat heartily once introduced to their new home. However, within a matter of weeks, the cyanide damage will take its toll, and most of these fish will perish. The poor unwitting aquarist is typically left wondering what went wrong and what could have been done differently to save the fish's life.

CHOOSE A CONSERVATION-MINDED DEALER

A good dealer is someone who encourages conservation programs by offering captive-bred fish and aquacultured invertebrates for sale instead of just specimens collected from the wild. In most cases, specimens propagated in captivity will cost more than their wild-caught counterparts, but they are well worth the added cost. Captive-bred specimens are better adapted to aquarium conditions and will greedily accept standard aquarium fare that wild-caught specimens may fail to recognize as food, and buying them helps to reduce collection pressure on wild populations, some of which have been sorely depleted over the years as a result of questionable collection practices.

SELECTING SPECIMENS FOR THE FISH-ONLY AQUARIUM

Once you've settled on a qualified dealer and armed yourself with information about the specific animals you'd like to keep, you're ready to purchase your first specimens. There are certain things to look for when buying fish. First, carefully examine each specimen for evidence of disease or parasitic infection, such as tiny white or black spots, velvety patches, cloudy eyes, ulcerations, warts or lumps, rotting fins, irregular or rapid movement, or scraping against objects in the tank. If any of these symptoms (or any other characteristics that seem out of the

Captive-raised specimens take collecting pressure off wild stock. You should seriously consider buying them.

ordinary) are present either on the fish you'd like to purchase or on other fish in the same tank, do yourself a favor and pass the specimen by. It may be frustrating to have to postpone buying your fish after having waited so long already, but it's even more frustrating to watch costly specimens die shortly after you purchase them—and most dealers do not offer guarantees on marine livestock.

It's also a good idea to make sure each fish is feeding properly before you buy. A malnourished fish will often have a pinched-in belly as opposed to a healthy, well-rounded belly, and may sulk or remain hidden from view behind the rockwork or decorations instead of swimming actively. A conscientious dealer will make sure each fish is actively feeding before putting it out for sale, but if you're uncertain whether a fish is feeding or not, ask the dealer to feed it in front of you. Most reputable dealers will be more than happy to oblige. After all, it's in their best interest to sell the fish in a timely manner. You can also take this opportunity to find out which particular foods are preferred by the fish you'd like to buy.

When Worlds Collide

My first real experience with species incompatibility involved introducing a pixie hawkfish, *Cirrhitichthys oxycephalus*, into a community of fish that happened to include a strawberry basslet, *Pictichromis porphyreus*. Prior to the hawkfish's arrival, the basslet was extraordinarily well behaved with its tankmates, all of which were markedly different from the basslet in coloration and body shape. But once the hawkfish came on the scene and attempted to establish a territory among the rocks (once the sole domain of the basslet), all bets were off. The basslet embarked on a ruthless crusade of harassment and seemed bent on destroying the newcomer.

Anytime the basslet caught a glimpse of the hawkfish, no matter how fleeting, it would go on the warpath, chasing and nipping the poor fish until it was nearly driven to distraction. The one-sided war finally ended one morning with the hawkfish leaping out of the tank and meeting his dusty end on the hardwood floor. The lesson? Use caution when adding new fish to an established community. Even seemingly dissimilar species can be incompatible if they happen to occupy the same niche in the aquarium.

PLAN YOUR PURCHASE, AND STICK TO THE PLAN!

The best approach to buying your first fish is to settle on a combination of hardy bread-and-butter species that you know will get along well in your aquarium and buy only those particular fish when you head for the aquarium shop. If your dealer doesn't have what you're looking for when you're ready to buy, he most likely will within a week or so. Don't be discouraged if you have to make repeated visits to your dealer to get exactly what you're after. Success is worth the wait!

Also, if at all possible, try to resist the temptation to purchase fish that you are unfamiliar with or that your dealer knows little about—no matter how beautiful they may be! Introducing a fish of uncertain deportment and dietary needs is almost always a recipe for disaster. Also, that tiny demure fish of uncertain origin that you just couldn't resist might eventually reach a mature size that is way beyond the dimensions of your aquarium, or it may become extremely territorial and declare war on every other fish in the tank. Worse yet, it may turn out to be a highly specialized feeder that won't settle for any of the standard foods you offer and ultimately wastes away before your eyes.

THE COMPATIBILITY QUESTION

It's not unusual for two marine fish of the same species (conspecifics) to battle to the death when confined within the same aquarium—even species that are known to congregate in massive schools in nature. Why? For one thing, even though certain fish tend to school in the wild, each individual may still stake out a small section of the reef for its own territory. In the aquarium, the available real estate is so greatly diminished that territorial disputes are almost inevitable between fish that naturally occupy the same ecological niche. Another reason is that a natural pecking order usually exists within wild fish populations, especially among harem-keeping species. But if two conspecifics collected from different populations are placed in the same aquarium, fighting will likely occur until a new pecking order is established. Unfortunately, the weaker or less aggressive fish often dies—either gradually as a result of the stress from constant bickering or quickly from actual physical trauma inflicted by the stronger fish.

As a general rule, it's best to keep only one member of a species in a given aquarium community. This rule also extends to fish of different species that are very similar in coloration, body shape, and/or the ecological niche they occupy. There are, or course, exceptions to this one-per-tank rule. For example, certain clownfish, *Amphiprion* spp., usually will tolerate conspecifics, as will jawfish, *Opistognathus* spp., firefish, *Nemateleotris* spp., and cardinalfish (family Apogonidae) to name but a few. Of course, the emphasis here should be on the word "usually." Aggression can vary from individual to individual within a species, so there's no guarantee that members of a supposedly peaceful species won't fight among themselves. Also, the size of the aquarium can have an impact on the frequency and severity of territorial disputes. Obviously it would be much harder for two feuding fish to stay out of each other's way in a 20-gallon (80-liter) aquarium than it would be in a 100-gallon (400-liter) aquarium.

THE QUARANTINE TANK

One of the most important steps you can take to ensure that your community of marine fish remains healthy and disease-free is to isolate, or quarantine, each fish for at least four weeks before introducing it to the main aquarium. This should be done with the first assortment of fish you buy after cycling the aquarium and with any specimens that are added later on. Quarantining the fish will give you a prolonged opportunity to observe them for any signs of disease that may not have been visible at the time of purchase. On the other hand, failure to isolate new introductions can lead to the aggravating loss of your entire fish community to disease.

Fish often carry disease-causing pathogens and parasites that do not immediately manifest themselves until a certain amount of time passes or the fish is placed under stress, such as being repeatedly netted, transported, and reacclimated. If a disease should develop after you buy a particular specimen, it's preferable and easier to treat the fish in isolation rather than in the main aquarium. Besides, isolating the sick fish will ensure that the disease does not spread to the healthy fish in the community.

The quarantine tank does not need to be especially large or elaborate. A 10- to 15-gallon (40- to 60-liter) aquarium will generally suffice. You don't need any substrate, decorations, or special lighting, and a simple, inexpensive sponge filter will suffice for water purification. A heater should be included in the setup along with an airstone and air pump to oxygenate the water. You might also want to provide a few rocks or an overturned terra-cotta pot for a hiding place. Of course, the water temperature, pH, and specific gravity of the quarantine tank should be the same as they are in the main aquarium so the quarantined fish will not be shocked by dramatically different water parameters when it is introduced to the main tank.

PROPER STOCKING RATE

Determining the total number of fish that can be maintained in good health in a given marine aquarium can be a tricky proposition, especially for those with no prior experience in fishkeeping. As you do your research and shop around for specimens, you might come across different rules you can use to determine the exact carrying capacity of your tank (a fancy way of saying the total number of organisms that your tank can accommodate). One that I've read or heard many times is that you can safely keep 2 inches (5 cm) of fish length for every

Oxygen!

If you have already kept freshwater fish, you might feel comfortable transferring your experience with stocking an aquarium to your marine tank. Don't. First of all, while only some freshwater species—typically ones from fast-flowing rivers and streams—require highly oxygenated water, our marine fish, thanks to the churning of waves crashing against a coral reef, all require maximum oxygenation. But wait. Salt water cannot hold as much dissolved oxygen as fresh water. This means that no matter how much aeration, current, and surface agitation you create in the tank, a marine aquarium will have a lower oxygen content than the same setup would with fresh water. This is why many knowledgeable aquarists recommend a protein skimmer even if for some reason a system wouldn't otherwise require it. All that swirling mixture of bubbles and water provides excellent gas exchange (oxygen in, carbon dioxide out) as well as waste removal, ensuring maximum oxygenation of the aquarium water. Even so, the saltwater tank will not be able to support as large a fish mass as a freshwater tank of the same size.

10 gallons (40 liters) of tank volume—or something to that effect. According to this rule, our model 55-gallon (200-liter) aquarium can accommodate approximately 11 inches (28 cm) of fish length.

The trouble is that this rule overlooks some very important factors, such as the overall height and thickness of a fish's body, its feeding habits, and, by logical extension, how much waste it produces. The bottom line is this: total body length doesn't really tell you much about the impact a fish or community of fish will have on your aquarium's biological filter. By means of illustration, one 11-inch (28-cm) Picasso triggerfish, *Rhinecanthus aculeatus*, which is a relatively greedy and sloppy carnivore, will place considerably more of a burden on your biofilter than will a small school of 2-inch (5-cm) cardinalfish. My suggestion is to use the 2-inches-per-every-10-gallons rule as a basic guideline only. Beyond that, a little common sense combined with the knowledge you've already acquired about the fish you intend to keep will help you to make sound educated stocking decisions.

In some ways, stocking a marine aquarium is more art than science. Start by introducing only two or three hardy specimens, and wait a few weeks to see how they adjust before adding more fish. If all goes well during that time, go ahead and introduce some more specimens, one at a time, testing diligently for ammonia and nitrite after each introduction. If you're adding specimens at the proper rate, the population of nitrifying bacteria should grow proportionally in response to the increasing biological load, and therefore no ammonia or nitrite should be detected.

As you add specimens to the aquarium, you'll notice that each fish will claim a certain area within the tank for its territory. One might stake out a cave in the rockwork. Another might dig a burrow in the substrate. Still another might routinely perch on a small ledge or outcropping, waiting for food items to float past. By carefully observing the interaction between the different fish, you should be able to approximate where one territory ends and another begins. Why is this important? Because an aquarium's carrying capacity is not just based on the population of nitrifying bacteria. Available real estate plays a major role as well. Once all of the available territories have been claimed, any further additions of fish may prove problematic, even if the biological filter is capable of handling more waste material.

TERRITORIALITY AND THE NEW FISH ON THE BLOCK

Inclusiveness is not a high priority among most reef fish, and oftentimes, even when there is plenty of space left in the aquarium to accommodate additional specimens, a newcomer will be ruthlessly harassed by one or more of the established fish in the community. In some cases

Saltwater fish must defend their territory on the coral reefs, and therefore many will be aggressive towards other fish in your tank, both conspecifics and fish similar in appearance. If you notice one fish bullying another, you must separate them immediately.

this may be because the newcomer is simply too similar in habit or appearance to the aggressor fish, in which case the best way to resolve the dispute is to return the new fish to the dealer and make a different selection. But in other cases you might be able to diffuse the aggression simply by rearranging the rockwork and decorations prior to introducing the new fish, thereby disrupting the established territories. The theory behind this approach is that the established fish will no longer feel as if they have "home tank advantage," and they'll have to focus their attention on finding new territories rather than tormenting the newcomer. Sometimes it works; sometimes it doesn't.

ACCLIMATING YOUR NEW FISH

Typically, your dealer will package your newly purchased fish in plastic bags filled with oxygenated aquarium water for the journey home. But you can't simply dump the fish and water out of their bags and into your new aquarium once you get them home. First you have to acclimate the fish to the water conditions in your aquarium, which will undoubtedly differ considerably from the water conditions in your dealer's tanks. Of course, if you intend to isolate your new fish properly, you'll need to acclimate them to the water in the quarantine tank first, but since the water parameters should be the same between your display tank and quarantine tank (and for the sake of brevity), we won't worry about making that distinction here.

In years past, the commonly accepted practice for acclimating fish was to float the bag containing the fish in the new aquarium for about a half hour to give it an opportunity to adjust to the change in water temperature. A major drawback to this method was that it didn't give the fish a chance to become acclimated to the other water parameters—pH, specific gravity, etc.—before being released into its new surroundings. Also, the original water was typically dumped right into the new aquarium along with any pollutants, parasites, or pathogens that might have been present in the dealer's tanks.

A better technique is to pour the fish and the original water gently from the bag into a separate plastic container. You might want to have some sort of makeshift cover handy in case the fish decides to jump. Next, begin to add small quantities of aquarium water to the container every 15 minutes or so, until the temperature, pH, and specific gravity of the water in the plastic container are the same as in the aquarium. Then net the fish out of the container and release it immediately into the aquarium. It's a good idea to thoroughly moisten the net in aquarium water ahead of time to minimize any trauma to the fish's body.

The first few weeks after acclimation and release will be a critical period of adjustment for your new fish. They won't be able to tell you whether they are being harassed constantly by their tankmates or that their dietary needs are not being fulfilled properly. It's up to you to monitor your new charges closely and to correct any problems that might develop before they get out of hand. It's also during this stressful adjustment period that disease or parasitic infection is most likely to occur, but if you continue to maintain excellent water quality and stable conditions overall, problems stemming from disease or parasites can be minimized.

DEALING WITH THE HUNGER STRIKE

Try not to be alarmed if a newly introduced fish refuses to eat for several days after arriving in its new home. This is a fairly common response, and it's understandable when you consider the cumulative stress a wild-caught fish has to undergo from the point of collection until it arrives in your aquarium. Essentially, each fish is netted and removed from its home on the coral reef, sent overseas in a bag full of less-than pristine water, retained temporarily in a holding facility tank, and shipped on to a hectic aquarium shop where it is placed in a display tank. From there the fish is netted yet again and transported to an aquarist's home where it is acclimated to different water conditions for the umpteenth time and then offered an assortment of unfamiliar food items. It's not surprising, then, that a fish might be a little reluctant to eat. Most people I know wouldn't eat under those circumstances either!

Given a little time to adjust, most marine fish will begin to accept standard fresh, frozen, freeze-dried, or flake foods within two or three days. However, a fish that continues to hunger strike much beyond this may need a little more persuasion. Live adult brine shrimp or mysid shrimp will often elicit a feeding response from finicky eaters. An offering that proves irresistible to many species is chopped clam or clam on the half shell. Feeder fish can also be offered to larger piscivores if nothing else seems to be working, but I would strongly caution you to feed them sparingly and to wean your fish off them as soon as possible. Feeder fish are problematic for several reasons, which we will examine in greater detail in Chapter 18.

Another method that is often successful in getting new fish to feed is to attach a strip of

Help With Feeding

It is a rare nonaquarist who can correctly feed your fish in your absence. Fish can easily go two weeks without being fed. Taken together, these two facts lead to the following conclusion: do not ask a nonaquarist friend to feed your fish for you while you are on vacation. If you will be gone for more than two weeks, either enlist the help of a hobbyist friend or, if you have to rely on a nonaquarist, pre-portion the amounts to be fed on a specified schedule (every few days is sufficient)—and then hide your regular food supply.

A school of Banggaii cardinalfish, *Pterapogon kauderni.* Buy only captive-bred specimens.

fresh fish or clam to the end of a feeding stick (available at any aquarium shop) and give it a little jiggle in front of the fish. The movement seems to send the message that the food item is alive, and the smell of fresh seafood permeating the water often proves irresistible to even the most stubborn fish. Not surprisingly, you can use this same technique to wean a large predatory fish off feeders.

SUMMARY

We've reviewed how to select fish for your tank, how to acclimate and quarantine them, and how to introduce them to your aquarium. You are now ready to start sifting through all of the available species to choose the ones you want to keep. You have to consider many things besides how much you like a certain fish, so, as always, research before you buy is very important. The next chapter will get you started.

Chapter 12

Some Excellent Beginner Fish

If you're like most people making their first foray into marine fishkeeping, you're hoping to establish a peaceful yet lively community of hardy and colorful specimens. But how do you know which species to start off with? Fortunately, there's quite a diversity of resilient marine fish that are perfectly suited for the beginner's tank, many of which are strikingly beautiful to boot! While there's no realistic way to chronicle every single marine fish that is desirable to beginners, there are several noteworthy examples that justify a closer look.

What Lies Ahead

- the best saltwater fish for beginners

BASSLETS

The basslets present troubled nomenclature. The name is applied to various fish in several families, and the common names "bass," "basslet," and "fairy basslet" are applied differently by different people. That aside, this group includes many delightful species for your aquarium.

Dottybacks

The fish in the family Pseudochromidae are sometimes called basslets as well, but most often go by "dottybacks." These fish are small, extraordinarily colorful, and hardy. They are also extremely territorial, especially but not exclusively toward conspecifics. You must not only keep just one dottyback in a tank, you should also not include any fish of similar size or color. Dottybacks are being commercially bred, and tank-raised fish are a little more forgiving of tankmates—but only a little! Without a doubt the best choice is also the one first bred in captivity, the orchid dottyback, *Pseudochromis fridmani*. This beautiful purple fish will fit into just about any setup.

Pseudochromis fridmani.

Grammas

Although the family Grammatidae includes several good aquarium candidates, only two are commonly available, but they are excellent choices. The royal gramma, *Gramma loreto,* and the blackcap basslet, *G. melacara,* are beautiful, the former being purple up front and yellow behind and the latter being a deep blue with (surprise!) a black head. These nook-dwelling fish will be forever darting in and out of caves in the live rock. They will defend their home against tankmates, but they are generally peaceful…except. Except with conspecifics. Keep only one per tank.

"Regular" Basslets

The bass family Serranidae includes some truly gargantuan fish like the giant grouper, *Epinephelus lanceolatus,* that grows to 9 feet (2.7 m)! That fish was once known as *Serranus abdominalis,* but a great many species still in the genus *Serranus* are downright petite, often called basslets or dwarf sea bass, and good aquarium candidates. While not as vibrantly colored as some other reef species, they are all pretty, and most are between 3 inches and a foot (7 and

Serranus baldwini.

30 cm). One delightful choice is the chalk bass, *S. tortugarum*, which is one of the smallest and has a beautiful pastel coloration. Also recommended are the orangeback bass, *S. annularis,* and the lantern bass, *S. baldwini.*

BLENNIES

Similar in many ways to gobies (more on these fish in a moment), blennies are another large and varied group. Although some species are extremely large, there are many suitably small ones, too. Many lack full swim bladders and stay on the bottom, but some have perfect swim bladders and live in the water column. They typically are extremely peaceful—as long as you don't keep more than one specimen of a given species.

Combtooths

The combtooth blennies of the genus *Ecsenius* are great choices for your tank. There are several species in the trade, all between 3 and 5 inches (8 and 13 cm). Most common is probably the Midas blenny, *E. midas*, but there are other equally satisfactory choices, some quite attractively colored.

Goby? Blenny?

The similarity between gobies and blennies leads to a lot of confusion, especially since those terms are not anchored in scientific definitions. Many fish not in the family Gobiidae are called gobies, and many not in Blenniidae are called blennies. Some fish are even known as both gobies and blennies!

The Engineer Convict

The species *Pholidichthys leucotaenia* is called by either name, either the convict blenny/goby for its dark and light stripes or the engineer blenny/goby for its digging proclivities. Juveniles are striped horizontally, while adults are striped vertically (barred). Since they are forever burrowing in the sand, make sure all rocks are placed on the bottom of the tank and then surrounded with sand so that their tunneling cannot cause disastrous cave-ins.

Pholidichthys leucotaenia.

This eel-like fish is a delightful aquarium choice on all counts, with one exception. It is peaceful toward any fish or invertebrate too large to swallow whole (and their small mouth really restricts this), it will live happily in small groups, it greedily eats absolutely any food you offer, it is hardy and disease resistant, and it is even an easy marine to breed. So what's the catch? Despite what you will see in some online sources, its adult size is 12 to 18 inches (30 to 45 cm). Being very slender and worm-like in shape, that is nowhere near the fish mass of, say, a foot-long angelfish, but it still needs ample tank space. A small group of three to five specimens can be housed in a 100-gallon (400-liter) or larger aquarium.

Fish in the genus *Nemateleotris* are known as wormfish, dartfish, or firefish, as well as fire or dart gobies. Even the scientists are not agreed, as some place them in the family Gobiidae while others put them in Microdesmidae. These fish are good for reef or peaceful FO setups. Many species stay under 4 inches (10 cm). They typically hover above a burrow, facing into the current, from which they strip plankton as it drifts by. Obviously they need frequent small feedings of appropriately sized foods. If introduced at the same time to a sufficiently large aquarium, pairs or small groups can be maintained, but they also can thrive as the only one of their species in the tank.

Meiacanthus grammistes.

Vampires

The recommended species include some—but not all!—of the fang, vampire, or saber tooth blennies, a group of medium small (4 to 5 inches [10 to 12 cm]) fish that are equipped with large canine teeth and a venomous gland that serves well to keep other fish at bay. Here is a case where you really need to do your homework. Some of these blennies are vicious sneak-attack artists that will constantly rip chunks off their tankmates, while those of the genus *Meiacanthus* are excellent aquarium candidates.

Meiacanthus blennies will not attack tankmates or your hand in the tank, but you should not try to handle them or hand feed them! Although not common in the trade as wild caught, they have been commercially bred, and tank-raised specimens are available. These are examples of blennies that do not stay on the substrate.

CARDINALFISH

There are several cardinalfish suitable for your marine tank. For the most part these fish are crepuscular, meaning that they are most active at twilight. They require an overhanging ledge of rock or similar retreats, but provided with this, they will often be out and about. Most species in the genus *Apogon* are colorful, and they often can be kept in small groups. Do research the adult size of a species under consideration, as some are significantly larger than others. The Banggai cardinal, *Pterapogon kauderni,* has become a favorite, so much so that it was severely overfished. Fortunately, not only is this fish a mouthbrooder like all other cardinals, its larvae are atypically not planktonic. The male holds the developing fry in his mouth until they are large enough to release, at which time they can already take foods such as baby brine shrimp and tiny prepared foods. Thus it is possible to raise them without the complications associated with most marine species. You should insist on captive-bred Banggais.

Apogon maculatus.

CLOWNFISH (ANEMONEFISH)

Close cousins to the damsels (more on these fish in a moment), the various clownfish species are also excellent beginner fish. Owing to their famous symbiotic relationship with anemones, clownfish have, perhaps, influenced more people to become involved in the marine aquarium hobby than any other marine animal. In fact, it was the common clownfish, *Amphiprion ocellaris,* that first enticed me into marine fishkeeping. You may not be familiar with this fish by its scientific name, but you'd undoubtedly recognize one if you saw it, especially since it starred in a popular animated children's film. For many marine aquarists, *A. ocellaris,* with its comical antics and its almost surreal orange, white, and black coloration, is the consummate clownfish. The percula clownfish, *A. percula,* sports coloration and pattering that are nearly identical to that of *A. ocellaris.* The only difference is that the percula clownfish

Premnas biaculeatus.

usually has slightly more pronounced black markings on its body and fins, but this is not a completely reliable diagnostic. Both species make equally delightful additions to the beginner's aquarium. Other excellent choices include the maroon clownfish, *Premnas biaculeatus*, Clark's clownfish, *A. clarkii*, and the tomato clownfish, *A. frenatus*. Many clownfish will coexist peacefully as pairs. If you get two small individuals, one will grow larger and become a female, while the smaller one will become a functional male. It is, however not a good idea in most cases to try to keep two maroon clowns in the same tank unless they are a mated pair, as these large and aggressive fish can be quite rough on any tankmates, including conspecifics. Clownfish often spawn in the aquarium, and the fry are among the easiest marines to raise, but with saltwater fish "easiest" is still difficult!

In spite of the fact that they seek refuge among the stinging tentacles of anemones in the wild, clownfish can be kept quite satisfactorily in captivity without an anemone. This is good news for newcomers to the hobby. While clownfish are relatively easy to keep, the same cannot be said for anemones. Even advanced reef aquarists have a hard time providing the exacting conditions that are necessary to keep anemones alive in captivity for any length of time. If you're new to the aquarium hobby in general and are considering keeping a clownfish and anemone together, I would strongly urge you to reconsider the anemone. In fact, anemones should be kept by expert reef hobbyists only, and then not by all of them.

Like the closely related damsels, territorial aggression can be a problem with certain clownfish species. In the case of my own percula clownfish, this aggression seems to be directed only at my hand whenever I'm performing some routine maintenance task in the aquarium. The little bugger ruthlessly nips at my fingers whenever I get too close to its little cave between the rockwork and substrate. Otherwise, it seems to get along just fine with its tankmates, one of which happens to be a yellow-tailed blue damsel. If clownfish territoriality should become a problem, you can generally overcome it using the same techniques as described for damsels.

DAMSELS

When it comes to tolerating the fluctuating water parameters that sometimes prevail in beginners' aquariums, no other group of fish can compare to the damsels (family Pomacentridae). These fish have several advantages that make them the ideal first fish for the novice marine aquarist. For one thing, most species do not grow larger than 3 to 4 inches (7 to 10 cm) in captivity, and they will readily accept all standard aquarium fare, including flake, freeze-dried, frozen, and live foods. Damsels also come in a wide range of dazzling colors, from the starkly contrasting white and black bands of the humbug damsel, *Dascyllus aruanus*, to the royal blue and bright yellow of the yellow-tailed blue damsel, *Chromis xanthurus*, to the iridescent green-blue of the green chromis, *Chromis viridis*.

The only drawback to this hardy and forgiving group of fish is that they can be extremely territorial and feisty toward their tankmates, especially toward other damsels. However, there are some simple steps you can take to help reduce their aggression. For one thing, avoid keeping more than one damsel of any given species in the same tank. Many aquarists have successfully kept a small school of green chromis in a large tank; this species is especially

Dascyllus aruanus.

tolerant of conspecifics and is the best choice if you want more than one damsel. Otherwise, protracted territorial disputes are virtually unavoidable. Exceptions can sometimes be made if the fish are housed in a very large tank with ample hiding places. It's also helpful to introduce the damsel after all the other specimens have had a chance to establish territories. That way the damsel will be the new fish on the block and won't be as likely to view the other fish as intruders. In the event that a damsel has already established its territory, and you'd like to introduce some additional fish, you can sometimes avert conflict by rearranging the rockwork ahead of time to disrupt the defined territorial boundaries.

DWARF ANGELS

Unlike the full-sized marine angelfish (the emperor angel, queen angel, French angel, etc.), which generally are considered too delicate for the beginner's aquarium (not to mention way too big), several dwarf (or pygmy) angels of the genus *Centropyge* (family Pomacanthidae) are terrific choices for the novice aquarist. These fish reach a very manageable size of only around 4 inches (10 cm) at maturity, and they adapt readily to aquarium conditions. Dwarf angels can be trained to accept a wide range of food items, including most standard flake, freeze-dried, and frozen foods, but most species also require a good amount of algae in their diets, which can be provided in the form of dried marine algae. Of particular interest to beginner aquarists are the coral beauty, *C. bispinosus*, the lemonpeel angelfish, *C. flavissima*, and the flame angelfish, *C. loricula*.

The coral beauty is an absolute delight to behold. The head and body of this exceedingly well-behaved dwarf angel are a bluish-purple. Its flanks are gold or reddish-gold interrupted

Centropyge loricula.

by a series of vertical purple stripes. The fins are blue to purplish blue, with the exception of the pectoral fins, which are transparent yellow. And this description hardly does justice to the coral beauty's coloration. In fact, there are subtle distinctions in coloration between individuals, depending on the location from which they were collected. You really have to see this fish to believe it.

The aptly named lemonpeel angelfish is almost totally bright yellow in color, which really makes this fish pop in the average community aquarium. The only variation from this monochrome is a light blue ring around each eye, a small blue streak on the edges of its gill covers, and an almost imperceptible pinkish tint on the outer margins of its dorsal, caudal, and anal fins. The lemonpeel angelfish is predominately a grazer, so don't hold back on the greens.

The flame angelfish gets its name from its dramatic orange-red overall coloration. Along its flanks are five or six dark vertical bands. The margins of its dorsal, caudal, and anal fins are tinged with blue. Like the lemonpeel angelfish, the flame angelfish's vivid color really makes it stand out from the rest of the fish in a community tank. This fish is just slightly more demanding when it comes to water quality than the other two dwarf angels we've discussed, but it shares their peaceful demeanor and willingness to accept a wide range of food items.

Each of these three species is commonly available at most marine aquarium shops (at a fairly reasonable price, I might add). Though they are relatively peaceful, they generally will not tolerate conspecifics and may square off with other species that are very similar in size, shape, or color.

GOBIES

With more than 2,000 species, the goby family has an enormous variety of fishes. Some are unsuitable for your first tank, but a great many are excellent choices. Many gobies stay small, and most are peaceful with tankmates other than conspecifics. Most fish called gobies are benthic, meaning they stay pretty much on the bottom. They lack a functional air bladder and typically hop or crawl along most of the time, though they are capable of swimming quickly when they have to. Two groups of gobies are particularly good choices for your first marine aquarium, the clown or coral gobies and the neon gobies.

Clowns

The clown gobies of the genus *Gobiodon* are attractively colored and quite small—most species are about 2 inches (5 cm). They are tadpole shaped and spend most of their time hanging around in the branches of stony corals, which is what gives them their other common name. The most often available species are the citron clown goby, *G. citrinus*, the blue-spotted coral goby, *G. histrio*, and a second yellow species, *G. okinawae*.

Elacantinus randalli.

Neons

The neon gobies of the genus *Elacatinus* sport a neon stripe along their bodies that is blue in some species and gold in others. They are all quite small and very peaceful, usually even with conspecifics. Furthermore, neon gobies are cleaners, meaning that they will pick parasites and dead flesh off their tankmates. Although the behavior is virtually absent among freshwater fish, reef species often visit cleaning stations served by cleaner fish or shrimps. Even the largest predators remain still, their fins spread and their mouths agape, while the tiny cleaners safely pick bits off their skin and even from inside their mouths and gills. Along with clownfish, neon gobies were among the very first marine fish to be bred successfully in captivity. Today many species are available as captive-bred specimens. There are even several hybrids of neon goby species available. Another species in the genus, *E. puncticulatus*, is sometimes called the red-headed neon goby, though it has traded most of its neon stripe for a bright red cap. It is also very hardy and an excellent choice for your tank.

HAWKFISH

If you're looking for small, peaceful fish with a little character and personality for your community, you can't go wrong with the various hawkfish (family Cirrhitidae). These fish get their name not so much from their appearance as from their habit of perching on coral outcroppings and swooping down on prey items as they swim by or drift past in the current. Because they lack swim bladders (an internal organ that allows fish to control buoyancy), they are generally poor swimmers and spend most of their time resting on the rockwork, propped up on their pectoral fins. When they choose to move, they typically get around by hopping comically from rock to rock.

The feature that is most appealing about hawkfish is their apparent awareness of everything that goes on around them. Their large, high-set eyes are always glancing about, keeping track of all the activity both inside and outside the tank. They'll even follow the aquarist with their eyes once they figure out from whom their daily "bread" comes.

Hawkfish are predatory by nature and should be offered plenty of meaty foods in the aquarium. They'll gladly accept most live, frozen, and freeze-dried foods and will even learn to accept flake food over time. The only food they'll completely ignore is marine algae and other greens. If you offer these items to a hawkfish, it will merely roll its eyes at you and flash you a little fishy expression that seems to say, "You don't honestly expect me to eat this, do you?"

The three most commonly sold hawkfish species are the scarlet (or flame) hawkfish, *Neocirrhites armatus*, the longnosed hawkfish, *Oxycirrhites typus*, and the pixie hawkfish, *Cirrhitichthys oxycephalus*, although other species sometimes make their way into dealers' tanks as well. The scarlet hawkfish is perhaps the most popular and attractive of the three, with its short, blunt body and its intense (you guessed it!) scarlet coloration. Unfortunately, since the supply of this fish is relatively short and the demand is relatively high, the scarlet hawkfish is the most expensive of the three.

The longnosed hawkfish has a more elongated body than the scarlet hawkfish, and, as the name suggests, it has a long pointy snout. The snout is perfectly designed for reaching into tight crevices on the coral reef for tiny crustaceans and other food items. Its overall coloration is white with a repeating square pattern made up of bright red lines. At the tip of each dorsal spine are little hair-like appendages called cirrhi, which are not as pronounced on the scarlet

My favorite of the three commonly sold hawkfish species is the pixie hawkfish. With its stocky body and short snout, this fish is closer in body shape to the scarlet hawkfish, but it is more similar in coloration to the longnosed hawkfish. Instead of a box pattern, it has dark rust-colored blotches ringed with orange against a white background. Cirrhi are also clearly visible on the dorsal spines of this species.

Cirrhitichthys oxycephalus.

TANGS

Most tangs and surgeonfish (family Acanthuridae) are touchy when it comes to water quality and diet, making them better suited for experienced aquarists than for beginners. And this is a real shame, since many of them are just drop-dead gorgeous. My personal favorite is the regal tang, *Paracanthurus hepatus*, with its stunning blue body, black painter's palette side markings, and bright yellow tail. Unfortunately, when I attempted to keep one of these fish in my first marine aquarium (before I knew anything about their specific dietary requirements and their need for near-pristine water conditions) it contracted a disease and wasted away in short order.

Yellow Tang

My own personal catastrophes aside, one particular species, the yellow tang, *Zebrasoma flavescens*, is fairly forgiving and will thrive under conditions that would not be tolerated by most tangs and surgeons. This is not to suggest that it can tolerate neglect or wildly fluctuating water parameters. On the contrary, it will likely become ill and perish if there are too many dissolved organic compounds in the water. A good protein skimmer is a must if you intend to keep this species, and, of course, it's important to keep up with those water changes. Also, since they are naturally found in relatively shallow water where wave action is heavy, they require highly oxygenated water and ample water movement such as that provided by a strong powerhead.

Like all other tangs and surgeons, the yellow tang has an extremely laterally compressed body and a scalpel-like spine on its caudal peduncle (the base of the tail). The spine can be erected, in switchblade-like fashion, whenever the fish feels threatened, so care must be taken when netting these fish. However, you don't have to worry about being attacked and injured by one of these fish whenever you place your hand in the aquarium. It will simply flee to the opposite end of the tank or hide within the rockwork when it sees your hand approaching. Yellow tangs are territorial with their own or similar species, but they are very peaceful otherwise.

Tangs are herbivores, preferring to graze throughout the day on algae, and the yellow tang is no exception. In order to keep this fish in good health, you must provide ample greens on a daily basis. Avoid feeding lettuce, spinach, and other terrestrial greens, as they cannot be digested properly. Instead, offer dried nori (the seaweed used to wrap sushi) or red marine algae. Both contain the necessary nutrients for marine organisms and will be accepted with enthusiasm.

WRASSES

The family Labridae is another enormous group. Known as wrasses, fish of this family range in size from under 2 inches (5 cm) for *Minilabrus striatus* to more than 7 feet (2.3 m) for *Cheilinus undulatus*. You may be surprised to find that this latter fish, called the Napoleon wrasse, though sofa sized, is often offered for sale as a cute juvenile! That is one of the reasons why it is so important to research any fish you are contemplating acquiring.

Wrasses are typically brilliantly colored, and the adult coloration is often strikingly different from the juvenile patterning. They are sequential hermaphrodites, taking on three or four different sexes in order: sexually undifferentiated juveniles, females, males, (and supermales), each of which is differently colored! All wrasses are spectacular jumpers and require carefully sealed tank tops. Many also dive completely into the sand to hide and to sleep. Unless these fish have a deep sand substrate, they will be nervous and stressed all the time. Many if not most wrasses simply get too big for most tanks, though there are many that are fine for systems of several hundred gallons. We'll look here at a few species that can be kept in aquariums of 100 gallons (400 liters) or less.

Coris Wrasses

There are a couple of dozen *Coris* species that make good beginner fish. The coloration as the fish transforms from juvenile to female to male is typically so different that the various forms have often been classified as completely different species. Although very readily available, most of the coris wrasses are simply too big for standard aquariums. They also tend to the nasty side. A few are "only" 8 to 10 inches (20 to 25 cm) and suitable for a large FO setup. Do your homework.

Bodianus bimaculatus.

Hogfish

The hogfish contain several possibilities, but they include some 3-foot (1-m) bruisers, too. The twinspot or yellow hogfish, *Bodianus bimaculatus,* is extremely peaceful and fine for reef or FO tank. At about 4 inches (10 cm), it is one of the smallest hogfish. The Cuban hog, *B. pulchellus,* is popular and quite peaceful, but it does top out at about 10 inches (25 cm).

Lined Wrasses

Several species in the genus *Pseudocheilinus* are found in the trade. They are all peaceful to the point of being shy and remain small—4 to 5 inches (10 to 13 cm). Most have horizontal lines, and all are colorful. These fish are fine for FO or reef systems, but they will eat ornamental shrimps. They are hardy and good choices for your tank. With sufficient hiding places like a wall of live rock they will make regular forays out into the open, especially at feeding time.

Maori Wrasses

The splendor or Maori wrasses of the genera *Cheilinus* and *Oxycheilinus* contain some promising aquarium candidates, but remember the behemoth Napoleon wrasse is also in this group! In fact, many of these fish, though considerably smaller than your furniture, are

What's With the Scientific Names?

You may be wondering why I list the scientific name of each fish species and not just its common name. The reason is that relying on common names when choosing animals for your marine aquarium can create lots of confusion and may even lead to disaster. Take the common name "powder brown tang" for example. You will find that two very similar-looking species, *Acanthurus nigricans* and *A. japonicus*, are both sold under this common name. They are so similar in appearance, in fact, that the layman would have a very difficult time telling them apart without seeing both species side by side. The only problem is that *A. nigricans* doesn't adapt well to life in captivity and usually dies within a few weeks of purchase, while *A. japonicus* is generally well-suited for the aquarium.

And this is only one example out of many. In some cases, the same common name is used to describe three or more different species, all of which might have radically different care requirements. Likewise, a fish may have several common names, some of which it shares with other species. The bottom line is this: if you arm yourself with the scientific names of the various marine organisms that interest you before heading for the aquarium store, you'll be much more likely to get the exact species you're after.

Cirrhilabrus rubrisquamis.

too large for most tanks. A beautiful exception is the red hogfish or snooty wrasse, *Cheilinus oxycephalus,* which grows to only 6 inches (17 cm). There are also several *Oxycheilinus* species that stay small and are good choices. If you find one, check out its maximum size before considering it.

Velvet/Fairy/Flasher Wrasses

The velvet or fairy wrasses in the genus *Cirrhilabrus* comprise many small, highly colorful fish that are great for the reef or FO aquarium. Ranging from about 2 to 6 inches (6 to 15 cm), these fish show a marked sexual dimorphism, with the males even more gorgeously colored than the females. If you introduce several juveniles all at once, they will form a harem; the dominant individual will become a male and protect his harem. Never place two males into the same tank. While the males often "flash" their fins and colors at the females, another group of very similar fish known as flasher wrasses have this behavior down to an art.

The flasher wrasses of the genus *Paracheilinus* get their name from their courtship display. A tiny, brilliantly colored fish with full, flowing, sparkling red or iridescent fins can easily attract females, but he would also be an easy target for predators. So the male hangs around the rocks, his fins closed. When he wants to display to a female or a rival male, he shoots up into the water column, quickly flashes his fins wide open, then drops back to the rock. Rivals are warned and interested females know where to find him, but predators don't have time to

*Paracheilinus
filamentosus.*

get a lock on him. With fins clamped, the males look similar to females, but when they spread their fins, the extra-colorful patterns are visible. Many different flasher wrasses are available in the trade, all small, hardy, and peaceful. They cannot stand up to aggressive tankmates. Single males often do not thrive, so it is best to include a small group of females.

Other Wrasses

There are literally dozens and dozens of species in the genus *Halichoeres*. With so many to choose from, it is not surprising that there are some suitable and some unsuitable for the aquarium. So, at the risk of giving redundant advice, research before buying. One prime candidate is the yellow or canary wrasse, often erroneously called the yellow coris wrasse, *Halichoeres chrysus*. At just 4 inches (10 cm), this peaceful fish is fine for reef or FO tanks with similarly unaggressive tankmates.

Halichoeres chrysus.

THAT'S NOT ALL

As I suggested at the beginning of this chapter, this by no means exhausts the list of marine fish that are suitable for the novice aquarist. Your dealer will be able to expand upon this list considerably and help you select a peaceful, compatible community of fish that will bring you years of pleasure. Just remember to research *before* you buy!

Chapter 13

A Sampler of Troublesome Fish

Okay, we've taken a good look at some species of marine fish that make great additions to the beginner's aquarium, but that's only part of the picture. When shopping for your first specimens, you'll undoubtedly come across species that are irresistibly beautiful or exotic-looking but don't really belong in the average novice aquarist's tank. In fact, some commonly sold species aren't suitable for any aquarium, regardless of how experienced the aquarist might be. That is why it is so important to research a fish before you purchase it. After you introduce it into your aquarium is not the time to find out that the fish will soon grow to twice the length of the tank!

What Lies Ahead

- salwater fish to be wary of
- fish to avoid

KEEP YOUR HANDS TO YOURSELF!

The first group of potentially troublesome fish consists of the various and sundry venomous species that are frequently offered for sale. By venomous I mean any fish capable of inflicting a painful toxic sting through sharp spines on its body.

Foxfaces

Just like the different species of lionfish, the foxfaces do not use their venomous spines offensively. Stings usually occur through accidental contact while netting or transporting one of these fish or while maintaining the aquarium.

Lionfish and Stonefish

The different species of lionfish (family Scorpaenidae) are all venomous, and they are widely available in the aquarium trade. In fact, I don't recall ever being in a marine aquarium shop that didn't have at least one lionfish (usually *Pterois volitans*) for sale.

A lionfish's sting, which is delivered by its beautiful, flowing, hypodermic-like dorsal spines, is not usually deadly, but it can cause excruciating pain. Some who have been stung compare the pain to that inflicted by a bee or a wasp sting, but other people have much worse reactions.

The bicolored foxface, *Siganus uspi.*

Another drawback to lionfish is that they can engulf any fish small enough to fit into their cavernous mouths and so are best kept alone in a large species tank. They also grow quite large.

Lionfish are generally nonaggressive (except to their prey items) and will not actively seek to sting an aquarist. More often than not, a sting results

A lionfish,
Pterois sp.

from accidentally brushing up against the fish while performing routine maintenance tasks in the tank. Some unwitting aquarists have even been stung through the plastic bag used to transport the fish home from the aquarium shop. Also, the fact that many lionfish and other scorpaenids have very cryptic coloration makes it easy to lose track of their location in the tank and hence to make inadvertent contact. Speaking of cryptic coloration, a relative of the lionfish that is completely inappropriate for the novice aquarist, and indeed for most advanced aquarists, is the extremely venomous stonefish, *Synanceia horrida*, along with its highly toxic conspecific *S. verrucosa*. These fish sport such outstanding camouflage that you can look right at them without discerning the outline of a fish. They're also armed with sharp dorsal spines capable of delivering a highly toxic venom that can cause intense pain, paralysis, and even death, depending on how many spines penetrate the skin of the unfortunate aquarist. Under no circumstances should one of these species be kept in a home aquarium. The potential for tragedy is just too great.

A close-up look at the venom-delivering dorsal spines of *Pterois volitans.*

Marine Catfish

A school of juvenile saltwater catfish, *Plotosus lineatus*, is a delight to behold in the wild. The young congregate by the hundreds in tight defensive balls that roll comically along the ocean floor, though this behavior seldom manifests itself in captivity unless a large number of these fish are kept together in a huge aquarium. Commonly available and inexpensive, these fish are nevertheless extremely unsuitable for your tank. Though they are strikingly colored as the little babies sold in the trade, they mature into drab adults that no longer school. In fact, they get rather nasty while growing to their full length of more than 1 foot (30 cm). They also possess venomous dorsal and pectoral spines and can be dangerous if not handled properly. Human fatalities from the sting have occurred.

OBLIGATE SPONGE OR CORAL FEEDERS

Even supposedly easy-to-feed fish species can sometimes turn their keepers' hair gray by refusing to accept standard aquarium foods. But when a fish requires a very specific food item in its diet that is difficult or impossible for the average aquarist to provide, the likelihood of that fish's surviving for long in captivity is minimal.

Angelfish

For example, certain large pomacanthid angelfish, including among others the conspicuous angelfish, *Chaetodontoplus conspicillatus*, the rock beauty, *Holacanthus tricolor*, and the blue-striped angelfish, *C. septentrionalis*, feed primarily on live coral polyps or sponges. Even if they eventually learn to accept standard aquarium fare in captivity, they generally will not thrive on it. Their rigid dietary requirements aside, most large angelfish are unsuitable for the beginner aquarium because they are extremely demanding when it comes to water quality and will often become ill and/or go on a hunger strike when water conditions begin to deteriorate. Most are also way too large.

Butterflyfish

As a general rule, what's good for the angels is good for the butterflies. That is, many of the same dietary and water quality concerns that apply to angelfish also apply to the closely related butterflyfish (family Chaetodontidae). While some butterflyfish can be kept successfully by advanced aquarists, most are poorly suited for the beginner's tank. Certain species, including the four-eyed butterflyfish, *Chaetodon capistratus*, the ornate butterflyfish, *C. ornatissimus*, the chevron butterflyfish, *C. trifascialis*, and several others, will fare poorly under even the most experienced aquarist's care. With so many similarly colored and patterned butterflyfish on the market, many dealers can't identify the different species with 100-percent accuracy, let alone provide their customers with accurate dietary information for each species offered for sale. It's best to pass on angelfish and butterflyfish, at least for your first marine aquarium.

Parrotfish

The parrotfish (family Scaridae) are totally unsuitable for any kind of aquarium because of their specialized diet, which consists mainly of algae-encrusted coral heads, which they chomp into with their tough, beak-like mouths. They digest the algae and any invertebrates

Most parrotfish need very large setups and will dine on your corals. These fish are best left in the ocean.

in the coral fragments, which they then excrete as sand. Yes, they defecate mostly sand! In fact, much of the sand substrate surrounding coral reefs has actually been produced by the digestive systems of parrotfishes. Apart from their destructive feeding habits, most species of parrotfish become much too large for the home aquarium.

FISH NEEDING A CONSTANT SUPPLY OF TINY LIVE FOODS

Some otherwise-perfect aquarium candidates starve in captivity because they simply cannot learn to recognize any usual fish food as edible.

Mandarins

Known as mandarins, mandarin gobies, and dragonets, fish of the genus *Synchiropus* are small, surrealistically colorful, extremely peaceful, commonly available, and inexpensive. So why are they in this chapter? Almost all of the mandarins purchased are dead within a few months. They die of starvation, as they will only eat tiny live crustaceans and worms. The general recommendation is that a 100-gallon (400-liter) tank that has been set up with live rock for over a year and that has no other fish that eat the copepods that live among the rocks can sustain a single mandarin. A scant few specimens have been trained to take nonliving foods, but even some of them fail to thrive. Hopefully soon someone will discover how to raise these fish commercially; the tank-raised babies will undoubtedly accept all kinds of prepared foods. At that time this beautiful fish can be moved into the preceding chapter, but for now do yourself and the fish a favor and avoid purchasing them.

Seahorses require a lot of small live foods.

Seahorses

Much like starfish, seahorses (family Syngnathidae) are considered by many to be true emblems of the sea. For this reason, along with their unique body shape and fascinating reproductive behavior, marine aquarists are often tempted to keep seahorses in their aquariums. Unfortunately, seahorses seldom live long in captivity unless their keepers go to great lengths to satisfy their specialized dietary needs and their demand for superior water quality.

Take one look at the tiny, tube-shaped mouths of these animals and you can tell right away that they're highly specialized feeders. Seahorses, along with the other syngnathids, the pipefish and seadragons, require an almost constant supply of very tiny live food items, such as marine rotifers and HUFA-enriched (HUFA is an acronym for highly unsaturated fatty acids) newly hatched brine shrimp. Standard offerings of flake, frozen, and freeze-dried foods a couple times a day simply will not suffice. Three to four (or even more) small feedings of live food a day would be more in line with what these fish require. Considering how hectic most of our schedules are these days, finding the time to provide four or more feedings a day seems highly unlikely—not to mention the impracticality of maintaining a steady supply of the live food items they need. Captive-bred seahorses that have been trained to eat frozen mysis shrimp are becoming available, but their food is expensive and not sold everywhere. Feeding these animals is still a chore, and their meekness requires that you keep them in a species aquarium—with no other fish. If you're still tempted, wait until you have kept a marine aquarium for a year or so, then set up another tank for seahorses *after* you do your homework and find out all you can about them.

FISH THAT DON'T SHIP WELL

Unless you're fortunate enough to live on an island in the tropical Pacific (or you only buy tank-raised specimens), the marine fish you buy for your aquarium are likely to have traveled a considerable distance in less-than-ideal water conditions prior to arriving in your dealer's tanks. Many species are hardy enough to survive this prolonged shipping period with no ill effects. Others almost always die soon after they are purchased. One of the worst choices for an aquarium specimen is the Moorish idol, *Zanclus cornutus*, a fish both notoriously difficult to ship and extremely difficult to maintain even if it survives shipping. Even public aquariums have a hard time keeping these fish alive for long!

The problem is that even though every single Moorish idol dies within the first few months in captivity, it is still prized by many aquarists for its exotic beauty and the characteristic

Countless Moorish idols have wasted away and perished in home aquariums.

long, flowing filament extending from its dorsal fin. Some find the Moorish idol so irresistibly beautiful that they will continue to buy specimens regardless of the outcome. And as long as a demand exists for these fish, collectors will continue to collect them, and dealers will continue to offer them for sale.

SHARKS AND MORAY EELS

It's the rare marine aquarist who hasn't at one time or another contemplated keeping a shark. There's just something about these top predators that seems to epitomize the mystery and wonder of the ocean, and the temptation to own one can

Moorish Idol Alternative

If you're really taken with the exotic beauty of the Moorish idol and feel you simply can't live without one, consider purchasing a bannerfish, *Heniochus acuminatus*, instead. The bannerfish (a.k.a. the poor man's Moorish idol) is almost identical in body shape and coloration to the Moorish idol and has the same graceful, flowing dorsal filament. The difference is that the bannerfish is very much hardier and more likely to adapt to conditions in captivity. The only real drawback to the bannerfish is its 10-inch (25-cm) size, but if your tank is at least 90 gallons (360 liters) and not overstocked, you can keep one successfully.

sometimes prove irresistible. The only trouble is that the odds rarely favor a shark's survival in the home aquarium. One obvious drawback is their ultimate size. Even some of the smaller bottom-dwelling species reach mature lengths that are way beyond the capacity of the average home aquarium. For example, the commonly sold gray bamboo shark, *Chiloscyllium griseum*, can reach a length of up to 30 inches (76 cm). Try fitting that into our model 55-gallon (200-liter) aquarium. No, don't! The popular peppered catshark, *Galeus piperatus*, is far more diminutive but still reaches the respectable length of 1 foot (30 cm)—no great white, perhaps, but still pretty large as aquarium specimens go.

Along with reaching tankbusting proportions, sharks are surprisingly sensitive to poor water quality and cannot tolerate even low nitrate levels. Sharks are extremely sensitive to even the mildest electrical signals in their environment and can be driven to distraction by the stray voltages that sometimes are produced by electronic filtration and heating devices. In addition, most of the commonly sold shark species prefer cooler water with a high dissolved-oxygen content, requiring chillers and high-powered water pumps. It is very common to see captive sharks with abraded or infected snouts; this is because they do not negotiate walls and corners very well. These animals not only require humongous aquariums, they need humongous *round* aquariums. Also, many species of sharks must keep swimming in order to breathe; even room-sized tanks are inadequate for their activity level.

Another sharp-toothed tank-busting predator that often stirs the imagination of marine aquarists is the moray eel. Most morays get way too large for the average beginner's aquarium. To illustrate how large some morays can get, consider one green moray, *Gymnothorax funebris*, that I observed once while diving in the Florida Keys. As a general rule, morays extend only about one-third of their body length out of their dens during daylight hours (at night, they emerge completely and swim around in search of prey). Taking diving mask magnification into consideration, the moray in question easily had 3 feet (90 cm) of its body exposed (with a "neck" resembling a linebacker's), suggesting that another 6 feet (1.8 m) of its body remained hidden in the den. That's a whopping 9 feet (2.7 m) of eel!

Granted, many of the species that are frequently sold to aquarists don't grow that large, but even "small" morays such as the snowflake moray, *Echidna nebulosa*, and the leopard moray, *Gymnothorax undulatus*, can reach lengths upwards of 3 feet and 5 feet (90 cm and 1.5 m) respectively. Along with reaching gargantuan proportions, morays are terrific escape artists and can wriggle their mucus-coated bodies through amazingly small gaps in the aquarium cover or lift the top completely with their considerable strength. Of course, when an escape goes undetected, the moray usually meets a dusty demise on the floor. When it is detected in time, the aquarist is faced with capturing a powerful, slimy, fast animal with razor-sharp teeth that does not want to be held—a recipe for serious injury of both human and fish.

Moray eels are generally good eaters in captivity and can be enticed with a broad variety of foods. However, since they're very nondiscriminating when it comes to diet, they'll be more than happy to devour any tankmates small enough to fit into their mouths. Morays also have very poor eyesight and may confuse an aquarist's hand for a prey item. When this occurs, the result for the unwary aquarist can be a painful, infected bite. Since many species have dagger-like teeth that angle backward to prevent seized prey items from escaping, it can be very difficult, once bitten, to break free of a moray's bite without causing serious injury to both of you.

Most moray eels grow too large for the average home aquarium.

Size Issues

There is considerable ignorance in the hobby about how large specific fish grow. Two aspects of this ignorance are very important for you to understand.

Aquarium Sizes

You will often find marine fish listed with two sizes, a size in the wild and a size in the aquarium. I hope this strikes you as odd. There is no evidence that suggests that smaller-than-in-the-wild specimens are anything other than stunted. They can be stunted by improper diet, intolerant tankmates getting most of the food, or poor water conditions. Some are not really stunted but simply fail to live long enough in captivity to reach full size. As aquarists, our goal should be to provide our pets with an environment compatible with a long, healthy life, and we should be dismayed if they fail to reach their species' full sizes for any reason. So if someone tells you that a given fish reaches 12 inches (30 cm) in the wild but only 8 inches (20 cm) in an aquarium, figure that its proper full size is the longer measurement.

Baby Giants

A surprising number of species of marine tropicals that are routinely sold in pet shops grow too large for most aquariums. Most fish are sold as juveniles, and people erroneously conclude that if a fish is for sale in an aquarium store it is suitable for keeping in a home aquarium. It is very common to see a tank stocked with a variety of juvenile fish, each of which would be too large as an adult to be kept alone in that aquarium.

Most angelfish, butterflyfish, tangs, wrasses, hamlets, and groupers are enormous, reaching lengths of 2 feet (60 cm) or more and requiring hundreds of gallons of tankspace. Most triggerfish are not only very large but also very aggressive and can bite tankmates in half with their small but powerful beaks.

So why are these fish sold in such quantities? Good question! They are sold because people buy them. If people stopped buying fish that have no way of surviving in their tanks, dealers would stop offering them, and collectors would stop catching them. With so many fantastic *and* suitable species to choose from, there is no reason even to consider fish that will soon outgrow your aquarium or, worse, soon die because your tank's volume is so small that the water becomes toxic from the enormous fish's enormous quantities of wastes.

Please, please do your homework and completely avoid those cute little fish that get so big they are popular food items—for large crowds!—in their native habitats.

Chapter 14

Stocking the Reef Aquarium

Stocking a reef tank presents its own challenges. Since the invertebrates are the focus, we will concentrate mostly on them. For the uninitiated reef aquarist, choosing healthy sessile invertebrates can be something of a challenge. This results largely from the fact that it's often difficult to know exactly what a healthy invertebrate is supposed to look like. To a certain degree, most of us can recognize an ailing fish. We might not be able to identify the exact cause or nature of the illness, but we can usually tell that something is wrong if a fish behaves in a peculiar fashion or has strange spots or growths somewhere on its body. But how is a sessile invertebrate supposed to look and behave?

What Lies Ahead

- how to select a healthy sessile invertebrate
- invertebrate compatibility concerns
- motile invertebrates
- invertebrate acclimation
- reef-safe fish

SIGNS OF A HEALTHY SESSILE INVERTEBRATE

As when purchasing fish, the first thing you'll want to look at when selecting invertebrates is the condition of the dealer's tanks. Are they choked with algae or detritus and reeking of decomposition? Are the inverts packed extremely close together? Are the tanks poorly lit? If any of these conditions applies to your dealer's tanks, your best bet is to shop elsewhere. Invertebrates kept under such conditions will most likely be in poor health and will have little chance of surviving in your aquarium.

Next, carefully examine the bodies of the invertebrates themselves. There should be no signs of tissue damage anywhere on the animals, as it can lead to bacterial infection and ultimately death. Pay special attention to the fleshy base of each animal or colony of animals to make sure it has not been injured during collection. Such injuries commonly lead to the rapid deterioration of the invertebrate. A healthy specimen will be attached firmly to a rock, the aquarium glass, or the substrate. Specimens attached to small portable rocks are preferable because it's easier to transfer them from tank to tank without the risk of injuring the base. Also, examine each animal for discolored lesions,

Research the corals that interest you so you have an idea how to tell if it is healthy or not. Pictured is *Parazoanthis gracilis*.

What to Look for When Buying Sessile Invertebrates

It can be extremely challenging for the novice reef aquarist to distinguish between a healthy sessile invertebrate and an ailing one. Here are some signs to look for:

- Specimens are displayed in a well-maintained, algae-free aquarium.
- There is no evidence of injury, tissue damage, or decay.
- Corals and anemones contract their tentacles rapidly when disturbed but are fully extended otherwise.
- Tridacnid clams have healthy-looking mantles that are not receding from the shell and snap shut when disturbed.
- Tubeworms have a full complement of feeding/respiratory tentacles that quickly withdraw into their tubes at any sudden movement.
- Animals exhibit their natural coloration (i.e., they don't look pale or bleached).
- The dealer demonstrates knowledge of proper handling/bagging techniques and can vouch for the fact that the animal has never been exposed to air.

powdery-looking areas, or slimy patches, which can be an indication of disease.

Healthy anemones and polyps should contract rapidly when disturbed but should remain fully expanded at most other times. Tubeworms should withdraw their feathery feeding tentacles into their tubes whenever they feel threatened, which is virtually any time they detect sudden movement either inside or outside their aquarium. Stony corals should be fully expanded with no evidence of decay or damage on their soft tissues. Also, avoid any stony coral specimens that appear to be receding or pulling away from their calcium carbonate skeletons.

It's extremely helpful to examine color photographs of the invertebrates you'd like to keep before heading for the aquarium shop. That way you'll have a better idea of how healthy specimens are supposed to look. Being familiar with natural coloration is especially important when selecting photosynthetic invertebrates that get their color from the symbiotic zooxanthellae residing in their tissues. When these invertebrates are ill or under stress, they'll often shed their zooxanthellae, causing them to lose their natural coloration and giving them a bleached appearance. Once they lose their zooxanthellae, these invertebrates are generally a lost cause in the aquarium, so having a color photo as a basis for comparison will help you avoid buying specimens that may already be in decline.

COMPATIBILITY AMONG SESSILE INVERTEBRATES

We've already discussed the importance of selecting compatible fish species for inclusion in your new marine aquarium. But what about sessile invertebrates? Is it possible that they, too, can make life miserable for one another? The answer is a resounding "yes!" The only difference is that the methods employed by certain invertebrates to keep their neighbors from encroaching on their individual territories are far more insidious than anything the average aquarium fish can inflict on its enemies.

For example, many coral species, such as the beautiful yet potent bubble coral, *Plerogyra sinuosa,* and elegance coral, *Catalaphyllia jardinei*, will ruthlessly sting neighboring invertebrates with their long feeding tentacles. Some also sting with specialized sweeper tentacles that are capable of extending well beyond the reach of their feeding tentacles. Several of the stony corals, especially members of the genus *Euphyllia* (e.g., frogspawn corals and vase corals), are equipped with these sweeper tentacles and are ready, willing, and able to put them to use to defend their territories in the aquarium. Because this stinging behavior typically occurs after lights out, it generally goes unobserved by the aquarist. On the other hand, it's hard to miss the injuries they inflict.

The sweeping tentacles of a *Euphayllia* sp. coral. These are extended to sting other invertebrates.

Preventing stinging deaths and injuries is a simple matter of spacing out your invertebrates properly. As a general rule, the space between two invertebrates should be approximately equal to the diameter of the larger species at maturity. This should provide ample room for each animal to grow to full size without coming into contact with its neighbors. However, certain rapid-growing corals may need to be pruned back routinely to keep them within reasonable boundaries.

Some corals, including the leather corals, *Sarcophyton* spp., and the pulse corals, *Xenia* spp., may actually wage a form of chemical warfare on their tankmates. That is, they are capable of releasing toxic compounds called

Territoriality Among Sessile Invertebrates

Don't let their sedentary lifestyles fool you. Many sessile invertebrates are completely capable of waging war on their neighbors when they perceive that their territories are being invaded. Some of their more sinister methods include:

- Rapidly overgrowing and shading out the competition.
- Ruthlessly stinging interlopers with their feeding tentacles.
- Launching nocturnal long-range strikes with specialized sweeper tentacles.
- Coral chemical warfare, the release of chemical compounds (terpenoids), to inhibit the growth of encroaching neighbors.

terpenoids into the water to discourage predation and to inhibit the growth of neighboring corals. On the coral reef, these compounds are quickly diluted by ocean water. However, terpenoids can have a major impact in the closed system of the aquarium, where dilution is minimal. The presence of these compounds may prevent corals from expanding or, in some cases, result in the stunting or death of specimens. Protein skimming, frequent partial water changes, and chemical filtration with activated carbon will help to remove terpenoids from the aquarium system. It's also helpful to maintain vigorous water movement throughout the aquarium so these compounds cannot accumulate around your invertebrates.

SELECTING MOTILE INVERTEBRATES

There is also a vast array of beautiful and exotic motile invertebrates, including various crustaceans, echinoderms, and mollusks that are often suitable for both reef and FO aquariums. When purchasing motile invertebrates, you should be concerned mostly with selecting specimens that are completely intact and moving actively about the tank in pursuit of food items. Lethargic specimens should be avoided as a general rule, but keep in mind that some are nocturnal and may be inactive during daylight hours.

Crabs, shrimps, and other crustaceans will attempt to evade capture by hiding amid the rockwork or behind decorations, a source of aggravation for the shopkeeper but a general indication of good health. You can also tell a lot about a crustacean's state of health by examining its mouthparts. If they aren't perpetually in motion, you should pass on the specimen because it is probably ill. Don't worry if a crustacean is missing a single claw or leg as long as it seems to be in good condition otherwise. The missing limb will be replaced when the animal molts (sheds its exoskeleton) again.

Determining the health of an echinoderm, such as a starfish (sea star), sea cucumber, or sea urchin, can be a little trickier, since many of them are extremely slow-moving by nature. Brittlestars, which are capable of surprisingly rapid bursts of speed, are an exception. Starfish should be plump and firm, with no sunken tissue on their central disks or along the margin of their arms. When disturbed, their tube feet should retract slowly but consistently. Sea cucumbers and the closely related sea apples should also be firm to the touch and plump, and they should retract their feeding tentacles promptly when bothered. Urchins should have a full complement of erect spines, and their tube feet should be in motion.

Snails, including the algae-munching turbo snails, and other univalve mollusks should have complete, undamaged shells, and they should be active in the dealer's tank. Of course, given the relatively slow pace of many univalves, you may need to spend several minutes observing a particular specimen before you can make a judgment concerning its health. Bivalves, such as the ever popular tridacnid clams, should snap their shells closed when disturbed. Otherwise, their siphons should be visible and their mantles should be fully expanded.

Motile invertebrates will be discussed in further detail in Chapter 17.

ACCLIMATING INVERTEBRATES

As with introducing new fish, invertebrates must also be carefully acclimated to the water conditions in their new home. In fact, gradual acclimation is even more critical for sessile invertebrates than it is for many fish species, as their delicate tissues can be damaged easily by a rapid change in specific gravity (osmotic shock). Rushing the process almost invariably leads to ailing or dying specimens.

In Chapter 11 I suggested acclimating marine fish in a separate plastic container in order to minimize the potential of introducing pathogens or parasites that might be present in your dealer's water to your aquarium. In most cases, you can use this same technique to acclimate invertebrates. Just be sure to acclimate them very gradually, preferably using the drip method.

For this technique (which works very well for fish, too, I might add), all you need is a plastic container and a length of flexible airline tubing. First, place your specimen in the acclimation container, fully submerged in its original water. Make sure the container is positioned below the level of the tank. Next, tie one or more loose knots in the airline tubing. Place one end of the tubing into the aquarium (you may need to clamp it there or wedge it beneath your aquarium cover) and the other in the acclimation container. Then either suck on the bottom end of the airline tubing to get the water flowing or force water through the top end by placing it in front of a powerhead or filter return. Once the water starts flowing, tighten the knots to slow the flow to a steady drip.

Allow the dripping to continue until the water volume in the acclimation container has doubled. Then gently pour or siphon out half of the water in the acclimation container and continue dripping. Repeat this process until the water parameters in your acclimation container match those of the aquarium. At that point you'll be ready to transfer the invertebrate to its new home in your tank.

Keep in mind that when introducing sessile invertebrates, there's more to consider than just acclimating them to different water parameters. You'll also need to acclimate photosynthetic specimens to the lighting in your system, which will differ markedly in both intensity and quality from the lighting (or lack thereof) they've been kept under during transportation and at the point of sale. Typically this involves starting them out at the bottom of the tank and gradually moving them upward to the appropriate level so they aren't shocked by a sudden change in light intensity. Less light-sensitive coral and anemone species can be placed lower down, as can tubeworms, which have no special lighting requirement.

Your invertebrates—both sessile and motile—have to be acclimated to your tank.

FISH IN THE REEF TANK

Many reef aquarists prefer to avoid including fish in their setups altogether, due to the fact that the fish's waste products tend to degrade water quality and because it can be next to impossible to capture and remove a sick or dead fish from a typical reef system. There are simply too many convenient bolt holes and hiding places to allow for easy netting. It's also undesirable to attempt to medicate an ailing fish in a reef aquarium, because many of the medications suitable for treating fish diseases are highly toxic to invertebrates and should only be administered in a separate quarantine tank. But in spite of the risks, some reefkeepers prefer the natural look of a reef aquarium that contains a few carefully chosen fish. In this chapter we will take a quick look at some of the types of fish that will work well in most reef tanks. For more information about them, see Chapter 12.

Reef-Safe *Centropyge?*

Are dwarf angels of the genus *Centropyge* safe in a reef aquarium? The answer is a firm "maybe." Some of these fish are true angels, never touching any of their sessile tankmates, while others see the aquarist's prize reef in miniature as a delightful smorgasbord. And we're not talking here about some *species* and other *species*—we're talking about individuals. You will meet some reefkeepers who condemn all *Centropyge* as invert eaters; once burned, a hobbyist is unlikely to try another dwarf angel in a reef. Others cannot understand their objections, having had only positive experiences. With this group of fish, the rule is definitely: your mileage may vary!

Count 'Em In

In order for a fish to be a desirable candidate for the reef tank, it must not put too much of a strain on the biofilter with its eating habits and waste and must not include sessile invertebrates as a routine part of its diet. The diminutive clownfish and damsels fit this requirement well. Several species of basslet and dottyback are also suitable for the reef tank, provided they are kept singly. Like the damsels, basslets and dottybacks can be extremely territorial and pugnacious with conspecifics, and their aggression may extend to any other fish that is similar in coloration or body shape.

The various cardinalfish are also generally well behaved, and you can usually house several together in the same tank quite peacefully.

Of course, this is just a small sampling of the fish species that are suitable for inclusion in a reef tank. With a little guidance from a trusted dealer, you should be able to assemble a small group of fish that are uniquely attractive and fascinating to observe without harming the invertebrates or heavily impacting the water quality in your aquarium. But remember, the key to success when combining sessile inverts and fish in the same tank is to choose your fish according to the needs of the invertebrates, not the other way around.

Count 'Em Out

On the flipside of the coin, there are various fish species that should be excluded from the reef aquarium with prejudice. For example, most triggerfish (family Balistidae) are totally unsuitable because they feed on invertebrates. Often they'll just sample a potential food item to determine whether it's worth eating, but because triggers have such impressive dentition, even curious nibbling can cause considerable damage or death.

Butterflyfish (family Chaetodontidae) are also problematic, as most species routinely include coral polyps and anemones in their diets. Unless you want to offer up your prized invertebrates as an incredibly extravagant smorgasbord, it's best to pass on the butterflyfish. One possible exception is the copperband butterflyfish, *Chelmon rostratus*, which is sometimes introduced to devour invasive *Aiptasia* anemones that occasionally stow away in live rock (as we mentioned in Chapter 6). But even this relatively innocuous species will sometimes turn its attention toward valued invertebrates.

Again, this is only a partial list of fish that are undesirable for inclusion in a reef aquarium. As a general rule, if you have any uncertainty about the behavior, feeding habits, or ultimate size of a particular species of fish—in other words, if you aren't absolutely certain that the fish has a proven record of being safe around invertebrates—it's best to leave it out of your reef tank.

A Sampler of Reef-Friendly Marine Fish

- anthias (family Serranidae)
- basslets and dottybacks (families Serranidae and Pseudochromidae)
- blennies (family Blenniidae)
- cardinalfish (family Apogonidae)
- clownfish and damsels (family Pomacentridae)
- dragonets (family Callionymidae)
- fairy basslets (family Grammidae)
- firefish (family Microdesmidae)
- gobies (family Gobiidae)
- hawkfish (family Cirrhitidae)

Chelmon rostratus.

Chapter 15

Are There Good Sessile Invertebrates for Beginners?

It's safe to say that many of the corals and other sessile invertebrates sought after by reef aquarists are highly sensitive when it comes to water quality and the spectrum and intensity of their lighting. However, there are some invertebrates that are slightly more forgiving when it comes to aquarium parameters, hence making them more suitable for an aquarist's first foray into the realm of the reef tank. This is not to say that any sessile inverts will thrive under wildly fluctuating water and lighting conditions. They won't. I'm merely suggesting that you'll be more likely to enjoy success with your first reef aquarium if you choose from hardier stock to begin with.

What Lies Ahead

- the best sessile invertebrates for beginners

So which invertebrates are best for beginners? To keep things simple, we'll focus our attention on some good choices from three tried-and-true groups, including (in no particular order) the soft corals, the polyps, and the mushroom polyps. The animals in these groups (along with the hard corals, sea anemones, and jellyfish) all belong to the phylum Cnidaria. All cnidarians have a similar radially symmetrical body plan with a central mouth/anus surrounded by numerous tentacles that are armed with harpoon-like stinging cells called nematocysts. But, as you'll see, there are quite a few variations on this one simple theme.

THESE CORALS ARE A BUNCH OF SOFTIES!

At this point, it might be helpful to explain the difference between soft and hard corals, because the foregoing watered-down descriptors don't really give you much to go on. Simply put, all hard corals (also called stony corals or true corals) manufacture calcium carbonate skeletons, whereas soft corals do not. Soft corals do have calcium carbonate in their tissues, but it is in the form of tiny spicules (called sclerites) rather than a large skeleton. You can also distinguish soft and hard corals from one another by the number of tentacles on each polyp. Soft corals have them in multiples of eight, while hard corals have six or more, but never eight. Another distinguishing trait of many (but not all) soft corals is the presence of small side branches (called pinnules) on the tentacles, which give the polyps a feathery appearance.

It is the hard corals, especially small-polyped varieties like the various species of *Acropora,* the elkhorn and staghorn corals, and *Montastrea,* the mountainous star corals, that are actually responsible for building tropical coral reefs. When hard corals die, their skeletons are left behind and serve as a foundation for other coral colonies. Over thousands of years, coral skeletons are continually deposited on top of one another, causing the reef to grow in turn. With few exceptions, hard corals are too touchy when it comes to water quality and lighting for the novice reef aquarist, so you're better off getting your feet wet with soft corals first.

Leather Corals

The leather corals, *Sarcophyton* spp., are some of the best soft corals for the novice reef aquarist. In the wild these animals will thrive under less-than-perfect conditions that prohibit the growth of hard corals. Leather corals come in two distinct forms. Some species are mushroom-like in appearance, with a stalk that supports a polyp-covered disk. Other species have a more prostrate, encrusting habit, with an abundance of tiny polyps emerging from a

Acropora sp. against the glass.

flattened broad base. These corals get their common name from the color (usually brown, beige, or yellow) and leathery texture exhibited by the main body mass when the polyps are withdrawn.

Don't be surprised if the polyps of a newly introduced leather coral remain withdrawn for several days. This is a natural response to changing conditions, not an indication of poor health. The polyps will re-emerge after having a chance to acclimate to the conditions in your aquarium. If given excellent water conditions, leather corals will grow rapidly in the aquarium and can even be propagated by taking cuttings and attaching them to pieces of live rock.

Lobophytum and *Sinularia* soft corals are very similar to the *Sarcophyton* leather corals in growth habit and appearance. *Lobophytum* corals are usually encrusting types, while *Sinularia* species are either encrusting, tree-like, or something in-between. Their colors range from pink to purple to beige. Species from both genera are very easy to maintain, even for the beginner.

Pulse Corals

The pulse corals of the genera *Anthelia* and *Xenia* are also excellent choices for the beginner's aquarium. These corals are so named because of the continuous pulsating

Leather coral, *Sarcophyton* sp.

Clavularia viridis.

movements that are exhibited by the polyps of certain species. Ironically, only a small number of these so-called pulse corals actually pulsate in this manner. Nonetheless, they are very beautiful and relatively easy to maintain. Pulse corals come in shades of beige, brown, white, and even purple. In some species, crowns of flower-like polyps are borne atop long, slender stalks. Other species spread horizontally along the substrate by means of runners (called stolons), with feathery polyps emerging along the length of each runner.

Like the leather corals, pulse corals will spread quickly, colonizing neighboring rocks if provided with excellent water conditions. Just be aware that the encrusting pulse coral varieties can be somewhat invasive and may inhibit the proper development of neighboring invertebrates. Fortunately, simply cutting back the offending coral or moving the affected animal to a different location in the aquarium will quickly reverse any adverse effects.

Star Polyps

The star polyps, *Clavularia* and *Cornularia* spp., are another group of soft corals well suited to the beginner's reef tank. Like the encrusting pulse coral species, these corals spread by means of horizontal runners, with polyps occurring along their length. Under optimal aquarium conditions, star polyps will grow rapidly, spreading out to adjacent solid substrates (i.e., the rockwork) with their runners. Of particular interest are the green star polyps, or starburst soft corals, *Clavularia viridis*. These extremely hardy corals have pale green polyps with bright green centers that are strikingly beautiful when fully expanded.

A PASSEL OF PERFECT POLYPS

Some of the easiest sessile invertebrates to maintain in captivity are the various zoanthid polyps (a.k.a. the button polyps or the sea mats). While not true corals, zoanthids exhibit many of the same fascinating characteristics, making them equally desirable to beginners and advanced reef aquarists alike. Most species of these anemone-like polyps are truly colonial. That is, groups of polyps are attached by their bases to a single encrusting membrane, through which they share nutrients and nervous impulses. They get their common name, sea mats, from their propensity to form enormous mat-like colonies on the coral reefs. In the wild, many zoanthid species thrive in very shallow waters and may even be exposed during periods of low tide, making them highly adaptable to changes in temperature and salinity.

In terms of body plan, zoanthid polyps are very reminiscent of true anemones, possessing a button-shaped oral disc that is surrounded with two rings of tentacles and attached to a stalk. The major visible difference is that true anemones tend to be more plump and robust in appearance. Zoanthids come in a wide range of colors, including different shades of brown, dark green, lemon yellow, and turquoise. Most species are relatively small, reaching a maximum size of approximately 1 inch (2.5 cm) in diameter.

In a well-maintained aquarium, zoanthids will spread prolifically (as their common name "mat" implies) either by budding from the base of an individual polyp or by sending out runners. In spite of the fact that they reproduce like rabbits, zoanthids generally will not attack neighboring invertebrates and, at the same time, seldom elicit aggression from other species. Of notable exception are the encrusting *Anthelia* pulse corals, which have been known to sting zoanthids.

Blue zoanthids, *Zoanthidea* sp.

Zoanthids seem to thrive in areas of high water turbulence, so be sure to provide ample water movement in your tank with a few strategically placed powerheads or filter returns. The only weakness to these relatively bulletproof invertebrates is that they can be smothered by heavy growths of filamentous algae. Deep-water species such as *Parazoanthus axinellae* (one of the noncolonial species) seem to be especially sensitive to algal overgrowth. To minimize this problem, it's important to keep the dissolved nutrient level in the aquarium low with a high quality protein skimmer and through regular partial water changes. It may also help to cut back slightly on the amount of time the lights are turned on each day.

One of the most commonly available species is *Zoanthus sociatus*, which is frequently sold under the name green polyp or green sea mat. These polyps are bright green overall, with yellowish-green at the center and on the margins of their oral discs. Other justifiably popular species that you may come across include, *Z. danae*, *Parazoanthus gracilis*, *Parazoanthus swiftii*, *Palythoa caribaeorum*, and *Palythoa tuberculosa*. And that's just scratching the surface!

MAKE ROOM FOR MUSHROOMS!

The mushroom polyps (order Corallimorpharia) have been an aquarium mainstay for many years and, like the zoanthid polyps, are supremely suited for the novice reef aquarist. As you've probably already guessed, their common name is derived from the mushroom-like

Actinodiscus sp. mushrooms.

shape of the individual polyps. Each animal consists of a flattened oral disc, which closely resembles a mushroom cap, attached to a short stalk. The stalk expands or contracts depending on the amount of available light. In a well-lit aquarium, the oral disc is almost flush with the substrate, but when lighting is more subdued, the stalk stretches out to bring the animal closer to the source. On some species the oral disc is covered with very short tentacles, while tentacles are absent altogether on others.

Like the zoanthid polyps, mushroom polyps are often sold in "colonies" on pieces of rock. However, they are not colonial in the true sense of the word. Several individual polyps may aggregate together in one small area, but there is no integration of tissue or sharing of nutrients. On the contrary, the base of each polyp is attached directly to the substrate. Mushroom polyps are more diverse in size and coloration compared to zoanthids. In size, they range from approximately 1 inch (2.5 cm) in diameter up to a whopping 12 inches (30 cm), and they come in various shades of brown, beige, red, blue, and green. Some even sport variously colored stripes, blotches, or spots.

Under excellent aquarium conditions, mushroom polyps will reproduce with abandon. This is achieved either by budding from the base or by the division of a single polyp into two separate polyps. The only drawback to their prolific reproductive habits is that whereas zoanthids are nonaggressive with their tankmates mushroom polyps pack a powerful sting and won't hesitate to use it on neighboring invertebrates. Surprisingly enough, however, they don't tend to show this aggression to zoanthid species.

The Downside of Zoanthids

Though zoanthids are among the hardiest invertebrates available to reef hobbyists, they do have one downside. Certain species (though not all) produce a potent neurotoxin, called palytoxin, which can cause illness or even death if it is ingested or enters the bloodstream through a cut or crack in the skin. Whenever handling zoanthids—for instance, when propagating them—it is imperative to take the precaution of wearing rubber gloves and washing your hands immediately afterward.

Wonderful Worms

Soft corals and polyps aren't the only easy-to-keep sessile invertebrates. The tubeworms (a.k.a., feather duster worms) are also well-suited to life in the beginner's reef tank. One of the biggest advantages of these animals, apart from their beauty, is that they don't require any specialized lighting.

Tubeworms of interest to aquarists fall into one of two categories, the sabellid worms and the serpulid worms. Sabellids encase their bodies in soft parchment-like tubes, revealing only their large and feathery feeding tentacles. The serpulid worms, on the other hand, produce small stony tubes and have much shorter, often conical, feeding tentacles that come in various shades of red, yellow, blue, black, or white. The tentacles of each are rapidly withdrawn at the approach of a perceived threat.

Tubeworms are filter feeders and will thrive on newly hatched brine shrimp, marine rotifers, or commercial liquid invertebrate foods. Take care when selecting tankmates, however, as many fish and crustaceans include tubeworms as a regular part of their daily diets.

Mushroom polyps also differ from zoanthids in that they don't seem to do as well in turbulent water conditions. When positioning them in the tank, try to find calmer areas with minimal water flow. If necessary, you can always rearrange the rockwork or redirect a powerhead in order to create such an area. So which mushroom polyp species are best suited for the beginner's reef tank? Actually, that's a question easier asked than answered. Most of the specimens offered for sale come from one of four genera: *Actinodiscus*, *Rhodactis*, *Discosoma*, and *Ricordea*. The problem is that it is often difficult to tell the different species apart with any degree of certainty, even for the experts. So it's highly unlikely that your dealer will be able to provide more than the generic name for any given specimen–if he even knows that much. But don't be too concerned about species identification. As long as you select healthy-looking specimens and provide excellent water quality and lighting, you'll get superior results with your mushroom polyps.

SUMMARY

There are several types of soft corals and coral-like animals that are very good choices for a first reef tank. It is best to leave the stony corals for later down the road, after you have proved your reefkeeping skills by successfully maintaining these hardier invertebrates for a while.

Chapter 16

Sessile Invertebrates for Advanced Reefkeepers

In the previous chapter I suggested that it's a good idea to start out with some of the hardier sessile invertebrates, such as soft corals and polyps, when stocking your first reef aquarium. Well, eventually your invertebrate husbandry skills and your confidence level are going to build to the point where you're ready, willing, and able to experiment with some of the more sensitive invertebrates. You'll master the subtle art of maintaining impeccable water quality, and you'll learn how to keep all of your critical water parameters, including (among others) the temperature, pH, specific gravity, nitrate level, and calcium concentration, in the optimal range. You can be proud of yourself at this juncture; you've reached a very significant milestone in the marine aquarium hobby!

What Lies Ahead

• corals to try once you have experience

STEP UP TO STONY CORALS

With few exceptions, reef aquarists eventually want to keep at least one or two stony coral specimens. Since they largely rely on the photosynthetic zooxanthellae residing in their tissues for survival, stony corals are extremely sensitive to lighting, even more so than the soft corals and polyps we discussed in the previous chapter (many of which are also photosynthetic, I might add). Excellent water quality is also of the utmost importance. These conditions being met, there are certain species among the large-polyp stony corals (LPS corals) that will do quite well under the care of a slightly more advanced reefkeeper. Most small-polyp stony corals (SPS corals), on the other hand, are really only suitable for expert reef aquarists.

Bubble Coral

One of the best stony corals for reef aquarists to cut their teeth on is the bubble coral, *Plerogyra sinuosa*. During daylight hours this aptly named coral looks very much like a mass of translucent velvety-white or fawn-colored bubbles. At night, however, the bubbles deflate slightly, revealing the polyp mouths and numerous stinging tentacles that the coral uses to capture plankton and to keep other invertebrates from encroaching on its territory. Give this fast-growing coral, and all the other corals in your reef tank for that matter, ample room to expand to its full dimensions and to prevent stinging injury to its neighbors. You may need to observe its nighttime behavior to get an idea of how far its tentacles can reach.

For the most part, bubble corals can derive all the nutrients they need from their symbiotic zooxanthellae, but occasional (weekly or biweekly) offerings of chopped fish, shrimp, or krill nestled gently between the bubbles will help keep these corals in superior health.

Frogspawn Coral

Another good choice for a first stony coral is the frogspawn coral, *Euphyllia divisa*. This animal has a very prominent, almost tree-like skeleton and thick, semi-transparent tentacles tipped with solid white dots—for all intents and purposes, looking like a mass of frog eggs (hence the common name). Take care when situating this coral, as it can expand its soft tissues to surprising dimensions. *E. divisa* is also very aggressive and can inflict a powerful sting. In addition, it possesses so-called sweeper tentacles that can

Frogspawn coral, *Euphyllia* sp.

extend well beyond the range of the feeding tentacles to sting competitors.

Like the bubble corals, frogspawn corals are photosynthetic and can get by with little or no supplemental feeding. If you do choose to feed this species, place small portions of krill or finely chopped fish among the tentacles. As a point of interest, frogspawn corals, in contrast to most other LPS corals, feed primarily during the day and retract their feeding tentacles at night.

Open Brain Coral

The last LPS coral I'd like to discuss (although there are many other species worth trying that we won't get into here), the open brain coral, *Trachyphyllia geoffroyi*, is certainly not the least when it comes to beauty. In fact, this coral sports almost surreal coloration, ranging from fluorescent green, pink, or purple to deep crimson. Its meandering soft tissues, which are delightfully convoluted and covered with numerous narrow ridges, emerge from a conical skeleton. Open brain corals do not firmly attach themselves to reefs. In the wild, the pointed end of the skeleton is typically buried in a sandy substrate. To keep from being buried in sediment, the animal can inflate its soft tissues with water to raise itself up out of the sand.

Trachyphyllia geoffroyi.

This ability to inflate the soft tissues also allows open brain corals, as well as many other LPS corals, to maximize their surface area, thereby maximizing the amount of light that reaches their photosynthetic zooxanthellae. It also helps to eliminate any detritus that may settle on the animals in their sandy natural habitat. At night the soft tissues deflate and short feeding tentacles emerge to capture plankton. Unlike the bubble corals and frogspawn corals, open brain corals are relatively slow-growing and have neither the propensity nor the capacity to aggressively attack and sting neighboring invertebrates.

As with the other two corals we've discussed, open brain corals can get almost all of their nutrition from zooxanthellae.

BEAUTIFUL BIVALVES: THE TRIDACNID CLAMS

The high-intensity lighting and pristine water conditions favored by stony corals are also required for the proper maintenance of a completely unrelated yet equally stunning group of invertebrates, the tridacnid clams (better known as giant clams). Like many corals and anemones, these beautiful bivalves have symbiotic zooxanthellae in their tissues, more specifically in their fleshy mantles, which produce the nutrients the clams need to survive. With tridacnid clams, the brightly colored mantles are the most attractive feature, although the deeply fluted shells of some species add interest as well. The brilliant mantles, which get

A tridacnid clam.

their color from specialized pigment cells called iridophores, come in shades of blue, green, purple, gold, and various combinations thereof, depending on the particular species. There may also be considerable color variation from individual to individual within a given species.

Since the mantle typically faces upward toward the light source, tridacnid clams are best viewed from above, which means they should be placed lower in the aquarium for the most pleasing aesthetic effect. In tanks over 18 inches (46 cm) tall, this may make it necessary to utilize metal halide lamps in order for an adequate amount of light to reach the clams. Full-spectrum fluorescent tubes or compact fluorescents may suffice for shorter tanks.

Most of the so-called giant clams belong to the genus *Tridacna*, and there is considerable diversity among the species when it comes to growth rate and ultimate size. To give you an idea of the potential size differential at maturity, consider that the smallest and most widely available species, *T. crocea*, reaches only 9 inches (23 cm) in length. *T. maxima*, another species that is commonly available to aquarists, grows to approximately 1 foot (30 cm). Moving up in size, we have *T. derasa*, maxing out at around 20 inches (50 cm). Then we get to the biggest of the bunch, *T. gigas*, the definitive giant clam, which can achieve an astounding 3 feet (90 cm) across!

In order to create their ponderous shells, tridacnid clams will extract a considerable amount of calcium from the aquarium water. For this reason it's very important to supplement routinely with calcium in order to maintain a constant level of around 450 mg/l. Otherwise these clams will never reach their true potential. Strontium and iodine are also important elements for tridacnid clams. The former promotes shell development, while the latter is used for the production of their iridophore pigments.

SEA ANEMONES

The sea anemones are another group of sessile invertebrates that almost all reef aquarists aspire to keep at one time or another. Most anemones have the typical cnidarian body plan—that is, a mouth surrounded by stinging tentacles atop a stout, fleshy base. They're sort of like coral polyps on steroids!

Unlike most corals, anemones do not permanently affix themselves to the substrate and can detach their basal disc to move about in search of more suitable surroundings if necessary. This mobility can be problematic in the aquarium, because wandering specimens can come into contact with—and sting—neighboring invertebrates or injure themselves by blundering into a powerhead or filter intake.

Anemone colors are highly variable depending on the species and the location from which they are collected, and they range in size from little more than a few inches in diameter to approximately 3 feet (90 cm) across. In common with many corals and the tridacnid clams, many anemones have symbiotic zooxanthellae residing in their tissues and thus cannot survive without intense illumination.

Oftentimes it's the desire to replicate the fascinating and iconic clownfish/host anemone symbiosis within the confines of an aquarium that drives the interest in buying anemones. Unfortunately, most of the anemones that host clownfish in nature tend to fare abysmally in the aquarium, with most specimens perishing within months of purchase. For an animal that essentially has an unlimited lifespan in nature (apparently *hundreds* of years) to die after just a few short months in captivity is unacceptable in my humble opinion. Not to mention that clownfish in the wild depend on their host anemone for survival, so removing a clownfish-hosting anemone from the natural reefs has a detrimental impact on the wild clownfish population.

But the good news for clownfish aficionados is that there's no requirement to keep anemones and clownfish together in the aquarium. Absent natural predators, clownfish will do just fine in captivity with no anemone present. In fact, they'll commonly adopt other invertebrates—even some decidedly non-anemone-like ones—as surrogate hosts, including various soft corals and long-tentacled stony corals. I once had a percula clownfish that would nestle in the mantle of a *Tridacna maxima* clam.

SUMMARY

Once you've succeeded with polyps and soft corals, you'll be ready to try some large-polyp stony corals, or LPS. After mastering their care, you can give in to the lure of small-polyp stonies, or SPS. Most species of anemone, however, are really not suitable for a reef aquarium. An aquarist who can keep an anemone for five years is considered highly successful, but these animals can live for centuries in the wild.

Fish Fact

Sound Asleep in a Bed of…Mucus?

Many nocturnal predatory fish are quite adept at sniffing out and snatching diurnal fish as they lie sleeping in the various nooks, crannies, and crevices of the coral reef. But many parrotfish (family Scaridae) have evolved a very peculiar defense mechanism against these night-raiding piscivores—they shroud themselves in a cocoon of mucus before they fall asleep! The transparent mucus pup tent does not actually conceal the parrotfish visibly, but it does mask their scent, making them extremely difficult to detect in the blackness that engulfs the coral reef at night.

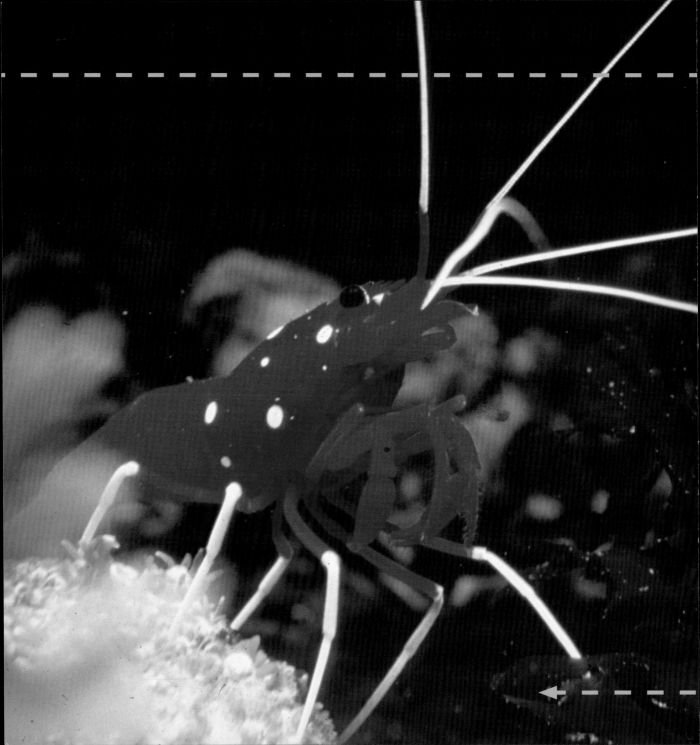

Chapter 17

A Mess of Motile Invertebrates

Regardless of the type of aquarium you decide to set up, you might want to liven things up a bit by adding a few motile (free-moving) invertebrates to your marine community. I'm talking about the various crustaceans, echinoderms, and gastropods that are routinely available to marine aquarists. Some of these organisms are ideally suited for inclusion in the FO system (okay, technically it wouldn't be "fish-only" anymore, but let's not get hung up on semantics!), while others will fare better in the reef tank. Still others can be kept in either system with no problems. But remember, as with selecting any other aquarium organism, it's important to research the needs and habits of any motile invertebrate before deciding to include it in your system so you can sidestep any compatibility problems.

What Lies Ahead

- the best free-moving invertebrates for beginners

A COCKTAIL OF SUPER SHRIMPS

Among the various shrimps that make their way into dealers' tanks, there are several species that are justifiably popular among aquarists because of their relative ease of maintenance, beauty, and fascinating behavior. Just keep in mind that shrimps are the natural food of many reef fish—and of each other! As extremely opportunistic feeders, larger shrimps will readily dine on smaller tankmates.

Banded Coral Shrimp

The first species that comes to mind is the banded coral shrimp, *Stenopus hispidus*, also commonly called the boxer shrimp. This shrimp has a slightly transparent white body disrupted by numerous red bands. It's long, arching, solid-white antennae sway gracefully in the current and make the shrimp seem much larger than it actually is. *S. hispidus* also wields absurdly oversized claws (also banded in red), which are typically longer than its 3-inch (7.5-cm) body.

When first introduced to the aquarium, *S. hispidus* will be quite shy,

Banded coral shrimp can be helpful in controlling bristleworm populations.

spending the daylight hours hidden within the rockwork and emerging only at night to forage. However, as it gets more accustomed to its surroundings, it will overcome its initial shyness and spend much of its time in plain view. These shrimps can be quite aggressive toward conspecifics and should be kept one to an aquarium. An exception can be made in the case of mated pairs, which are often sold together. Feeding is easy for this species, as it will gladly accept just about any standard aquarium fare.

S. hispidus will do equally well in both the FO tank (as long as crustacean-crunching species, such as triggerfish, aren't included) and the reef tank.

Cleaner Shrimps, *Lysmata* spp.

The various cleaner shrimps of the genus *Lysmata* also make terrific aquarium inhabitants and can usually be kept in same-species groups. These shrimps, which are being captively bred, are so named because of their propensity to clean large (and often predatory) fish of parasites and dead tissue. Fish will even line up at coral reef cleaning stations for an opportunity to be picked clean by these shrimps and other cleaning organisms. In keeping with their nature, these shrimps will clean the fish in your aquarium and will even attempt to clean your hands if you allow them to. They're also relatively easy to feed, accepting most dry, freeze-dried, and frozen foods.

Perhaps the most popular, as well as most frequently sold, cleaner shrimp is *L. amboinensis*. This shrimp has a yellow body and a prominent red stripe overlain with a narrower white stripe running the entire length of its back. *L. amboinensis* has gracefully arching antennae, but it lacks the oversized claws of *S. hispidus*.

The peppermint shrimp, *L. wurdemanni*, is another cleaner worth keeping. It gets its name from its rather surreal red and white coloration, which is somewhat reminiscent of peppermint candies. This shrimp makes a great reef inhabitant due to its propensity to devour *Aiptasia* anemones. However, whereas *L. amboinensis* tends to be fairly outgoing, *L. wurdemanni* spends much of its time in hiding, especially when kept with a lively community of fish.

Of all the cleaner shrimps, my personal favorite by far is the blood shrimp, or fire shrimp, *L. debelius*. This species has a blood-red body with pure white legs and antennae. A few small white dots appear along its back as well. This is an animal that must be seen to be believed. With its snow-white legs it looks almost as if it's wearing white stockings, and its flowing antennae are perpetually in hypnotic motion. In my experience, *L. debelius* (see this chapter's opening photograph) tends to be somewhat

Lysmata amboinensis.

more delicate and sensitive (especially to excessively high water temperatures) than the other shrimp species we've discussed, but in terms of beauty it beats the rest hands down.

CRABS WITH CHARACTER

For the most part, crabs get too large and rambunctious to make good aquarium inhabitants. However, certain crab species have become aquarium mainstays because of their generally peaceful deportment and fascinating (sometimes comical) behavior. Among these are the arrow crab, the Sally Lightfoot crab, and certain hermit crabs.

The Arrow Crab

As you might guess, the arrow crab, *Stenorhynchus seticornis*, is so named because of its arrowhead-shaped body. This crab gets around on exceedingly long and spindly legs (up to 6 inches [15 cm]), giving it a rather spider-like aspect. (Note: those with arachnophobic tendencies might find this crab's appearance somewhat startling.) But whatever you might think of its looks, the arrow crab is generally well behaved in both FO and reef aquariums. The only desirable invertebrates this crab will torment include other arrow crabs, which it will fight to the death, and possibly tubeworms. To the delight of many reef aquarists, they've also been known to devour predatory bristleworms, a common plague.

Hermit Crabs

Hermit crabs are widely available at very reasonable prices to hobbyists, and many species make terrific additions to the marine aquarium. There are also many species sold that are dubious additions. Some of them are touted as algae eaters, but all crabs are opportunistic omnivores, and many will eat algae only if there is nothing else available. In addition, many are predatory on other invertebrates, including other hermit crabs. Often an aquarist starts out with a large group of hermits and eventually winds up with just one big fat one! The typical stocking recommendations are excessive. The leftover food and algae in a well-maintained reef tank might support a few crabs, not a few dozen. As most people know, hermit crabs have no shell to protect their elongated bodies and so must borrow (or steal) the shells of other invertebrates—usually univalve mollusks such as snails. You must supply empty shells in various sizes so that as the crabs grow they can find an appropriate home.

Care must be taken when selecting hermit crabs because they range considerably in size and disposition in the aquarium. Some of the larger species can be very destructive to sessile invertebrates as they roam around the tank in search of food. Smaller species such as *Calcinus tibicen*, *Phimochirus operculatus*, and *Paguristes cadenati,* are generally better choices, especially for inclusion in a reef tank. *P. cadenati*, the scarlet hermit crab, with its bright red legs and

distinctive yellow face, is perhaps the most commonly sold of the three. The drawback to this species (among others) is that it is largely nocturnal and may remain hidden in its shell during the day, although these crabs have been known to shift to a more diurnal lifestyle when that is the only time food is made available.

The Sally Lightfoot Crab

The little Sally Lightfoot crab, *Percnon gibbesi*, is another excellent choice. More genuinely crab-like in appearance, the Sally Lightfoot may be a better option for arachnophobes than the arrow crab. This crab is typically a drab greenish brown in coloration, but what it lacks in color it certainly makes up for in character. Its two front claws are in perpetual motion, continually plucking algae and food scraps from the rockwork and placing them in its mouth, looking very much like a greedy little child with a plate of French fries. It also has two tiny appendages, one over each eye, that continually flick up and down in comical fashion. Its herbivorous tendencies make the Sally Lightfoot crab an excellent addition to either the FO or reef tank.

Molt-Induced Panic

If you decide to include crustaceans in your aquarium, be aware that all crustaceans molt. That is, they shed their rigid exoskeletons as a normal part of the growing process. Immediately after molting, a crustacean is extremely vulnerable to predation and will go into hiding for a couple of days while its soft new exoskeleton hardens off. While this is a completely normal occurrence, it can lead to panic when an inexperienced aquarist finds the animal's molted exoskeleton (which, at first glance, looks very much like a complete animal) and, seeing no evidence of the living crustacean, assumes it has died.

EXCELLENT ECHINODERMS

Among the invertebrates known as echinoderms, there are several animals worth keeping in a marine aquarium, including certain starfish (now often called sea stars), brittlestars, sea urchins, and sea cucumbers. Another major group of echinoderms, the crinoids (or feather stars), tends to fare poorly in the aquarium. These animals are best left to live out their fascinating lives on the natural coral reefs. Echinoderms (members of the phylum Echinodermata) are characterized by a pentamerous radially symmetrical body plan (the body can be divided into five parts around an axis), spiny skin, the presence of tube feet (tiny appendages that aid in locomotion, predation, and respiration), a simple internal skeleton made up of calcite crystals, and a unique water vascular system. However, as with the cnidarians, there are ample variations on this simple theme from one group of echinoderms to the next.

Brittlestars

With the brittlestars or brittle starfish we get into another group of invertebrates that are best left out of the arachnophobe's aquarium. Most brittlestars are shy and retiring filter feeders or scavengers, but some species are efficient predators and will rush out of hiding with alarming speed to grab food—much too spiderlike for some tastes. However, for the rest of us, brittlestars are a great option. They are especially useful in the reef aquarium, where they earn their keep by scavenging uneaten food items from hard-to-reach places. They are inoffensive to corals and other sessile invertebrates as they roam about in search of food.

Like starfish, brittlestars have five limbs, but these limbs are generally longer in relation to the size of the central disc, more slender, and more flexible than the arms of a starfish. Some species have pronounced spines along the length of each arm, while others have smooth, almost serpent-like arms. Their limbs also have the tendency to break off easily if these animals are handled aggressively, which accounts for their common name. A lost or damaged limb is no cause for concern, however, since brittlestars will quickly regenerate any lost appendages. Most brittlestars are fairly subdued in coloration, but red or orange specimens are sometimes offered for sale.

Brittlestars of interest to the marine aquarist include, among others, the Caribbean sponge brittlestar, *Ophiothrix suensonii*, the giant red brittlestar, *Ophiocoma wendtii*, and the banded brittlestar, *Ophioderma brevispinum*. Each will do quite well in the confines of the aquarium under the same high-quality water conditions favored by other starfish.

Of Cucumbers and Apples

The last group of echinoderms we'll look at is the sea cucumbers. With this group, the kinship with the starfish is even more difficult to discern, but all of the necessary echinoderm traits are present. For all intents and purposes, most sea cucumbers look like stretched-out sea urchins with the spines removed. Obviously, one could also argue that they look like shriveled terrestrial cucumbers (sea pickles?).

Like the sea urchins, sea cucumbers feed in different ways depending on the species. Some, such as the black cucumber, *Stichopus chloronotus*, sift through the substrate swallowing gravel, digesting detritus, and ejecting any indigestible material from their rear ends. Others are filter feeders that capture plankton from the water with the tentacles (actually modified tube feet) surrounding their mouths. The filter-feeding species can be very difficult to maintain in captivity, as they require several daily feedings of live brine shrimp or rotifers to survive.

One significant characteristic of sea cucumbers that aquarists should consider before buying a specimen is their propensity to discharge their viscera into the aquarium when disturbed. This sticky, threadlike substance can entangle fish and other marine organisms with fatal consequences. Some species, when agitated, will even exude a toxic substance into the water that is capable of killing everything in

Some brittlestars make good aquarium residents, while others should be left in the ocean. Only research will help you learn which is best for your tank.

the aquarium. Not all species will do this, however, so it's important to do your homework on a given species before deciding to take it home.

The Spiniest Echinoderms

At first glance you'd never make the connection between sea urchins and their starfish cousins, but the two are closely related. These pincushions of the sea are typically spherical in shape, with numerous spines covering their bodies. Anyone who has ever had the misfortune of treading upon a sea urchin while wading in shallow water will likely never forget the experience. Protruding between the spines are tube feet and pincer-like organs called pedicellariae that are used to clean the animals and to defend against predation.

Sea urchin species feed in one of several ways. Some are purely herbivorous and graze on algae, while others scavenge dead animals and detritus. Some species are actually solution feeders, which means they absorb the nutrients they need to survive directly from the water. All require excellent water conditions and will waste away rapidly if conditions begin to deteriorate. Promptly remove any urchin specimen from the aquarium if its spines begin to droop or shed. This is a sure sign that the animal is in poor health and will likely die, and a decomposing sea urchin can really wreak havoc on your aquarium's water quality.

Urchins with long needle-like spines, such as the long-spined urchin, *Diadema antillarum*, and the blue-spotted urchin, *Astropyga radiata*, should be handled with extreme care, since their spines can easily puncture the skin. Also, they can do considerable damage, albeit unintentionally, to the tissues of soft corals, anemones, and LPS corals, so take care when choosing their tankmates. Better choices are short-spined species, such as the pencil urchin, *Eucidaris tribuloides*, and the rock-boring urchin, *Echinometra lucunter*. The common urchin, *Echinometra mathaei*, is also well suited to aquarium life, but it can inflict a painful sting if handled improperly.

Star Power

The sea stars, or starfish, are probably the most widely recognized of the echinoderms. Most have five arms radiating out from a central disc, but some have more. The crown-of-thorns star, which has gained notoriety in recent years for the devastating impact it has had on coral populations, has upwards of 23 arms at a time. Most starfish have amazing regenerative abilities. That is, they have the capacity to regrow limbs lost to predation or some other injury. In fact, a starfish can survive as long as the central disc and part of one limb are left intact.

These animals feed primarily on other invertebrates or detritus, depending on the species. Those that actively hunt invertebrates tend to favor clams, scallops, and other bivalves, worms, and fellow echinoderms. The way in which a sea star devours a bivalve is really quite bizarre. First it seizes the shell with its hydraulic tube feet. Then it pries the two halves of the shell apart

The underside of a starfish, *Protoreaster* sp.

and actually extrudes its stomach into the shell. At that point it secretes a digestive enzyme onto the soft parts of the bivalve, which breaks down the tissues and makes them easier to consume.

In the aquarium, offerings of chopped fish, clam, scallop, shrimp, and large particulate foods are adequate. However, as starfish require excellent water quality and very low nitrate levels, care must be taken to avoid overfeeding and polluting the water. Most species will get along well with a community of fish, but specimens for the reef tank must be chosen with care. Otherwise, many of your prized invertebrates may be served up as costly entrees.

A good rule of thumb when selecting starfish for the reef aquarium is to leave out specimens that have knobby backs, such as the common knobbed starfish, *Pentaceraster mammillatus*, and the red-knobbed starfish, *Protoreaster lincki*. Knobbed species tend to be omnivorous and so cannot be trusted around valued sessile invertebrates. On the other hand, smooth-skinned detritus feeders, such as the blue starfish, *Linckia laevigata*, and inoffensive small species, such as the red starfish, *Fromia elegans*, and the orange starfish, *F. monilis*, will do quite well in the reef aquarium.

ALGAE-GRAZING GASTROPODS

Most marine aquarium dealers offer a varied assortment of snails at a fairly reasonable price, primarily for the purpose of algae control in the aquarium, and some species really earn their keep in this manner. Certain species also possess very beautiful shells, which makes them doubly attractive. While there are literally thousands of gastropods inhabiting the world's oceans, we'll limit our discussion to a few commonly sold herbivorous kinds that are safe for inclusion in both FO and reef systems. You should make certain that you are getting appropriate snails. Some snails are carnivorous and will dine on all your invertebrates—including other snails! Sometimes estuary tideflat species are sold; they will forever be trying to climb out of the tank, and most will eventually succeed.

The Limpets

The limpets (family Acmaeidae) are a group of marine gastropods that will rid an aquarium of irksome algae in short order. Limpets' shells lack whorls and have a low dome shape. They also vary considerably in color, pattern, and texture, depending on the species. Limpets are commonly found adhering to rocks in tidal pools. In the aquarium they will exhibit this same behavior, seeking out protected areas within the rockwork. Since limpets are nocturnal feeders and tend to return to the same site after feeding each night, their keepers often wonder whether they are feeding at all. But such concerns are soon dispelled once the rocks are cleaned of algae.

Turbo-Charged Snails

Marine snails of the genus *Turbo* are some of the best choices when it comes to algae control. These snails feed almost exclusively on undesirable film and filamentous algae, and one or two large specimens can literally strip an aquarium's rockwork clean of algae within a few days. Turbo snails typically have top-shaped shells with only a few whorls that are often encrusted with coralline algae. This tends to camouflage them perfectly against the backdrop of the aquarium's rockwork, making them difficult to discern without close inspection. *T. fluctuosus*, with its green to orange coloration, is both attractive and efficient and is well worth keeping. Snails of the genera *Astraea*, *Arene*, and *Cyclostrema* are also good choices, as they are close relatives of the turbo snails and share their algae-munching propensities.

The Tops in Algae Control

Like the turbo snails, the so-called top shells have a (you guessed it!) top-shaped shell. However, they exhibit more spirals and a subtle iridescent sheen. *Tegula rugosa*, with its attractive checkered brown shell, is one good option for algae control, as is *T. mariana*, which is

Turbo snails are excellent algae eaters and will help keep your tank clean.

smaller and has a mottled pattern on its shell. Top shells from the genera *Solariella, Margarites,* and *Lischkeia* are also excellent algae eaters. Members of the genus *Calliostoma* are best avoided; they will consume algae but may also choose to sample certain sessile invertebrates.

SUMMARY

Shrimps, crabs, starfish, snails, and other motile invertebrates can work in many FO and reef systems. As always, you just need to know the exact needs and habits of any animal before acquiring it.

Chapter **18**

Strapping on the Feedbag

Apart from maintaining impeccable water quality at all times, the most important role played by marine aquarists is providing the right types of foods in the right proportions to the fish and/or invertebrates in their care. This can be a challenge, considering the fact that most marine specimens are still wild-caught, and many of them have very specific dietary requirements that must be met if they are to adapt successfully to life in captivity. Simply put, providing proper nutrition can mean the difference between enjoying healthy and naturally long-lived specimens and continually having to replace animals that succumb to diseases.

What Lies Ahead

- how and what to feed your fish and invertebrates

Not only is feeding important from a health and longevity standpoint, but it is also the only real opportunity we aquarists have to interact directly with our aquatic pets. The more intelligent fish species will soon recognize that their food always comes from one particular human and will reward him or her with almost puppy-like begging at mealtime. Some species may go so far as to feed directly from their owner's hand. This may seem insignificant in the grand scheme of things, but interacting with different aquatic species is one of the many rewards of keeping a marine aquarium.

FEEDING OUR PISCINE PALS

When it comes to feeding fish, variety is definitely the spice of life. The average community of tropical marine fish combines species with markedly different dietary requirements—some are primarily herbivorous, some are carnivorous, and others are omnivorous. Therefore it's critical to offer an assortment of both meaty and plant-based foods in order to satisfy the different palates of the fish in your aquarium, and considering the incredible diversity of flake, frozen, freeze-dried, fresh, and live foods available on the market today, it's never been easier to provide a varied selection of food items.

How Much and How Often?

As a general rule, fish should be fed no more than they can completely consume in just a couple of minutes. Give them just a little, much less that you think is right. If there is any food left over, it should be promptly removed with an aquarium net or vacuumed up with a siphon hose, and you should feed less next time. Uneaten food that settles into the substrate or gets trapped in the rockwork will quickly decompose and degrade your water quality, so it's important to monitor the amount your fish are actually eating and make any necessary adjustments in the quantity you feed.

You'll also want to make sure that all the fish in the aquarium are getting enough to eat. It's not uncommon for larger, more aggressive fish to grab up all the food, depriving more passive species of sustenance, or for the mid-water feeders to gobble up the food before it reaches the bottom feeders. In other words, not only is it important that you familiarize yourself with the types of food a given species of fish will eat, but you should also be aware of its typical feeding behavior and the portion of the water column it tends to occupy.

So how often should you feed? Since reef fish are accustomed to browsing throughout the day, it's recommended that you offer multiple small feedings each day rather than one or two large feedings. Of course, once you factor in hectic work schedules and the various social commitments that most of us are bound by, two medium-sized feedings, one in the morning and one at night, might be more realistic. But whichever feeding schedule you adopt, keep in mind that you can do much more harm, to both the health of your fish and the quality of your water, by overfeeding than you can by underfeeding.

Foods for the Herbivore

Fish that are primarily algae grazers in the wild, such as the tangs and many angelfish, often suffer in captivity because they don't receive an adequate amount of plant-based food in their diet. Or if they are given plant material, it's usually in the form of terrestrial greens like spinach and romaine lettuce, which they can't digest properly (as we've already mentioned). A better choice for tangs and other marine herbivores is marine algae. This can be provided in the form of dried green or red marine algae. Both of these products come in paper-thin sheets that can be cut into appropriately sized portions, depending on the number of grazers.

To feed dried algae, simply clamp a pre-cut section in a lettuce clip and place it on a rock in the aquarium, or secure the piece between the two sides of an algae-cleaning magnet (with the aquarium glass in between) and slide the magnet down into the desired location. Remove and discard any portions that are left uneaten after 24 hours, and replace them with fresh algae. Herbivorous fish prefer to graze continually throughout the day, so make sure an algae portion is always available in the tank.

It is better to underfeed your fish rather than overfeed.

Another way to provide algae to marine grazers is to place a glass container or a small aquarium filled with salt water in front of a window that receives full sun. Place a rock from your aquarium into the container and wait for it to develop a nice shaggy coat of algae. Then place the algae-encrusted rock back into the aquarium for your herbivores to graze, and put a different rock into the container to keep the process going. If you play your cards right, you'll always have a rock with a full complement of algae ready to replace the one that's been grazed.

Yet another way to satisfy the dietary needs of marine grazers is to feed them one of the frozen formula foods that are specially geared for herbivores. These formulas combine an assortment of marine algae, vegetable matter, and several types of seafood in one easy-to-feed product. I should add that there are similar frozen products on the market specifically formulated to meet the dietary needs of carnivores and omnivores as well.

Fish Fact

Of Bright Eyes and Bacteria

Bioluminescence (the emission of light by living organisms) plays an important role in the "after hours" coral reef community. One of the most dramatic examples of this is the flashlight fish from the Western Pacific. Flashlight fish possess special pouches filled with bioluminescent bacteria underneath each eye. When visible, these pouches serve to attract the tiny crustaceans that make up the flashlight fish's diet. These fish can cover the bioluminescent pouch with a skin flap whenever they wish to extinguish the light. When a school of flashlight fish is kept in a dark aquarium, the aquarist will see only a group of white lights, flitting about the tank and blinking on and off at random.

Foods for the Carnivore

The dietary requirements of meat-eating marine fish can be satisfied with any number of fresh, frozen, freeze-dried, and live foods. Suitable fresh foods include almost any seafood items you can buy from your local grocer, including fish (with the exception of oily species such as salmon, mackerel, and herring), shrimps, scallops, mussels, and clams. These items can be cut into bite-size portions for small- to medium-sized fish or served whole to larger predatory fish. If you buy fresh seafood in bulk quantities, you can store it in the freezer and thaw out small portions as needed.

Also, your aquarium dealer should have various frozen food items for sale, including brine shrimp, bloodworms, *Mysis* shrimp, and the previously mentioned formula foods, that are ideal for smaller carnivorous fish. These products will be either frozen in a slab, from which you can break off the desired amount, or in small easy-to-feed cubes. To feed any of these products, all you have to do is drop the food into the tank. The fish will pick it apart as it thaws.

Plankton, krill, brine shrimp, and bloodworms are some of the better freeze-dried foods for supplementing the diets of carnivorous marine fish. The freeze-drying process completely dehydrates these foods while retaining most of their essential nutrients. If properly stored (i.e., protected from moisture, heat, and light), freeze-dried foods have a relatively long shelf life compared to fresh and frozen foods. The only drawback to freeze-dried foods is that they can take a long time to rehydrate and are best soaked for several minutes prior to feeding—not a problem if you have time to kill, but a bit of an obstacle when you're rushing off to work.

Several live foods are irresistible to carnivorous fish as well. Some of the better choices for small- to medium-sized fish are adult brine shrimp, bloodworms, and *Mysis* shrimp. Each will be accepted with gusto.

Larger predatory fish are often fed feeder fish (goldfish, guppies, mollies, etc.) in captivity. This would seem like the most appropriate type of food to offer them, but, ironically, it isn't. Feeders are bred for only one purpose—to feed other fish. Little effort is made to keep them in good health or even to keep them fed, so they tend to be sorely lacking when it comes to nutritional value. Also, it has been shown that marine predators that are routinely offered nothing but freshwater feeder fish end up dying prematurely of liver disease. This is a common occurrence with lionfish, which are often difficult to wean off feeders. Every effort should be made to start lionfish and other large predators on frozen brown silversides, lancefish, or other marine-based meaty foods as soon as possible. Remember also that even a fish that eats nothing but other fish in the wild is still getting algae in the guts of its prey. In addition, almost any species will take an occasional nip of algae, so training a predator to take food pellets or sticks with an algae component will help keep the fish healthy.

Foods for the Omnivore

Although we discussed the various feeding options for herbivores and carnivores first, most tropical marine fish are technically omnivorous, which means they require both meaty and plant-based foods in their diet. Their needs are relatively easy to meet because most staple flake and pellet foods are formulated for omnivorous fish. However, that doesn't mean that a constant diet of nothing but flakes or pellets will keep these fish in optimal health. Just like obligate herbivores and carnivores, they prefer a varied diet and will be healthier, more active, and more colorful if given some alternatives. A good approach to feeding omnivores is to offer one or two feedings each day of flake or pellet food and one supplemental feeding of a meaty item like frozen brine shrimp, frozen bloodworms, freeze-dried plankton, or chopped fish. When available, you can also present them with some live foods. Try to alternate the supplemental foods you offer so your fish won't get bored with their menu. It's even a good idea to offer different varieties of flake or pellet food to make sure your fish are getting all of their nutritional needs met. Remember, not all prepared foods are necessarily created equal when it comes to ingredients.

Since most reef fish are mid-water or bottom feeders, it's a good idea to swish your flake food around in a cup of aquarium water for a few seconds so it becomes saturated and will sink readily. Flakes floating at the surface are generally useless to the fish and will be skimmed off quickly into the wet/dry prefilter chamber if such a system is in use. If you prefer to feed pellets, buy the sinking kind, as floating pellets are equally useless to most marine fish.

Make sure you distribute the fish's food across the entire length of your tank, giving each fish a chance to eat. If you drop all of the food in one spot, you run the risk of one fish gobbling up all of the food and its tankmates getting nothing.

FEEDING SESSILE INVERTEBRATES

One of the most perplexing issues confronting both the beginner and experienced aquarist alike is determining the most appropriate way to feed sessile invertebrates in a reef aquarium. Fish we understand. To a certain extent, they're very much like us in that they'll thrive if given two or three balanced meals a day. And when they're hungry, they'll generally let you know it through their body language. But the feeding habits of sessile invertebrates (especially the photosynthetic species) are definitely beyond the realm of human experience, and if they exhibit any hunger cues, they're certainly not perceptible to people. So what's an invertebrate fancier to do? Once again, the key is research. It's very important to learn the natural feeding habits of any sessile invertebrate before attempting to keep it, let alone feed it.

Should You Feed Light-Hungry Invertebrates?

The waters surrounding tropical coral reefs are very nutrient-poor, prompting the evolution of the unique symbiosis that exists between light-hungry invertebrates and the photosynthetic zooxanthellae residing in their tissues. Though they get much of the nutrition they need from their zooxanthellae, some—perhaps all—of these invertebrates will also feed actively on plankton or absorb nutrients directly from the water. Photosynthetic invertebrates therefore will usually benefit from supplemental feeding in captivity.

Your corals need to eat too!

Before offering any food to corals or other invertebrates, however, you must do some research to determine which foods, if any, would be appropriate for the animal in question. The food must also be of the correct particle size for the invertebrate or it will be of no benefit. After all, watermelon fits well into a human's diet, but you can't swallow one whole!

Marine rotifers, brine shrimp nauplii, cyclops, finely chopped fish, crustacean, and mollusk flesh, and commercial liquid invertebrate foods are some examples of foods that can be used for the supplemental feeding of reef invertebrates. But again, don't offer any food without first doing your homework to ensure that it is appropriate for your invertebrates. Also, just as with feeding fish, be sure not to feed with too heavy a hand. Any benefit these animals will derive from supplemental feeding will be undermined extremely quickly if water conditions begin to deteriorate as a result of overfeeding.

Feeding Nonphotosynthetic Filter Feeders

In contrast to their light-hungry neighbors, nonphotosynthetic filter-feeding invertebrates, including (among others) certain soft corals, sponges, feather duster worms, and flame scallops, depend upon regular feeding in the aquarium. A daily feeding of marine rotifers, newly hatched brine shrimp, or a liquid invertebrate food is necessary to sustain most filter feeders. During feeding it's a good idea to shut off the aquarium's filtration system so the tiny suspended organisms aren't filtered out before the invertebrates have a chance to capture them. One way to ensure that each animal gets enough food is to dispense it directly onto its feeding tentacles (or over its siphon) with a turkey baster. Again, err on the side of feeding too little, especially when feeding commercial liquid invertebrate foods, to avoid fouling the water.

CRUSTACEAN CUISINE

Small crustaceans, such as the hermit crabs, banded coral shrimps, and cleaner shrimps, will generally fare quite well on the same cuisine offered to omnivorous fish and may be able to get by on the food scraps left over by the fish. However, this should not be taken as justification to overfeed. Most small crustaceans consume very little food and will not fill the role of aquarium vacuum cleaner. In other words, uneaten food can still accumulate on the substrate and in the rockwork, causing your water quality to crash, even when several scavenging crustaceans are present.

Of course, you don't want to go to the other extreme either, feeding such small portions to the fish that no morsels are ever left over for your crustaceans. Though considering the fact that most of us tend to overfeed rather than underfeed, I would suggest that this is a highly unrealistic scenario in the FO aquarium. In the nutrient-poor environment of a reef tank, on the other hand, you may need to go the extra mile to ensure that your crustaceans are getting enough to eat. The best way to achieve this is by placing sinking food items in the same easily reached location each day. And don't worry, it won't take your crab or shrimp long to figure out where to go for regular feedings. Remove any uneaten portions after about one hour so they don't have a chance to decompose and degrade your water quality.

SUMMARY

In the closed system of an aquarium, the livestock are totally dependent on you for the water quality and their nutrition. Those two are closely linked, since overfeeding will quickly degrade the water quality. At the same time, your fish and invertebrates have no way of supplementing their diets. Choose carefully what, when, and how you feed them.

Chapter 19

Aquarium Health Care and Maintenance

Though this chapter is dedicated primarily to disease and health care in the marine aquarium, it also includes a section on routine aquarium maintenance. This is because the two subjects are inextricably bound together. Marine fish typically become ill and die as a response to declining environmental conditions or fluctuating water parameters. These stressors have a tendency to inhibit the natural disease-fighting mechanisms of marine animals, making them more susceptible to infectious agents, including various bacteria, fungi, viruses, and parasites. Disease can also rear its ugly head when a specimen is consistently fed the wrong foods or is fed too much of the right foods.

What Lies Ahead

- quarantine
- common saltwater fish diseases
- freshwater dip
- tank maintenance

Of course, in some instances marine fish die as a result of the combined stresses of collection (including unethical collection practices, such as poisoning with sodium cyanide) and prolonged shipping, which in no way reflects on the skills or diligence of the aquarist. For example, if a fish dies shortly after purchase and testing reveals that all of the aquarium's water parameters are correct, you can usually assume that the fish was in poor condition when you purchased it. If you should experience this at some point, don't be discouraged, because it happens to the best of us. Just be sure to inspect the next specimen thoroughly before buying to verify that it looks healthy, eats well, and exhibits the appropriate coloration.

DON'T FORGET THE QUARANTINE TANK!

We've already discussed the importance of quarantining newly purchased specimens before releasing them into your main aquarium (see Chapter 11), but it's something that bears repeating. A quarantine tank will allow you to isolate and monitor new acquisitions for several weeks to determine whether they are harboring harmful pathogens or parasites that could infect the rest of the fish in your community, potentially causing the death of all your valued specimens. While quarantining fish is no absolute guarantee that dangerous microbes won't make their way into your aquarium, it will certainly decrease the odds. A quarantine tank will also make it possible to administer any necessary medications directly to a sick animal without having to subject your healthy specimens to a battery of potentially toxic chemicals. When a fish that is kept in a reef tank becomes ill and requires medication, a separate quarantine tank is essential because sessile invertebrates generally cannot tolerate the chemicals used to treat fish diseases.

ARE YOU A VET?

The only way to identify most fish pathogens is through microscopic and laboratory analysis. Would you want a physician to prescribe medication or perform surgery based on just looking at you? Well, a veterinarian wouldn't treat a fish based just on looking, either. Many different fish pathogens produce identical symptoms. Examining samples under a microscope and culturing microbes assist a veterinarian in choosing the proper medications to use, if any. In addition, the purchase and use of fish medications is coming under increased scrutiny, regulation, and legislation. Aside from the difficulties in diagnosing fish diseases, many traditional treatments for aquarium fish contain chemicals that are now known to be harmful to the person using them! For these reasons what follows is a very cursory look at some of the afflictions fish can face. Before treating any problem, it is always best to seek professional help.

BACTERIAL INFECTIONS

Pathogenic bacteria can always be found in aquarium water, but they tend to cause disease only when a fish's immune system has been suppressed as the result of some form of stress or physical trauma. Injury from rough handling or fighting, poor water quality, and inadequate nutrition are just some of the possible stressors that can predispose a fish to bacterial infection. Also, fish with pre-existing diseases will commonly contract secondary bacterial infections.

Bacterial infection can manifest itself either externally or internally. External manifestation typically is in the form of fin-and-tail rot or body ulcers. With fin-and-tail rot (as you might guess), the soft tissues and rays of the fins begin to deteriorate or take on a tattered appearance. It's easy to distinguish bacterial rot from mechanical injury—such as that caused by fighting—because rotting fins are typically red or brown in color at the margins. Body ulcers are red, swollen lesions that often start in one area and then expand to other parts of the fish's body. Keep in mind that if left unchecked external infection can spread to the fish's internal organs and bloodstream, sometimes with fatal consequences.

The most troublesome internal bacterial infection experienced by marine fish is fish tuberculosis.

Signs and Symptoms of Fish Disease

As you observe the day-to-day behavior of your fish, be on the lookout for these common warning signs of disease (possible causes are included in parentheses):

- scraping or rubbing on rocks, substrate, or decorations (parasitic infection)
- white or black spots/gold-brown dusting (external parasite infection)
- frayed or disintegrating fins (bacterial infection or mechanical injury)
- body ulcers (bacterial or parasitic infection)
- warty growths (viral infection, usually lymphocystis)
- cloudy eyes (physical injury, bacterial infection, parasitic infection)
- bulging eyes (bacterial, viral, or parasitic infection)
- distended abdomen (overeating, internal bacterial infection, parasitic infection, tumor)
- excessive secretion of body slime (protozoan parasitic infection, presence of ammonia, excessively high pH, presence of copper)
- increased respiration (parasitic infection, low dissolved oxygen level, high water temperature, presence of ammonia)
- long-term change in coloration (many diseases and water-quality problems can cause this)
- refusal to eat (improper diet, aggression from tankmates, many infectious diseases)
- listlessness (most infectious diseases, low water temperature, poor water quality)

An angelfish with an advanced case of saltwater ich.

The best way to treat bacterial infections is to take all necessary steps to prevent them from happening in the first place. This means using the best possible protein skimming and filtration equipment and adopting outstanding aquarium water management practices in general. Of course, the most important step you can take is to stay on top of those regular partial water changes.

There are proprietary medications and various antibiotics that can be used to treat bacterial infections after an outbreak occurs, but typically they are effective only when the disease is caught in the early stages. In addition, just dumping an antibiotic into the water is a poor way of delivering it to the fish. It is much more effective to administer drugs in food or by injection. Always keep in mind that all medications should be used judiciously and in strict accordance with local laws and the manufacturer's recommendations. Administering an improper dose can have an adverse effect. Remember that antibiotics kill bacteria, and that includes the bacteria in your system's biofilter. Worse yet, if you fail to complete a full course of treatment you may inadvertently be selecting for antibiotic-resistant strains of bacteria. It is always best to consult a fish veterinarian for any treatment.

FUNGAL AND VIRAL INFECTIONS

Fungal diseases are relatively uncommon in marine fish, but occasionally they do occur after an injury or a parasitic infection, especially when water conditions are poor. The spores of pathogenic fungi are always present in marine aquariums, and they are surprisingly resilient. When the spores begin to grow on an ailing fish's body, they send out numerous thin threads that actually penetrate deep into the tissues and organs of the fish. All that the aquarist can see at this point is a thin film or discoloration on the fish's body or gills.

Diagnosing a fungal infection is difficult, since the symptoms often mimic those presented by certain parasites. Proper identification is confounded even further by the fact that parasitic and fungal infections tend to occur together. As with preventing bacterial infection, the best way to deter secondary fungal infection is to improve the environmental conditions in the aquarium. However, if an outbreak should occur, treating the infected fish with one of the various proprietary fungicides will eradicate the problem successfully.

Viral diseases are relatively uncommon among marine aquarium fish, though there is one—called lymphocystis—that you should be aware of. There is both good news and bad news concerning this disease. The good news is that it progresses very slowly and is rarely fatal. The bad new is that the disease is disfiguring, and there is no medication that will cure it.

Lymphocystis affects the fish's connective tissue, creating hard, warty growths on the trailing edges of the fins, on the body, and around the mouth. In severe cases, the growths that occur in the area of the mouth can prevent the fish from feeding properly, but normal behavior is unaffected otherwise. Unfortunately, the symptoms of lymphocystis can take so long to manifest themselves—up to ten days after infection—that all of the fish in an aquarium may be infected before the disease is detected.

Any fish exhibiting symptoms of lymphocystis should be removed promptly from the aquarium and placed in quarantine. While there are no drugs that you can use to treat the fish, it may rid itself of the virus after several months. Of course, you should monitor the rest of the fish in the community to determine whether any have been infected, and no new fish should be added until you're certain that the aquarium is disease-free.

PARASITIC INFECTIONS: WHO SPRINKLED SALT ON MY FISH?

While fungal and viral diseases may be relatively uncommon, parasitic diseases are almost inevitable. If you keep tropical marine fish, you'll most likely, at one time or another, have to combat parasites. And there are lots of parasitic critters out there, including various protozoans, copepods, and flukes and other worms. To keep things simple, we'll limit our discussion of parasites to the two that you are most likely to experience: marine velvet, *Amyloodinium ocellatum*, and white spot disease, or saltwater ich, *Cryptocaryon irritans*. These protozoans share a similar life cycle and *modus operandi*, and both are introduced into the aquarium through infected (usually nonquarantined) fish.

Fish TB?

Your fish can fall victim to the bacterium *Mycobacterium marinum*, which causes the disease called fish tuberculosis or wasting disease. It is a close relative of *Mycobacterium tuberculosis*, which causes human TB. While it does not cause tuberculosis in humans, there have been cases of aquarists being infected with this bacterium or others through cuts in the skin when they immersed their hand into the tank. The resultant infection can cause local swellings and other discomfort. While very rare, this does happen; most aquarists ignore the risk and never suffer, but the most cautious use latex or vinyl gloves whenever they must put the hands into an aquarium. As always, if you develop symptoms of infection on your hands or arms, see your doctor immediately. If you believe a water-borne pathogen might be involved, make sure to mention that possibility.

Fish that succumb to this disease are usually older fish, especially those that are kept in overcrowded aquariums with inadequate filtration and generally poor water quality. Symptoms vary depending on the stage of the disease and the particular species of fish that is infected, though some of the more common signs include change in body color, emaciation, and bulging eyes.

A tang with head and lateral line erosion, or HLLE. Research has show that foods rich in Vitamin C can help prevent this disease from ever occurring.

With marine velvet, tiny parasitic protozoans attach themselves via a root-like structure to the body, fins, and gills of a host fish and live off its tissues. To the naked eye the parasites look like a fine white- to gold-colored dust. Once they reach maturity, they detach and settle to the bottom of the aquarium, where they form cysts. Inside each cyst, cell division starts to take place, producing over 200 spores (called dinospores). Eventually, the cysts rupture, freeing the dinospores, which then swim off in search of a host fish to infect.

Fish infected with marine velvet will express their discomfort by scraping their bodies against the rockwork and substrate. Other obvious signs of infection include pale coloration, excessive body slime production, and increased respiration. If not treated in a timely manner, marine velvet can cause the death of the infected specimen in short order.

Saltwater ich is virtually identical to marine velvet when it comes to the life cycle of the associated protozoan. The physical symptoms of the disease are also very similar. The only difference is that saltwater ich is characterized by larger white spots instead of a dust-like coating. The white spots are actually cysts produced by the fish in an attempt to reduce the impact of the parasites. Like marine velvet, this disease will kill its host fish if not treated promptly.

Treating both of these parasites can be a challenge because most medications are only effective against the protozoans in the free-swimming and adult stages. The encysted parasites are unaffected. For this reason, it's necessary to maintain a therapeutic level of medication in the tank long enough for any cysts that remain on the substrate to release the free swimmers into the medicated water. This takes a minimum of 14 days for marine velvet and 21 days for white spot disease.

The most commonly recommended course of action for both marine velvet and white spot disease is to dose the water with a copper-based medication. If left in the system long enough, copper is very effective at eradicating these parasites. However, copper does have its drawbacks. For one thing, it is lethal in even minute concentrations to any invertebrates that aren't protected by a hard exoskeleton, and even some fish are quite sensitive to it. For another, copper can be precipitated out of the water by various calcareous materials (e.g., the rockwork and substrate) and small amounts can be dumped back into the aquarium water for many years to come. This is no big concern in an FO aquarium unless you intend to convert it to a reef tank someday. But keep in mind that even the glass itself can retain enough copper to be lethal to invertebrates years later.

THE FRESHWATER DIP

A good alternative to copper for treating marine velvet, white spot disease, and a host of other diseases is to give the infected fish a freshwater dip. This is a very simple procedure that is surprisingly effective, and if it is done correctly your fish will experience minimal stress.

So how does fresh water kill parasites? Actually, it's a very simple process. Water tends to flow from areas of lower salt concentration toward areas of higher salt concentration. When a marine parasite (say, for example, the *Cryptocaryon irritans* protozoan) is placed into fresh water, the salt concentration is higher within the body of the parasite than it is in the surrounding water. Therefore water will flow rapidly into its body, causing it to burst from the osmotic shock—a fitting end for such an irksome pest, I think.

To perform a freshwater dip, fill a 1-gallon (4-liter) glass or plastic container with fresh tap water. Remove the chlorine or chloramine from the water with an appropriate liquid product, and make sure the temperature and pH are nearly identical between your main aquarium and the treatment water. Then, as carefully as possible, net the infected fish and place it into the freshwater bath. Leave the fish in the bath for no more than ten minutes, and monitor it closely during the entire treatment. The fish may become disoriented at first and possibly lie flat on its side. This is a normal response and no reason for concern. However, if the fish begins to behave extremely erratically, you'll want to put it back into salt water as quickly as possible. After all, you don't want the cure to be worse than the disease.

Just as most freshwater organisms won't survive long in salt water, marine organisms, including pathogens that infect saltwater fish, won't last long in fresh water. Employ a series of freshwater dips to combat illnesses before you resort to the various chemicals, medicines, and antibiotics that are available.

A FEW WORDS ON USING AQUARIUM MEDICATIONS

If I had to sum up my feelings about aquarium medications in a single, succinct statement, I would have to say, "Don't use them unless it's absolutely necessary." Whenever possible, try to find an environmental solution to a disease outbreak rather than a medicinal one. It's very difficult for the average aquarist to precisely diagnose the various ailments that can afflict fish without having access to a battery of laboratory equipment. And using the wrong drug to treat a disease or using the right drug incorrectly will only make matters worse for your fish.

If you decide that it is necessary to medicate the tank, be sure to follow the drug manufacturer's dosing instructions to the letter, and don't fall into the "if a little is good, more is better" trap. Also, keep in mind that you'll need to remove any activated carbon from your aquarium system before dosing the aquarium, as it will adsorb many dissolved medications from the water before they have a chance to do any good.

A SCHEDULE OF AQUARIUM CHORES

I've emphasized the importance of maintaining a stable environment in the marine aquarium repeatedly through the pages of this book. But if you'll indulge me, I'll state it one more time and then shut my mouth about it. (Did I just hear a collective sigh of relief?) The coral reef habitat is one of the most stable environments on earth, and the ultimate key to keeping reef organisms successfully in captivity is to approximate that stability as closely as possible in the aquarium. To achieve this, you'll need to commit yourself to a set schedule of routine aquarium maintenance chores. Following a set maintenance schedule will ensure that any problems are caught before they reach crisis proportions. In other words, you'll be more likely to notice them in the early stages when you'll still be able to correct them through small incremental adjustments rather than through extreme measures.

The schedule I've outlined here is one that I at least try to adhere to. I'm presenting it to you as one possible option. Feel free to modify it as you see fit or as your particular circumstances dictate. You may find it helpful to write out your maintenance schedule in the form of a checklist so you can mark off each chore once it's been completed.

Daily Duties

- Check the water temperature.
- Check specific gravity.
- Make sure all heating, filtration, protein skimming, and lighting equipment is functioning properly.
- Empty the accumulated waste from your protein skimmer collection cup.
- Clean salt creep from various aquarium surfaces.
- Top off water lost to evaporation; use fresh, not salt, water.
- Check over your animals for signs of stress, injury, or disease (and, of course, to make sure none has died). This is best done at feeding time when the more skittish fish will emerge from hiding.
- Remove any uneaten food or other organic debris with a net or siphon.

Weekly Duties

- Test for ammonia, nitrite, and nitrate.
- Check calcium level and add any necessary supplements or trace elements (especially with a reef tank).
- Rinse off any prefilters to eliminate trapped gunk and uneaten food that could decompose and degrade your water quality.
- Scrape algae from the front pane of the aquarium.

Biweekly Duties

- Perform, at the very minimum, a 10-percent water change (even better if done on a weekly basis). Gently vacuum the substrate to remove detritus.
- Remove and replace any mechanical filtration media. This should be done a few days before or after the water change to avoid disrupting the biological filter too greatly.
- Clean the cover glass. This is especially important in a reef aquarium, since salt buildup, calcium deposits, and dirt on the glass can reduce the amount of light that reaches photosynthetic invertebrates.
- Check all of your power cables and electrical connections to verify that they are free of salt creep and in good condition.

Regular water changes are essential for the overall health of your saltwater charges.

Every Six to Eight Weeks

- Replace airstones. They will undoubtedly be getting clogged, and therefore losing efficiency, after six weeks of use.
- Replace used-up carbon so it doesn't dump adsorbed pollutants back into the aquarium.
- Clean your protein skimmer and all filter housings, pumps, tubes, and hoses with aquarium brushes.
- Gently rinse your biological filtration medium/media in aquarium water.

Per Manufacturer's Recommendation

- Replace the fluorescent tubes or metal halide bulbs used to illuminate your reef. This is usually recommended every six to nine months, depending on usage.

SUMMARY

Disease prevention is much easier than treatment. Quarantine is the foundation of a healthy marine aquarium. If illness strikes, an accurate diagnosis and appropriate treatment may save your fish. Treatment does not necessarily mean chemicals—a freshwater dip is highly effective in many cases. It is always best to consult a professional when treating sick fish.

Chapter 20

Current Trends in Saltwater Aquaria

By David E. Boruchowitz

As the marine hobby matures and more people become involved, it is natural that we are starting to see some unusual—or at least different—trends in the types of systems that people are setting up. In this chapter we'll take a quick look at some of these systems to give you an idea of where the cutting edges are and the plethora of directions in which you can head once you've used this book to help you set up your first successful marine aquarium.

What Lies Ahead

- big tanks
- small tanks
- predators
- different habitats and shapes

Warning: Large reef tanks can become habit forming.

SIZE TRENDS

The aquarium hobby in general has experienced an explosion in the types, sizes, and shapes of fish tanks available. Marine aquarists are taking full advantage of the bounty, making it harder and harder to define the most common or typical setup.

Bigger Is Better

A variety of factors has fueled the growth in larger and larger home aquariums, and a major one is the trend toward bigger and bigger reef setups. Aside from the fact that reef aquarists find it difficult to stop acquiring more and more corals and other invertebrates, the stability of larger systems and the opportunity they provide for the inclusion of extremely territorial species or those with special habitat needs make mega tanks very appealing. Tanks as big as several hundred gallons are now routinely stocked by specialty suppliers, and custom aquariums can be made to fit any dream or decor in glass or acrylic. In addition, aquarium maintenance companies permit people to enjoy the beauty of a huge marine aquarium in their homes or offices without having to do any of the work.

And it's not just reefs. Many mega tanks are FO setups. There are plenty of beautiful marine fish that are hardy and personable but that simply grow too big for standard tanks. An aquarium of 300 gallons (1,100 liters) or more, however, can often accommodate these desirable species.

Micro Is Best

At the opposite end of the spectrum, very small reef tanks, often called nano reefs, are also rapidly gaining popularity. Not many years ago the idea of a desktop reef was laughable, but today you'll find that reef aquariums as small as 1 gallon (4 liters) are prevalent. What's changed?

Nano tanks can help you appreciate various small saltwater beauties.

Part of the answer is that husbandry techniques have been perfected and equipment like hi-intensity lights and protein skimmers have been designed for tiny tanks. But make no mistake, a small reef tank can still crash extremely quickly, and these setups are most often successful when a long-term reef aquarist is maintaining them. Fish are never included in the littlest versions, and in larger nanos, say from 10 to 30 gallons (40 to 115 liters), at most one small fish shares its home with the live rock and one or two inverts.

One way in which these tanks are maintained is through water changes. A 50-percent weekly change on a 2-gallon (8-liter) reef requires only a gallon of new salt water, of course, so water stability can be kept up with massive (relatively) water changes. One of the nicest things about these systems is that a few pieces of live rock rubble, a couple of coral fragments, and maybe a shrimp, all of which would quickly be lost to sight in a large reef setup, can be the center of attention. In fact, a nano tank stocked only with live rock can be a fascinating display. The tight focus on such a small area will enable you to notice the day-to-day changes as the life brought in on the rock grows and becomes visible.

LIVESTOCK TRENDS

The popularity of certain species waxes and wanes, and there are many reasons for this.

Increased Availability

Obviously, an animal has to be readily available for it to become popular. Improved collecting and shipping practices have joined with mushrooming technology and information about keeping marine species alive to enable aquarists to maintain an enormous variety of species. Invertebrates that 20 years ago were doomed to certain death are now routinely kept and propagated in hobbyists' tanks. The successful rearing of a spawn of many species of marine fish is no longer a notable event, and there actually are some aquarists making a living from breeding marines. Captive breeding can also make available species that are not abundant or that are difficult to catch. When such a species is a good aquarium candidate and its availability goes from sporadic to reliable, it can become a popular animal.

A recent example involves the Banggai cardinalfish, *Pterapogon kauderni*. Unlike most other reef fish, this species has an extremely limited distribution, being found only in the Banggai islands in Indonesia. This is because its larvae do not have a planktonic stage and are brooded in the male's mouth until they are large enough to make it on their own on the reef. Without the pelagic planktonic distribution of most species, the Banggai's range is quite restricted. The fish took the hobby by storm, and within a few years the species was pushed to the brink of extinction by over-collecting. The price jumped, and some controls were put in place. Unfortunately, reports heralding this fish as "the marine guppy" were premature, and although raising the fry is relatively easy, the species does not procreate in captivity as prodigiously as the famed "millions fish." Nevertheless, captive-bred specimens are available, and you should insist on them.

Maintaining and breeding once-difficult organisms obviously leads to a greater choice for hobbyists and eases pressure on wild populations, but sometimes people get so excited about this idea that they fail to read the fine print: many faddishly popular species are not once-difficult, but instead *still* difficult. I hope that through education we can curb the capture and sale of animals that have no realistic hope of surviving in captivity. At this time, however, finding a marine fish for sale, even by the thousands, is not an indication that it is well suited to the home aquarium. At the risk of abject redundancy: research before you buy!

Keeping Large Predators

One of the factors behind so many mega tanks is people's desire to keep large marine predators. Many conscientious fishkeepers enjoy these big fish, but there is always a small group that exploits the fish to show off or to satisfy some bloodlust by feeding live animals to the predators. Not surprisingly, these same people often keep them in poorly filtered tanks that are way too small. They also often provide an inadequate diet. Lionfish die by the hundreds from malnutrition or digestive obstruction brought on by an unnatural steady diet of live goldfish that their owners are forever plopping into the tank for a show whenever anybody visits.

If you truly appreciate large predatory fish and can provide a sufficiently large tank with adequate filtration and a proper diet, one or more of these animals might be right for you. But make sure that you research thoroughly any species that interests you, and make sure that you have a large enough aquarium for the adult fish *before* you purchase it, no matter how small the fish might be at the time. I cringe whenever I see a panther grouper, *Cromileptes altivelis,* in a dealer's tanks. This fish attracts the way a clownfish does—it has attractive coloration and an appealing, almost comical method of swimming. The tiny babies normally offered for sale are irresistible time bombs. Time bombs? Yes. Unlike a clownfish, a panther grouper will top 28 inches (70 cm). That means that a 100-gallon (400-liter) tank is too small for one of these fish. Even a 240-gallon (900-liter) aquarium, at 24 by 24 by 96 inches (60 by 60 by 240 cm), is inadequate, since the animal could not position itself front to back without bending its body. I have also seen juvenile Napoleon wrasses, *Cheilinus undulatus,* and baby nurse sharks, *Ginglymostoma cirratum,* for sale in retail stores. Yes, that 7-foot (2-m) giant we've already

The Napoleon wrasse, *Cheilinus undulatus.* Definitely *not* an aquarium species!

discussed, along with a 14-foot (5-m) monster that has no place in a home aquarium under a million gallons, minimum!

SHARKS

Perhaps the most common large fish on people's wish lists are sharks. Unfortunately, the proper care of sharks goes way beyond having a big enough aquarium. Even many public aquaria cannot provide satisfactory quarters for large pelagic sharks. There are a few small shark species that can survive in systems of several hundred gallons, but to thrive even the tiniest sharks need truly humongous tanks. In addition, the potential shark keeper must consider the shape of the tank (circular is best), the possible need for a chiller, and the paramount need for truly gargantuan skimming and filtration systems. Feeding a shark is not always easy, and it can be very expensive. In fact, the annual cost of just the salt mix for the necessary water changes on a single shark tank can easily exceed what even dedicated hobbyists spend on their entire collection! There are many other fish much more suitable for a mega home aquarium, but if you simply must have a shark, procure a tank of at least 500 gallons (2,000 liters) and stick to one of the species that are under 2 feet long (60 cm) when full grown.

TAME CEPHALOPODS?

Although fairly closely related to snails, octopuses and their kin have no external shell and are smart, fast, agile, dexterous, and consummate predators. In recent years the popularity of cephalopods for the home aquarium has soared. The Internet is central to much of the attention being given to octopuses and cuttlefish as pets, and an excellent website is www. tonmo.com. Unlike most other invertebrates, such as snails, shrimps, and crabs, cephalopods are very intelligent and playful, and an increasing number of hobbyists are keeping these shell-less mollusks. There is a great deal of variation by species and by individual, but many become hand tame and are truly interactive pets. They also have several specific needs and are almost never suitable for keeping in an aquarium with any other animals. Thus cephalopod tanks are typically single-specimen setups.

Octopuses are escape artists with the strength to lift heavy tank covers, often even if they are weighted down, and the slippery flexibility to squeeze through tiny openings. In fact, any hole large enough for the animal's parrot-like beak is large enough for the entire octopus to slip through. But the major downside to cephalopod keeping is their extremely short life spans—less than a year in many cases and rarely more than two years. Couple this with their affable personalities and you have a recipe for grief and disappointment. Many aquarists make up for this by keeping cephalopods in succession, obtaining a new pet when the previous one dies, and some are perfecting protocols for breeding their cephalopods, maintaining successive generations of these fascinating creatures.

If you are interested, make sure you read up on these fascinating but hard-to-keep animals before deciding to get one.

HABITAT TRENDS

In the same way freshwater aquarists create biotope aquariums modeled on various habitats, such as jungle streams, swift rivers, lakes, and swamps, marine aquarists are increasingly trying to set up tanks that mimic marine habitats. While most marine tanks are still based on the coral reef, some aquarists are venturing beyond.

Coldwater Tanks

There is no doubt that tropical coral reef fish and invertebrates are riotously colored and highly diverse, but there are fascinating and beautiful animals from temperate oceans as well. Modern aquarium chillers make it possible—even easy—to maintain an aquarium for specimens that require cooler-than-room-temperature conditions. If you are already familiar with maintaining a tropical tank, or even a room-temperature goldfish system, the idea of an aquarium on which you have to wipe off the condensation is certainly exotic, to say the least.

The major drawback to a coldwater system aquarium is that you will likely have to collect your own specimens, as appropriate animals are rarely offered for sale in the aquarium trade. This can add to the fun of your hobby, but make sure that it remains fun by researching and obeying all local laws and regulations regarding taking living organisms from the wild.

Deepwater Tanks

Another ocean region just beginning to be explored, collected, and exported to the trade is the deep reef. Advancements in

Cephalopods are fascinating invertebrates. The most commonly available ones in the aquarium trade are octopuses and cuttlefishes. Seen here is a cuttlefish, *Sepia* sp.

re-breathers, exotic air mixes, and other equipment enable divers to investigate reefs at depths of 400 feet (120 m) or more. Some of the animals down there are also found in shallower water, but many species are endemic to the deep water. Right now the few specimens that make it into the trade command outrageous prices, but this will change as more collecting is done of these habitats.

Some reef aquarists are experimenting with deepwater invertebrates, most of which rely little if at all on photosynthetic zooxanthellae, so the possibility exists of putting together an entire reef system of corals and other invertebrates without having to provide high intensity lighting.

Tidepool Tanks

Most tropical marine ornamentals are reef associated, but there are many interesting fish and invertebrates that inhabit tidepools—pools of water left behind when the tide recedes that are completely flooded by the next high tide. Since they are normally exposed to rapid large swings in temperature, current, and sunlight, sometimes being left high and dry for a while, these creatures are typically very hardy and forgiving of variations in aquarium conditions. Many different fish and sessile and motile invertebrates (inluding some octopuses) make tidepools their home.

Stocking a tidepool setup, like stocking a coldwater setup, will probably require collecting your own specimens. Remember to check and comply with local laws and regulations. You may be able to purchase some specimens by meeting local fishing boats or by making arrangements with professional fishermen to set certain species aside in a bucket of sea water for you.

TRENDS OUTSIDE THE GLASS BOX

Just when you think you've seen it all, someone will come up with a marine aquarium system so novel that it almost seems bizarre. Still, most of these exceptions may eventually become rules.

Coral Reef Ponds

I've seen only one saltwater pond, and that was indoors, but it has given me much to think about, and I can imagine many variations on the theme. The roughly circular pond was made from a liner supported all around with a wall of those concrete "rocks" that are sold for building retaining walls. In the center was a "reef island" of live rock, and a single mangrove propagule sprouted out of the water toward a pendant light fixture. A few brightly colored fish lived among the rocks. They would dart out for an instant, then zip back to safety. An anomalous "saltwaterfall" provided excellent aeration as it returned water from the filtration system. Hardly a biotope-accurate display, but it was very interesting!

Strange Shapes

In addition to the cylinders, pentagons, spheres, and other unusual shapes, aquariums have been constructed in some truly outside-the-box designs. One idea for which I have seen several variations is the concept of linking two or more tanks with transparent swimways so that the fish can visit from one tank to another. One particularly ambitious setup encompassed an entire room, with clear pipes stretching around all fours walls, joining several aquariums at various places in the room. An intriguing application of such a system would be to allow the aquarist to keep several specimens with a kill-any-conspecific-I-see attitude, since when one attacks an interloper, the victim can quickly escape across the room, leaving the aggressor unwilling to leave its territory to continue the chase. This could be one way to eventually breed some species that obviously need to be in the same confines to mate but are too belligerent to keep in groups in normal systems.

Another design that permits this type of partial segregation is large U-shaped aquariums that are engineered to fit on both sides of a wall through an archway or doorway. The two large rectangular tanks along the walls are joined by a narrow connection that goes through the opening in the wall. Figure 1 shows this design from above. Fish on one side cannot see tankmates on the other side, and, again, territorial specimens will be unlikely to leave their territory, make two right or two left turns, and hazard entry into someone else's territory with their own now out of sight.

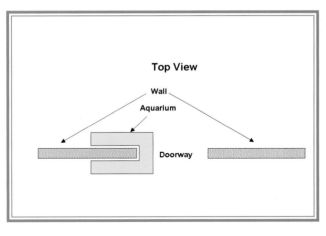

Figure 1.

Top View

Wall

Aquarium

Doorway

SUMMARY

As you can see, there are multiple directions that marine aquarists are taking with innovations in their hobby. Whether you choose to follow one or more of them or remain in a more traditional mode is completely up to you. You might even set off in a new direction, blazing a path that other people can follow. Once you have mastered the basics of a marine aquarium, as this book has prepared you to do, the sky… or, should I say, the *ocean* is the limit! Enjoy!

Conclusion

Now that you've taken the plunge into the fascinating realm of the marine aquarium, you'll soon discover that the rewards and challenges that lie ahead are almost limitless. Once you've mastered the basics and gotten that first critical taste of success, you'll be ready to expand your horizons to include the care of more sensitive and exotic species. And like almost every marine aquarist before you, you will eventually succumb to the temptation (or should I say compulsion?) to set up multiple aquariums to accommodate an ever-growing population of fish and/or invertebrates.

But getting the most out of the marine aquarium hobby is not completely automatic. It requires a significant amount of effort and a willingness to learn on your part. The more effort you put into maintaining your aquarium and the more time you invest researching the characteristics and needs of various marine organisms, the more you'll succeed in your endeavors, and the more likely you'll be to stick with the hobby for the long haul.

So what steps can you take to keep your interest level high? For one thing, you can get connected to your local aquarium society, which will allow you to exchange ideas, information, equipment, and even specimens with aquarists of all different skill levels. Also, there are numerous Internet chat rooms and forums you can frequent to share your thoughts with fellow aquarists. I've found that this is an excellent way to get timely responses to healthcare issues and other problems I've encountered along the way. Of course, don't forget your trusted aquarium dealer. He or she can give you lots of friendly advice as well as keep you apprised of exciting new trends in the marine aquarium industry. In addition, you can continue to read every piece of marine aquarium literature that you can lay your hands on, including textbooks, magazines, newsletters, and journals. With the continued support of these influences, along with your own enthusiasm and ingenuity, you're sure to enjoy a lifetime of wonder and success in the marine aquarium hobby. Good luck!

RESOURCES

Magazine

Tropical Fish Hobbyist
1 TFH Plaza
3rd & Union Avenues
Neptune City, NJ 07753
E-mail: info@tfh.com
www.tfhmagazine.com

Internet Resources

Aquaria Central
www.aquariacentral.com

Aquarium Hobbyist
www.aquaiumhobbyist.com

Marine Aquarium Advice
www.marineaquariumadvice.com

Microcosm Aquarium Explorer
www.microcosmaquariumexplorer.com

Reef Central
www.reefcentral.com

TFH Magazine Forum (formerly Tropical Resources)
http://forums.tfhmagazine.com

Wet Web Media
www.wetmedia.com

A World of Fish
www.aworldoffish.com

Associations and Societies

Federation of American Aquarium Societies (FAAS)
E-mail: Jbenes01@yahoo.com
www.faas.info

Marine Aquarium Council (MAC)
E-mail: info@aquariumcouncil.org
www.aquariumcouncil.org

Marine Aquarium Societies of North America (MASNA)
E-mail: secretary@masna.org
www.masna.org

Books

Boruchowitz, David E. *Mini-Aquariums*. TFH Publications, Inc.

Brightwell, CR. *Marine Chemistry*. TFH Publications, Inc.

Brightwell, CR. *The Nano-Reef Handbook*. TFH Publications, Inc.

Dunlop, Colin and Nancy King. *Cephalopods*. TFH Publications, Inc.

Fatherree, James W. *The Super Simple Guide to Corals*. TFH Publications, Inc.

Fenner, Robert M. *The Conscientious Marine Aquarist, 2nd Edition*. Microcosm/TFH Publications, Inc.

Goemans, Bob and Lance Ichinotsubo. *The Marine Fish Health & Feeding Handbook.* Microcosm/TFH Publications, Inc.

Hellweg, Michael R. *Culturing Live Foods.* TFH Publications, Inc.

Hemdal, Jay F. *Advanced Marine Aquarium Techniques.* TFH Publications, Inc.

Kurtz, Jeff. *Saltwater Aquarium Problem Solver.* TFH Publications, Inc.

Kurtz, Jeff. *The Simple Guide to Mini-Reef Aquariums.* TFH Publications, Inc.

Michael, Scott W. *Adventurous Aquarist Guide™: The 101 Best Marine Invertebrates.* Microcosm/TFH Publications, Inc.

Michael, Scott W. *Adventurous Aquarist Guide™: The 101 Best Saltwater Fishes.* Microcosm/TFH Publications, Inc.

Michael, Scott W. *A PocketExpert™ Guide to Marine Fishes.* Microcosm/TFH Publications, Inc.

Michael, Scott W. *A PocketExpert™ Guide to Reef Aquarium Fishes.* Microcosm/TFH Publications, Inc.

Michael, Scott W. *Reef Fishes, Vol. 1-5.* Microcosm/TFH Publications, Inc.

Shimek, Ronald L. *A PocketExpert™ Guide to Marine Invertebrates.* Microcosm/TFH Publications, Inc.

Ward, Ashley. *Questions and Answers on Saltwater Aquarium Fishes.* TFH Publications, Inc.

Wilkerson, Joyce D. *Clownfishes.* Microcosm/TFH Publications, Inc.

Wittenrich, Matthew L. *The Complete Illustrated Breeder's Guide to Marine Aquarium Fishes.* Microcosm/TFH Publications, Inc.

Photo Credits

Lynsey Allan (Shutterstock): 175

G.R. Allen: 157

Konovalikov Andrey (Shutterstock): 167

Laurence Azoulay: 220

Joe Barbarite (Shutterstock): 202

Eugene Berman (Shutterstock): Front Cover

CR Brightwell: 44, 69, 232

Luis Fernando Curci Chavier (Shutterstock): 119, 144

Stephen Coburn (Shutterstock): 230

Colin Dunlop: 128

James Fatherree: 17, 46, 48, 49, 112, 114, 168, 180, 198, 211

Tyler Fox (Shutterstock): 43, 176, 218

U. Erich Friese: 85

Ilya D. Gridnev (Shutterstock): 5

Markus Holcomb: 80

Johnny Jensen: 161

Jeya (Shutterstock): 102

Stephan Kerkhofs (Shutterstock): 9, 169

Justin Kim (Shutterstock): 164

Jeff Kurtz: 75, 97, 243

Gary Lange: 30, 178, 190 (top & bottom), 197

Dan Lee (Shutterstock): 25

James Lee: 186, 191, 196

Oliver Lucanus: 227, 229

Yuriy Maksymenko (Shutterstock): 143

MaxPhoto (Shutterstock): 40

Dermot McMahon: 77, 101

Stephen Mcsweeny (Shutterstock): 241

Michael Metheny (Shutterstock): 91

Aaron Norman: 71

Khoroshunova Olga (Shutterstock): 133

John O'Malley: 147, 154

Michael S. Paletta: 13

MP. & C. Piednoir: 35, 59, 72, 98, 122, 151, 200, 203, 212

Daniel Pon: 57

Kristian Sekulic (Shutterstock): 38

Craig Sernotti: 113

Elisei Shafer (Shutterstock): 6

Asther Lau Choon Siew (Shutterstock): 194

Egidijus Skiparis (Shutterstock): 130

Dr. Dwight Smith: 62, 83, 93, 171, 183, 207, 215, 237

Mark Smith: 11, 27, 67, 107, 148, 150, 152, 153, 156, 159, 163, 166, 189, 205, 209, 217

Specta (Shutterstock): 20

Walter A. Stark II: 140

Russell Swain (Shutterstock): 125, 235

Morozova Tatyana (Shutterstock): 124

Iggy Tavares: 19, 37, 162, 185

Terence (Shutterstock): 170

Nikita Tiunov (Shutterstock): 105, 120

Paul van Eykelen (Shutterstock): 52

Nicholas Violand: 233

Matthew L. Wittenrich: 87

All other photos courtesy of the TFH Photo Archives

The World's Leading Aquarium Magazine
from the publishers of the world's finest aquarium books

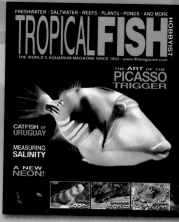

FRESHWATER • SALTWATER • REEFS • PLANTS • PONDS • AND MORE!

FREE Gifts With Your Subscription:

• **FREE** *TFH* Aquatic Life Calendar • **FREE** Access to *TFH* Digital
• **FREE** book with 2-year subscription
Choose either *The 101 Best Saltwater Fishes* or *The 101 Best Tropical Fishes*
from the Microcosm/TFH Professional Series

Call for a **FREE** Trial Issue! 1-888-859-9034
www.tfhmagazine.com